Bradford's Indian Book

UNIVERSITY PRESS OF FLORIDA

Florida A&M University, Tallahassee
Florida Atlantic University, Boca Raton
Florida Gulf Coast University, Ft. Myers
Florida International University, Miami
Florida State University, Tallahassee
New College of Florida, Sarasota
University of Central Florida, Orlando
University of Florida, Gainesville
University of North Florida, Jacksonville
University of South Florida, Tampa
University of West Florida, Pensacola

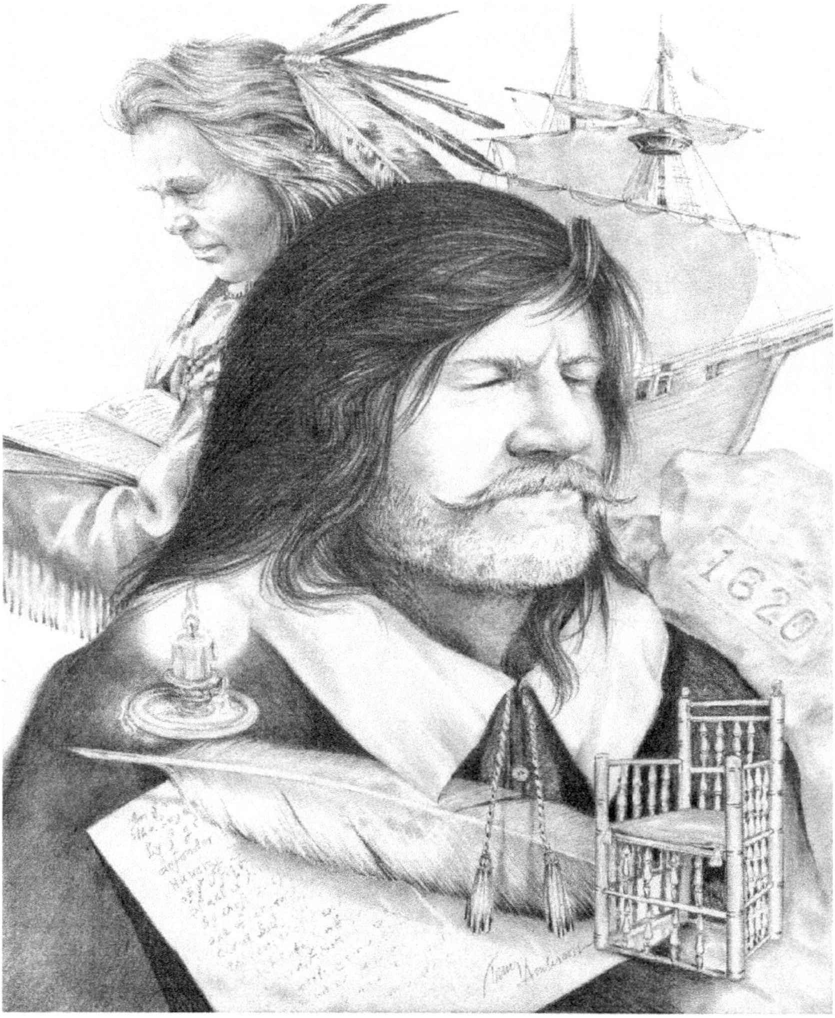
1620

BRADFORD'S INDIAN BOOK

Being the True Roote & Rise
of American Letters as Revealed
by the Native Text Embedded in
Of Plimoth Plantation

Betty Booth Donohue

ᏬᎫ ᏇᎫ ᎱᏇᎢ

University Press of Florida
Gainesville · Tallahassee · Tampa · Boca Raton
Pensacola · Orlando · Miami · Jacksonville · Ft. Myers · Sarasota

The frontispiece illustration is reproduced from an original pencil drawing (12" x 16") created for this volume in 2011 by Cherokee artist Troy Anderson of Siloam Springs, Arkansas. It depicts William Bradford with the Mayflower and Squanto behind him.

First cloth printing, 2011
First paperback printing, 2014

LIBRARY OF CONGRESS CATALOGING-IN-PUBLICATION DATA
Donohue, Betty Booth.
Bradford's Indian book : being the true roote & rise of American letters as revealed by the native text embedded in Of Plimoth Plantation / Betty Booth Donohue.
p. cm.
Includes bibliographical references and index.
ISBN 978-0-8130-3737-0 (cloth: alk. paper)
ISBN 978-0-8130-6088-0 (pbk.)
1. Bradford, William, 1590-1657. History of Plymouth Plantation. 2. Bradford, William, 1590-1657—Criticism and interpretation. 3. Indians of North America—Massachusetts—Plymouth—History. 4. Indians of North America—Massachusetts—Plymouth—Social life and customs. 5. American literature—Indian authors—History and criticism. 6. Indian literature—History and criticism. 7. Massachusetts—History—New Plymouth, 1620-1691. I. Title.
F68.B80733D66 2011
974.4'02092—dc23
2011018981

The University Press of Florida is the scholarly publishing agency for the State University System of Florida, comprising Florida A&M University, Florida Atlantic University, Florida Gulf Coast University, Florida International University, Florida State University, New College of Florida, University of Central Florida, University of Florida, University of North Florida, University of South Florida, and University of West Florida.

University Press of Florida
15 Northwest 15th Street
Gainesville, FL 32611-2079
http://www.upf.com

For **DhBΘꙍ ꞏꝆꙅET DꞆꙍꝆ Dꞇ ꙍꝆ ꝆꙅϯꙅꙍꝆ**,
the People of the Eastern Light, and Bradford

CONTENTS

ACKNOWLEDGMENTS

For seeing me begin this journey, I want to thank the late Paula Gunn Allen, Michael Colacurcio, and Eric Sundquist of the University of California, Los Angeles. Their belief in the validity of the undertaking and their material assistance were invaluable. For bibliographic support, I want to thank Sue Tircuit of Cody's Bookstore formerly in Berkeley, California. In the age before online texts, Sue was able to locate rare and out-of-print volumes and get them to me quickly and happily. For those who have stood by me for the last leg of the trek, Joanna Brooks, Matt Cohen, Jason Murray, Harry Oosahwee, Karen Wallace, and Hilary Wyss, I owe a great debt of gratitude. From the heart, G V.

PREFACE
BGᴧE AⱭPCʹCʹ

When Massachusetts Natives met English settlers in 1620, literary events took place. The American Indian oral tradition confronted English-speaking immigrants and changed their discursive propensities. As the English-speaking immigrants wrote, they produced a new literature that would eventually be designated American, and **BGᴧE AⱭPCʹCʹ**, or American literature, is different from continental British. It is a literature that reveals an American Indian presence, a characteristic that British literature does not have. American Indian words, characters, and actions entered America's written works at Contact, and these words, characters, and actions have become a part of a continuing European American literary tradition. Remove the Indians, and the literature is no longer American.

Bradford's Indian Book asserts that American Indians brought forces to bear on the new nation's developing literature and helped shape it. Trace evidence of these formational dynamics can be found in most of the early documents produced by English speakers in seventeenth-century America, but the highest concentration of forensic markers aggregate in William Bradford's history of Plymouth Colony.

OP ⱭJ JStᴣⱭJ began writing his history in 1630, and he worked on it intermittently until 1650. He produced a vellum-bound manuscript measuring approximately 11 ½ inches by 7 ¾ that contained 270 pages of inaccurately numbered text. The manuscript has several blank flyleaves on which he wrote Hebrew grammar exercises and a plea to "see" the language of God, angels, and the Patriarchs. The manuscript's later handlers, perhaps to establish control of the document or to emend it, added their own comments to these pages and thus created a palimpsest. After Bradford's death, the volume passed to his son William and later to his grandson

John and then to his great-grandson Samuel. During this great passing, the manuscript was borrowed by Nathaniel Morton, Increase and Cotton Mather, William Hubbard, Samuel Sewell, Thomas Hutchinson, and Thomas Prince. When Prince completed his *Chronological History of New-England* (1736), he colonized the history. After pasting in his personal bookplate, underlining certain passages, inserting marginalia, and correcting Bradford's spelling, he appropriated the manuscript for his own collection. He then named his holdings the *New England Library* and deposited them in the bell tower of the Old South Meeting House in Boston. After Prince's death, what happened to the manuscript is conjectural. Either the very disgruntled Tory Thomas Hutchinson or a nameless bibliophilic British soldier bivouacking in the Old South took the manuscript to London after the Revolutionary War, and by some miraculous means the document made its way to Fulham Palace, the residence of the Bishop of London. It lay there in oblivion until a passage of it was quoted by the Right Reverend Samuel Wilberforce, Bishop of Oxford, in his *History of the Protestant Episcopal Church in America* (1844). An American scholar recognized the quote and reported it to the president of the Massachusetts Historical Society, Charles Deane. After learning of its whereabouts, Deane had an English scholar transcribe the manuscript and send the copy to him and, in 1856, he published it in the Fourth Series of the *Collections* of the Massachusetts Historical Society. For slightly more than forty years, however, Bradford's original manuscript remained in London, the subject of a protracted, bilateral struggle. Finally the manuscript was repatriated to the United States in 1897 but only after it had been reclassified as the *Mayflower's Log,* and thus by a legal technicality released.[1]

Even though *Of Plimoth Plantation* is a work of non-fiction, it is important to American literary theory because it contains many themes, stylistic devices, archetypal characters, and narrative techniques that later surface in European American fiction, and these rhetorical strategies can be traced to American Indian poetics. Why an English settler named William Bradford became a conduit for the American Indian literary power informing a new national literature will probably never be understood, but what is certain is that his history left proof of the process.

When the passengers on board the *Mayflower* settled at Patuxet, they did not find themselves in a literary or intellectual wilderness. The Newcomers had entered a land that was filled with people, thoughts, stories, and ceremonies. Narrative, or ᎧᏃᎮᎵᏙᎭ, is in the earth and it was here before time was counted. Prior to the influx of Europeans into what is now called the United States, literature, in oral form, was everywhere there were people.[2]

Before Contact, American Indians employed most of the genres known to Europeans. Natives produced creation accounts, histories, orations, lyric poetry, lullabies, fables, love songs, elegies, epics, and dramatic rituals. In addition to these familiar literary modes, American Indians composed songs or poems designed to effect protection or success for a designated undertaking. They composed hunting, fishing, and planting songs, traveling songs, war chants, and battle narratives. Native life began and ended with poetry. Naming songs introduced infants to the Creator; vision recitations revealed a person's life-plan or obligations, while death songs prepared the singer for his spirit journey and identified him to his Maker once again.[3] The most important of all tribal compositions, however, were the oral formulae designed to effect change or bring about healing. I call these sacred chants medicine texts, and it is this genre with which *Bradford's Indian Book* is concerned.

At the time of Contact, literature in the Western Hemisphere was alive and dynamic. Literature was "practiced" or engaged in by laymen and by literary specialists who were referred to as DhᎫᏝᏓᎣᎤᎥ, persons-who-know-things, or medicine people. Literature was an action that had medical, religious, social, aesthetic, intellectual, and didactic properties. It was an all-encompassing part of life. American Indian literature did not need print in order to exist. Logocentric in the extreme, Native literature served to instruct, to delight, and to effect. Generative rather than mimetic, it was, and is, vital and puissant. Simply put, it makes things happen.

There were several paths that the oral tradition took to make its way into American letters. One of the most common trajectories of influence was that moving from a medicine man and his associates to the Christian divine and from there to the writing society at large. In the Plymouth paradigm under consideration here, this trajectory is traced from Passaconaway and the Massasoit Osamequin to Tisquantum and Hobomok and then to William Bradford and Edward Winslow, who, although not ordained clergymen, were devout believers and exegetes of their faith. Bradford's poetry and Winslow's essays, *Hypocrisie Unmasked* (1646) and *New-Englands Salamander* (1647), exhibit theological polemics. Since Bradford and Winslow were part of the second British settlement in North America, they are two of our earliest writers. Of course, there were many other trajectories.

Another common course of influence was from Indian guide or Indian society to European explorer, visitor, or immigrant. This trajectory produced works like the Dermer letter (1620), which is embedded in Bradford's history, William Wood's *New Englands Prospect* (1634), and Thomas Morton's *New English Canaan* (1637).

Indianization is another method by which Europeans absorbed Native culture. It has been a long-standing custom for American Indians to take in strangers and remake them. Captives taken from other Nations were changed to conform to the captors' norms.[4] Similarly, the Natives who interacted with European immigrants attempted to Indianize them. Recent epidemics had decimated their populations, and they needed to attract energetic people who would contribute to the general welfare, refresh the gene pool, and not disrupt the social order.

At Plymouth, Indianization was easily accomplished because Natives and Newcomers lived as neighbors and got into each other's minds. The Principal Patriarch enjoyed a close relationship with Hobomok and Tisquantum (Squanto), a Patuxet headman who had been kidnapped by Europeans, taught to speak English, and returned to his native land. In *Saints and Strangers* (1945), George Willison relates that Squanto "had been more or less adopted by Bradford."[5] It is probable that the two shared living quarters for a time, since housing was extremely limited during Plymouth's early years. Bradford's inclusion into his history of several pages of sympathetic biographical information about Tisquantum indicates that he had a genuine affection for the man. Tisquantum's political, diplomatic, and theurgic powers, perhaps exemplified by his escaping the plague that decimated most of his village and his breaking free of several European captivities, must have touched Bradford to some degree. Both men had survived political exile, social alienation, and the loss of close relatives and friends to devastating diseases and sudden deaths. Each had been a stranger in a strange land, dependent upon the kindness of persons unknown for succor and support.

Bradford's history invariably refers to Tisquantum as "Squanto," and whether that designation was a nickname or title is uncertain. The "-[h]*anto*" at the end of the name, however, indicates that Squanto was a "'Wonder Worker,'" meaning that he had "mysterious, magical, . . . [and] miraculous'" powers.[6] Like Hobomok, who joined the Colony later and quartered with Miles Standish, Tisquantum was a *pniese,* or apprentice-level medicine man, dream interpreter, conjurer, and diplomat.[7] Jessie Little Doe, a

Wampanoag linguist, doubts that the northern Narragansett or Kaweesuc term "pniese" actually means medicine man in the way it is generally used today, but the term does designate someone who defends the people, a foot soldier, or a kind of protector.[8] Of course, protection in Native societies often refers to medicine.

Another reason that Indianization was quickly accomplished at Plymouth was that, at Contact, Europeans were an infinitesimal minority. Russell Thornton estimates that there were approximately seven million people living in what is now the United States while Henry Dobyns puts the figure at ten million.[9] America was not "the Lord's waste" as John Winthrop occasionally styled it, but was instead a heavily populated country.[10] There were hundreds of complex civilizations here with well-organized governmental systems. The Southwestern Pueblos, the Algonquian Confederacies of New England, the Mid-Atlantic Powhatan Confederacy, and the Iroquois League were four such bodies that wielded influence over the first European settlers in what is now the United States. The infrastructure of American Indians provided the colonists with knowledge of the essentials of daily life—foods, hunting methods, roads, water routes, fighting techniques, medicines, land management, and democratic political structures. As colonists learned the tangible details of life in the New World, they also unknowingly absorbed the intangible aspects associated with the acquired knowledge and were subtly changed.

To reveal the Native influence in *Of Plimoth Plantation*, I read closely and give hermeneutical attention to ambiguities. Passages resistant to only one interpretation are designated *seemingly unintentional narratives*. Gerald Prince's assertion that narratological analyses of texts sometimes must include issues of "psychology, anthropology, history, literary criticism, or esthetics" partially undergirds my approach.[11]

My primary methodologies, however, derive from examining the Navajo sacred chants translated by Father Berard Haile; from heeding the principles of American Indian literary theory as understood by Native medicine people, scholars, and storytellers; and by analyzing the works of modern Native writers. I use the Navajo chants as prototypical examples of medicine texts only because they are intact, reliable, and accessible. It is unlikely that similar materials from the eastern Nations now exist in written form, but given the compositional propensities of various nineteenth- and twentieth-century Native writers it is possible to hypothesize that most Native ceremonial chants shared certain characteristics. The formularies that appear in the Navajo chants also inform nearly all modern Native inscriptive practices regardless of a writer's tribal affiliation. That is to say, narrative strata observable in Louise Erdrich's works are also visible in Pauline Johnson's, Alexander Posey's, Linda Hogan's, James Welch's, and David Seals', to name only a few. Erdrich is Turtle Mountain Chippewa; Johnson is Mohawk; Alexander Posey is Mvskogee; Hogan is Chickasaw; Welch is Blackfeet/Gros Ventre; David Seals is Huron.

Even though the works of the above-mentioned writers are quite different and span two centuries, they nevertheless share discursive characteristics. These stylistic devices are not the sole property of Mohawks, Mvskogees, Chippewas, Chickasaws, Blackfeet/Gros Ventres, or Hurons, but can be designated American Indian as opposed to European. Because these narrative strata are found in recorded Navajo chants, I use them as examples of archetypal sources. Certainly, there is no connection between Bradford and *Beautyway*. There is, however, a significant connection between the narrative dynamics functioning in *Of Plimoth Plantation* and American Indian poetics demonstrable in a wide variety of healing chants like *Beautyway*. The same poetics are discernable in recitations of vision quests such as Black Elk's relation of his experience recorded in *Black Elk Speaks* (1932).

In the best of all possible worlds we would have hard evidence, full texts, and indisputable facts with which to work, but the post-Contact American Indian world is fragmented. Scholars working in Native studies must reconstruct from shards. Much cultural knowledge has disappeared. A significant amount of what remains is closely guarded and unavailable to scholars or tribal outsiders. The paucity of comprehensive, authenticated, and accessible materials about the many issues that concern Northeastern tribal customs forces some upstreaming, or working back into time from the cultural knowns of the present. Because Native influence entered American letters by means of social contact, I cite ethnohistorical and anthropological data. Even so, this volume is primarily a work of literary criticism, and upstreaming is done only to make plausible illustrations for literary explication. My procedure will be to use what is accessible and presently knowable without encumbering the text with constant qualification.

American Indian history and culture is large and indeterminate in scope, and everything that bears on American Indian exegesis cannot possibly be contained in one theory or one volume. Paul Chaat Smith (Comanche), in

"The Terrible Nearness of Distant Places" (2007), recognizes this problem and points out additionally that the issue is magnified because presently we do not have a "framework with defined meanings in which to ground our discourse."[12] That pronouncement, however arguable, does underline the many controversies surrounding a significant number of issues stemming from American Indian cultural exposition. Some of these controversies are vexed by what often appears to be semantic hairsplitting while others are enhanced by the exploration of genuine concerns.

For example, a current trend in publications dealing with American Indian subject matter stridently calls for tribal specificity when working with Native materials. That highly appropriate and well-intentioned demand is reasonable for critical, historical, anthropological, or ethnographic research regarding a clearly designated Nation or tribal person, but *Bradford's Indian Book* is about an Englishman's history, not indigenous writing. As apposite as the concept of tribal specificity is, the practice has very real constraints. Comprehensive, tribally specific data for many indigenous entities, and especially for those among the Eastern Woodlands people, is limited given the ravages of colonization. Because Bradford dealt with Algonquians, Algonquians figure prominently in this discussion. Scholars can be fairly certain about superficial aspects of Algonquian material culture: foods, hunting techniques, housing, weapons, utensils, and legends. The more abstract or metaphysical aspects of the culture cannot always be discovered and substantiated. I try whenever possible to use Algonquian data, but when it is impossible to find Algonquian material pertinent to a critical issue, I use what is Native, accessible, plausible, and illustrative. Even though American Indians differ, we also hold many ideas and customs in common. Respect for the natural world, belief in the power of the spoken word, the ritual use of corn and tobacco, and the employment of cedar and sage in purification rites are four shared attributes. After five hundred years of colonization, many of us have come to realize that our commonalities unite us as much as our differences divide us.

By bringing pan-tribal understandings to this discussion, I emphasize the fact that many American Indian intellectual systems operated throughout the continent. These systems did not function in tribally specific vacuums; they interfaced. America's indigenous people mingled with others; they conversed, intermarried, exchanged information, and borrowed each other's customs and technologies. The continent was not static but in constant motion. More important, America was not a wilderness inhabited by non-communicative savages. It was a vibrant civilization of heterogeneous, enlightened human beings who had intellectual curiosity and complexity. It was filled with people who displayed scientific knowledge, artistic abilities, engineering capabilities, pharmacological expertise, and agricultural understanding. American Natives also had at their disposal rich oral compositions that were not confined to space and time. Some of this tradition was/is dream-inspired or divinatory, and its range and capacity are infinite. Smith's contention that at Contact American Indians were not victims, but "actors on a world stage" is one I share.[13]

Tribal specificity is also often problematic when applied to Bradford's history.[14] In regard to this volume, Bradford had contact with Wampanoags, Abenakis, Micmacs, Narragansetts, Nausets, Nipmucks, Massachusets, Niantics, Pequots, Mohegans, Patuxets, and Pokanokets, to name a few. The weight of tribal specificity here, could it be determined, would burden an encyclopedia. Important also is the note that nomenclature can be slippery. For instance, the designation Algonquian refers to people who share a language, but it includes Nations as disparate as Wampanoag, Cree, Arapaho, Shawnee, and Miami. When using the term Algonquian in this volume, I am referring primarily to the Eastern Algonquian Nations who interacted with the Saints and Strangers.

Even though Bradford dealt with Eastern Algonquians, it must also be emphasized that this book is not "about" Algonquians. It is "about" the American Indian presence in American letters. The presence can be traced to Bradford's history and to the fact that Bradford was surrounded by Algonquian Indians. The operative word here is Indians. Had Bradford been surrounded by Natives from the Southeast culture group, the same thing would likely have happened. He would have absorbed certain elements of "Indianness," which would have modified his thinking and writing. Referentially here, Gertrude Stein's observation that "a rose [Indian] is a rose is a rose" is humorously meaningful. Mentioning Algonquians in this volume honors them, and they deserved to be honored. In Native societies, the gift of knowledge must be returned.[15] Referring to Algonquians, however, does not restrict the discussion to Algonquian material.

Using multi-tribal concepts to elucidate American Indian thought is not new. Fiction writer N. Scott Momaday, a Kiowa/Cherokee, brings into play materials deriving from Navajo and Jemez sources as well as the Native American Religion to fill out his novel, *House Made of Dawn* (1966).

Non-Indian scholars Dennis Tedlock and Barbara Tedlock, editors of *Teachings from the American Earth* (1975), compile data from several tribes to produce their work. Peggy Beck, Anna Lee Walters (Pawnee), and Nia Francisco (Navajo) co-authored *The Sacred* (1992), a book that includes spiritual traditions from myriad Nations. Clara Sue Kidwell (Choctaw), Homer Noley (Choctaw), and George Tinker (Osage) elucidate several tribal religious concepts in *A Native American Theology* (2001), and Vine Deloria Jr. (Standing Rock Sioux) continues the practice in *The World We Used to Live In* (2006). Penelope Myrtle Kelsey (Seneca descent), in *Tribal Theory in Native American Literature* (2008), incorporates two Native intellectual systems in her discussion. Most of the volumes cited above are concerned with delineating facets of an American Indian experience as opposed to a non-Native experience.

I am a Cherokee scholar and I occasionally use the Cherokee language in this volume for several reasons. As Daniel Heath Justice has noted, "Our fire survives the storm," and our language, despite centuries of assaults, does also.[16] For reasons of respect and gratitude, Cherokee speakers should be remembered and appreciated. Using the old language recalls our forebears and the dark days following Removal just as it testifies to our endurance and our hopes for the future. Equally important, writing in **G W Ᏼ**, or in any Native language, brings the American Indian intellectual tradition into focus and gives it immediacy; furthermore, **G W Ᏼ** offers epistemological insights into Native thinking that English cannot. Finally, *Bradford's Indian Book* offers a red reading of a white book, and the Cherokee language underscores that point.

Another salient and essential component of this treatise is the fact that traditional American Indians do not think or act like European Americans. Worldviews and social values are often disparate. Richard West (Cheyenne), the first director of the Museum of the American Indian, in an address to the Society of Early Americanists meeting at Purdue University in 2008, reminded his audience of that reality.[17] American Indian epistemological systems are not like Western methodologies. The Native mental processes determining conclusion-reaching will deviate from accepted Western norms. Native and Western responses to identical givens will differ. The reader who sincerely wishes to learn from this volume will do well to buy into American Indian literary conventions in the same way that he accepts Western dramatic conventions when he attends a theatrical production. The object is not to believe that what a theatergoer sees on stage is "real," but it is to appreciate, or not, the play's philosophic content and enjoy the performance.

Bradford's Indian Book will bring to light Of Plimoth Plantation's Native characteristics. My purpose is to illuminate, and that intent leads to the second prong of my methodology. The Reverend Mr. Randolph Jacob (Choctaw), Cumberland Presbyterian minister, storyteller, and educator, asserts that the well-composed American Indian text is designed to mystify the hearer or reader. In the oral tradition, good storytellers do not tell all of a story and they do not spell out a narrative's meaning. The hearer/ reader must supply the missing parts of a narrative and comprehend the point of the work by means of his own intellectual efforts. As his personal experiences and perspectives change, the hearer/reader then "grows" into the narrative. Since a narrative assumes different meanings as the interpretative abilities of the hearer/reader presumably broaden, narrative, like the hearer/reader, stays in a constant state of interpretative motion. The Reverend Mr. Jacob admonishes us not to strive so hard to get the "point" of a work that we miss its wisdom and its intent.[18]

As the hearer/reader/critic of the Bradford narrative, I have been given only part of the story. The Bradford text raises questions. Of Plimoth Plantation incorporates more than one cultural code. It "writes" in an English linguistic code, but it occasionally signifies or "means" in a Native rhetorical mode. Of Plimoth Plantation occasionally presents us with narrative mysteries, especially in regard to Plymouth's dealings with American Indians, but it also provides possible answers to those mysteries.

Because I rely on American Indian literary interpretative techniques, I will occasionally refer to the erudition of American Indians who have never been published. Much of what has been recorded about American Indian epistemology, cosmology, and teleology has been collected by non-Indians, so that it often appears that American Indians have no organized system for preserving and transmitting their own cultural practices and beliefs. This non-Indian work is excellent and most helpful, and it has certainly paved the way for my studies; however, there is a centuries-old American Indian intellectual tradition in this country, and there are systems in place for its transmission. It is my feeling that Native sources should be consulted for research into works that concern American Indians; furthermore, American Indian epistemological constructs should be relied upon when they are relevant to the matters under discussion.

The documents this book considers are William Bradford's *Of Plimoth Plantation*; *Mourt's Relation* (1622), a compilation of works thought to be written by Bradford, Edward Winslow, and anonymous others; and *Good Newes from New England* (1624), written by Winslow while in England. The central focus of the work is *Of Plimoth Plantation*. *Mourt's Relation* and Winslow's text are used primarily to fill in background the Bradford history omits. Conclusions drawn from these early texts are mine alone and do not necessarily represent the thinking of other American Indians.

All references to and quotations from *Of Plimoth Plantation* come from the 1901 facsimile edition, a work of 544 pages, fascinating spelling, and compelling narrative. Because Bradford's spelling is occasionally humorous and often telling (Oldham is "Old Dame" and Indians are "Indeans"), perhaps as in academia, I neither update it nor call attention to it with *sic* since that practice seems unnecessarily intrusive. When quoting Bradford and Winthrop within my own prose, I usually retain his use of the past tense in which *Of Plimoth Plantation* is written. The exact words of the Principal Patriarchs are frequently woven *without citation* into the text because, from a Native perspective, the meaning is in the sound, and it is therefore necessary to "hear" the utterance. (The same concern informs my decision to use endnotes to document secondary sources, as in-text citations would interrupt the word flow.) Bradford's style is eloquent and powerful, and American Indian literary tradition favors repeating passages exactly, not shortening or modifying them to meet the modern preference for brevity or for keeping textual discussions in the historical present. The designation "Mourt" is used to identify quotes from Dwight Heath's 1963 edition of *Mourt's Relation*, while the notation "Winslow" signals quotations from *Good Newes from New England* found in Alexander Young's *Chronicles of the Pilgrim Fathers* (1844), where it is designated *Winslow's Relation*. When it is necessary to situate a date precisely, I use NS or New Style, to differentiate Bradford's Julian calendar from our Gregorian; otherwise his dates stand.

The Algonquians frequently described by the early European writers are members of the Northeast culture group. In the seventeenth century, the word Pokanoket was used to designate the entire Wampanoag Nation as well as the Pokanokets who were the Massasoit's band of Wampanoags living at Sowams. *Massasoit* is a Wampanoag title that means *great leader*. The Massasoit who befriended the Pilgrims was Osamequin, Yellow Feather. Because the early writers tended to refer to American Natives as Indians, I will also use that designation since most American Indians have grown accustomed to it and do not consider it pejorative.

In *Beyond 1492: Encounters in Colonial North America* (1992), James Axtell restates Paul Horgan's observation that "we must take the raw material of our searches . . . 'through the crucible fires of our own achieved awareness.' Like poets and novelists, we must . . . imagine what we know."[19] Explaining one teleological system in the language and terms of another is a daunting task. In the absence of incontrovertible facts and in the face of antithetical worldviews, this work will raise questions. There will not always be conjectures or answers that will satisfy all readers, especially those trained in the rationale of Western civilization, but American Indian literary scholars must begin somewhere, and for better or for worse, this is an emergence point. The notion that American Indians influenced American literature requires more explanation than one volume can contain, and to that end more monographs dealing with works of other periods will follow.

Bradford's Indian Book does not call into question any of the earlier critical work that locates the headwaters of the American literary tradition in Europe, particularly Great Britain. Because the works of what Michael Colacurcio calls the Perry Miller paradigm are quite familiar to Americanists, this volume will not restate them.[20] It is to be expected that British immigrants of primarily Christian persuasion, people educated in systems derived from the erudition of prominent thinkers of Western civilization, will write from their inherited cultural perspectives. Even the non-Christian immigrants, the multitudinous "Strangers," write out of much the same Western European context. This volume seeks only to suggest that *in addition to* the very obvious and well-documented European influences working on American literature there are American Indian contributions that should finally be recognized and understood.

My hope is that this work will allow the reader to find in American literature additional insights, awareness, and new awe, unexplored yet sound, ethnologically grounded understandings, and a recognition that American literature is not primarily bifurcated into racial issues of black and white, but is quite red in many ways. I further hope the task of reading this work is lightened by the book's occasional humor. Despite the best efforts of Will Rogers (Cherokee) and Sherman Alexie (Spokane/Coeur d'Alene), American Indians are rarely, if ever, portrayed as humorous people, but we often are. Humor has sustained us over the centuries, and it is a shortcut to insight. As we proceed to the center of American literature, humor will help us preserve the integrity of American Indian intellectual strategies just as it will replicate certain American Indian storytelling techniques in the oral tradition. It goes without saying that a little humor will certainly make Brownist documents livelier. In short, this volume will try to make American Indian thought engaging and accessible to the European American academic community and give that community yet another way of appreciating our national literature and the DᏎBᎾꭲ upon whose literary traditions it rests.

Bradford's Indian Book

PRELUDE

The Beginning They Told

ᏗᎶᎯᏁᎬ ᎤᏂᏃᎮᎵ

Ꭰ *Stories came first. They spun the earth into being and gave it shape. When their work was completed, they disappeared into what they had just created. After the stories were safely hidden, Holy People and animals appeared on the earth's surface and made everything useful and good. Finally humans arrived. Some of them found their way here by tunneling up from the dark narrative worlds below. Others fell to earth's surface from the overcrowded upper stories. That is how narrative, earth, people, and other living creatures became one. The primal stories, which are indistinguishable from the earth they formed, still exist and can be found in sacred rocks, mountains, caves, and trees because such land monuments are their dwelling places.*

The first humans on this land called themselves **ᎠᏂᏴᏫᏯ**, *the Aniyvwiya, or the original People, because they were here before others like them.* **ᎠᏗᎳ** *or* **ᏝᎦᎻᏸ** *(Water Beetle) and* **ᏕᎵ** *(Buzzard) helped them settle in. The* **ᎠᏂᏴᏫᏯ** *later became known as* **ᎠᏂᎦᏬᏯ**, *Chalakees or Cherokees, for the reason that their new neighbors, the* **ᎠᏂᏗᏣᎻ** *or Creeks, could not pronounce* **ᎠᏂᏴᏫᏯ** *easily and, furthermore, had no desire to pronounce it.*

Because the **ᎠᏂᏴᏫᏯ** *are the Original People, they have perfect knowledge.*[1] *They can see beyond mimetic forms. Since their language is first among all human tongues, they speak the truth for they are closest to it. It follows, therefore, that* **ᎠᏂᏴᏫᏯ** *have intellectual authority, and intellectual authority, like Kiowan memory, is in the blood. That is simply the way it is as the old people have repeatedly told it.* Ꭰ

PART THE FIRST

PREPARING
THE GROUND

1   LAND AND MEDICINE
JOUET

Of Plimoth Plantation exhibits certain characteristics of Native healing narratives, the most powerful of all Native genres. These ceremonial texts, designed to effect change, incorporate narrative, song, poetry, dance, and sacred objects in a prescribed form. The chants are composed of many interwoven narrative strands, and each strand is a complete story with a beginning, a middle, and an end. More important, each constituent narrative is essential to the ritual protocol.

The most critical of these strands are narratives featuring ancient tribal gods, hero warriors, plants, animals, tricksters, and the land. All of a chant's several narratives project a kaleidoscopic sense of constant motion intensified by seemingly countless transformations of characters. One life-form instantly melds into another and then another, and all life-forms are imbued with vivid colors. Embedded within these texts are special songs or combinations of powerful words that enable the chant to do its intended work, which is to restore balance and thereby effect change. Humans, if they appear at all, are minor players in the narratives. The colors, numbers, characters, and symbols used to enrich these works are usually tribally specific, while the narratives of landforms, gods, animals, tricksters, heroes, and plants, especially corn and tobacco, are common to most. All significant action takes place at highly specific geographical sites that the hearer must remember and venerate. Of all the narrative strands, the land narrative carries the most interpretative weight.

In addition to particularizing sacred landforms, the land narrative calls up the winds, the directions, and vegetation, all of which are personified and take part in the action. The land is the only trustworthy "character" in a medicine text. Others dissemble, but the land is constant. In American

Indian works, the land narrative never corresponds to the European idea of "setting." In Native works, the land is not a background for the plot; to a large extent it informs the plot.

Properly recited by medicine people, medicine texts do not simply delineate the restoration of order; they bring it about. These chants, usually recited in their entirety, can be performed only for specific purposes by persons who not only have learned them but can correctly interpret and employ them. Various passages, however, can be taken out of context and recounted at certain times of year, but only when the thunder ceases and the snakes are asleep.

Several ancient Navajo ceremonials have been recorded, translated, and transliterated, and various versions of them have been collated and are available to study. *Blessingway,* and to some extent *Emergenceway,* are rites used for home blessings, puberty ceremonies, weddings, protection, and life events not concerned with illness. *Blessingway,* and again to lesser extent *Emergenceway,* contains the metanarrative from which the healing chants such as *Ghostway, Deerway, Beautyway,* the several *Shootingways,* and the *Mountainways* descend. These oral compositions begin with a recitation of a mythic tale, which either contains or alludes to a creation account that is part of the patient's cultural knowns. This core narrative includes references to legendary heroes, corn, animals, the major gods, and land-forms. The principal narrative contextualizes the ritual that accompanies it and effectuates the healing portion of the ceremony. Some rituals may last as long as nine days and require months of preparation.

In its performance, the ritual incorporates the colors, directions, characters, and symbols itemized by the central narrative. The purpose of the contextualizing narrative and accompanying ritual is medicine, which connotes healing, magic, power, and restoration of balance. To understand Native literature one must accept this vital nexus: the "story" generates the ceremony that effectuates the desired change. Just as classical Western tragedies theoretically seek to restore the social order, Native sacred works actually seek to restore cosmic balance.

The traditional Native convention is that these texts either create reality or modify it. They also fully explicate American Indian literary theory.[1] In order for American Indian literary theory to penetrate the Newcomers' minds and modify their literature, the immigrants first had to be initiated and taught to read the Native First Text, the earth. Because the earth is animated by spirits, it can think and act.

The earth began the initiation, or the Indianization, of the English settlers on November 11, 1620, the day the *Mayflower* passengers first set foot in Massachusetts. Because the land is both text and spiritual entity, when the Newcomers invaded this organism, they were metaphorically absorbed into it and transformed. The Newcomers became characters in a narrative extant long before their arrival and, at the same time, they began to take in the narrative techniques of the system that embraced them. Since the settlers of New Plymouth found themselves planted in American Indian literary theory as well as in the New World, it is not surprising that their writing immediately began to show evidence of Native compositional techniques.

Bradford relates that the Newcomers first sighted land, which they took to be Cape Cod, on November 9, 1620. After a two-day search for a suitable port, they dropped anchor in what is now Provincetown Harbor on November 11 and made their first trip ashore to pick up firewood and fresh water. Mourt tells us that the ship's chosen explorers returned to the *Mayflower* laden with "juniper, which smelled very sweet and strong and of which [they] burnt the most part of the time [they] lay there."

Mourt's commentary suggests to the American Indian critic that the Indianization process was under way, since the Newcomers were beginning their venture in America with an Indian-like spiritual cleansing. Juniper is an evergreen that symbolizes eternal life and is often used by American Indians, and present-day Wampanoags, to open ceremonies, purify people and habitats, and lift prayer words to the heavens.[2] William Bradford, soon to become the primary writer of the Plymoutheans, was touched by these Native fumes. In Indian terms, he was "smoked" or purified. Bradford was thus made ready for the ceremonial entrapment that awaited him.

As weather permits during the days that follow, the Newcomers continue to make short trips to the land to explore and to look for a place to settle. The Indianization of William Bradford, which began with the smoking, intensifies on November 17, 1620, with the Newcomers' third foray into the land. Mourt recalls that while still at anchor, the Pilgrims, with the Strangers, commissioned sixteen men to spy out the area and find a suitable place for settlement. The exploration party, led by Miles Standish, was "adjoined, for counsel and advice, [by] William Bradford, Stephen Hopkins, and Edward Tilley." On their first day out, November 15, the explorers spot five or six Indians walking along the beach with a dog. When approached by white men with weapons, the Indians flee and the English track them in hopes of discovering a village. Unsuccessful in this venture, the exploration party makes camp when evening falls, and the men spend their first night away from the ship.

November 16 sees the party continuing the search for a Native town. As they continue tracking the Indians, whose footprints turn into a thicket, the English "soone lost both them & them selves." Even though the search for Indians fails, the English do find a source of good drinking water, cleared fields, and the remains of a house. Further investigation reveals heaps of sand containing caches of corn stored in baskets and several graves filled with human remains and artifacts. At this point, the reticent Bradford narrative remembers that the men returned to the ship, but Mourt recalls another scenario.

With his usual candor, he confesses that by evening they were unable to locate the ship and were forced to spend another night on land. Mourt writes that the morning of November 17 found them still "shrewdly puzzled, and lost," and it is at this point in the exploration of the New World that William Bradford is caught in an Indian net, both literally and metaphorically.

As the Englishmen make their way through a wooded area, Bradford is walking in the rear of the exploration party and happens upon a deer trap that consists of a bowed sapling, a rope, and a scattering of acorns. He steps on a hidden spring, which "gave a sudden jerk up, and he was immediately caught by the leg." Mourt resists the impulse to tell us that Bradford found himself swinging helplessly in the air, but, gentleman that he is, comments instead upon the "pretty device" that snared the Pilgrim father and the artfulness of the rope's construction. Mourt directs our eyes to the trap itself and alludes neither to the physicality of the action that moved Bradford off his feet nor to the metaphorical import of the catching. Mourt writes only that the trap was "made with a rope of their [the Indians'] own making . . . [and that it was] as artificially made as any roper in England can make."

Bradford fails to mention the event. The omission of an occurrence that made the Governor look silly or foolish is characteristic of the man who prided himself on solemnity and dignity. What a critic reading from an American Indian perspective finds important about this incident is that, for one brief moment, Plymouth's Principal Patriarch was at the mercy of an Algonquian mechanism. His normal operations were interrupted, and his perspective was involuntarily changed. The Algonquians had momentarily given Bradford an opportunity to observe the earth from the air, and from this unaccustomed elevation, he could see the juxtaposition of New World ingenuity and colonial naïveté. The Indians had turned his position as counselor and advisor upside down. They had moved his feet to the sky and pointed his head to the earth. In metaphorical terms, the writer of Plymouth's first history was directed to a page of American Indian narrative. American Indian culture was forcing itself into his consciousness and literally redirecting his mind. Bradford, alone of all the others, was touched by an unseen Algonquian hand and imprinted.

Bradford's amused companions considered the trap ingenious, but it is doubtful that he shared their view. Calvinist and believer in Providence that he was, Bradford no doubt saw the incident as some kind of a sign, but what kind of a sign is unclear. For the believer in the works of Providence, there are no random events in the world. Things happen for a reason, and everything is part of a plan. The trap may have reinforced Bradford's earlier expressed fears of Indian barbarity, or it may have engendered notions of Satan at work. Unquestionably, the snare was a representation of very present danger for them all, and the accident was certainly an embarrassment. Bradford had been enjoined to accompany the group in the capacity of an advisor, but instead found himself swinging helplessly in the air above his companions' heads. It is fair to conjecture that he considered the event unsettling. While this event may be considered an accident, an American Indian critic could look at this incident as a singling-out occasion. In Puritan terms, it was a "calling," albeit a Native one.

Even though the Indianization process during the First Exploration was focused upon Bradford, it was not limited to him. As they explored their new surroundings, all the Englishmen put their hands into the source of Eastern Algonquian culture and were touched by the American Indian ontological and teleological systems operating there. Mourt relates that on November 16, again their second day of exploration, the Englishmen found many springs in small valleys that were stocked with "fine vines, and fowl and deer." They also found a great amount of sassafras and "much plain ground, about fifty acres, fit for plow, and some signs where the Indians had formerly planted their corn." Further observation revealed "a little path to certain heaps of sand" that contained the Natives' winter rations.

The Newcomers may have been unaware that Eastern Woodland tribes moved seasonally over vast tracts of land, each set aside for specific purposes. Some seasons and regions were for spring planting, others for fall hunting, while certain other places were good for summer or winter fishing. When the people moved among their seasonal homes, they often left the frames of their wigwams standing. They took the mats that covered them and their most essential household goods, leaving their heavy furniture and much of their harvested corn crop in the area that was their assigned planting ground and alternate home. The Eastern Woodlands people did not live in municipalities that were recognizable to the English as "towns," with paved streets and permanent structures. Eastern Woodlands people did, however, live in villages or camps that were recognizable as settlements of people. For Algonquians, large geographical regions were their "towns," and each family had several home sites scattered over these provinces.

Mourt goes on to write that as the English resumed their exploration on November 16 they came to yet another recently harvested corn field, and there they "found where a house had been, and four or five old planks laid together; also . . . a great kettle which had been . . . brought out of Europe." What the Englishmen probably saw was a temporarily empty house, a plank sleeping platform, and a large iron pot. Nearby was a sand heap containing a cache of maize, which they "digged up," and in it they came across "a little old basket full of fair Indian corn, and . . . a fine great new basket full of very fair corn." Mourt exclaims that they marveled at the basket, which "held about three or four bushels . . . and was very handsomely and cunningly made." Aware that their pillaging was reprehensible and likely to bring reprisal, the Englishmen encircled the site and guarded it while two or three of them dug up the corn. Mourt explains that "we were in suspense what to do with it [the corn] and the kettle, and at length, after much consultation, we concluded to take the kettle and as much of the corn as we could carry away with us; and when our shallop came, if we could find any of the people, and come to parley with them, we would give them the kettle again, and satisfy them for their corn."

Bradford summarizes this incident similarly but attaches a Providential significance to it:

Ther was allso found 2. of their [the Indians'] houses covered with matts, & sundrie of their implements in them, but yᵉ people were rune away & could not be seen; also ther was found more of their corne, & of their beans of various collours. The corne & beans they [the Pilgrims] brought away, purposing to give them full satisfaction when they should meete with any of them (as about some 6. months afterward they did, to their good contente). And here is to be noted a spetiall providence of God, and a great mercie to this poore people, that hear they gott seed to plant them corne yᵉ next year, or els they might have starved, for they had none, nor any liklyhood to get any till yᵉ season had beene past. . . . (100)

What is important to my reading of this passage is that Bradford's account of the corn discovery attributes a sacred or Providential quality to the event. His ability to connect corn with the sacred creates an unintended narrative that puts Bradford tenuously in line with much American Indian thinking that recognizes the hallowed nature of corn. In American Indian societies, corn is a sacramental as well as a food. William Bradford is a quick study.

During this expedition, the Englishmen not only came across homesteads from which they borrowed corn, but they also found grave sites, which they pillaged for funerary artifacts that were intended to serve a purpose in the spirit world. The explorers' acts made winter subsistence more difficult than normal for the living Algonquians, just as the disturbed graves distressed them.

Bradford limits his account of the days between November 11 and November 17, 1620, to three and one-half pages, but Mourt gives that period more space and greater description. He itemizes the contents of the second grave they excavated in some detail and provides a close look at the corpses, which are not yet fully decomposed:

We found a place like a grave, but it was much bigger and longer than any we had yet seen. It was also covered with boards, so . . . we . . . resolved to dig it up, where we found, first a mat, and under that was a fair bow, and there another mat, and under that a board about three quarters [of a yard] long, finely carved and painted, with three tines, or broaches, on the top, like a crown. Also between the mats we found bowls, trays, dishes, and such like trinkets. At length we came to a fair new mat, and under that two bundles, the one bigger, the other less. We opened the greater and found in it a great quantity of fine and perfect red powder, and in it the bones and skull of a man. The skull had fine yellow hair still on it,[3] and some of the flesh unconsumed; there was bound up with it a knife, a packneedle, and two or three old iron things. It was bound up in a sailor's canvas cassock, and a pair of cloth breeches. . . . We opened the less bundle likewise, and found . . . the bones and head of a little child. About the legs and other parts of it was bound strings and bracelets of fine white beads; there was also by it a little bow, about three quarters long, and some other odd knacks. We brought sundry of the prettiest things away with us, and covered the corpse up again. (27–28)

The grave contents reveal much about the Algonquians and their world-view. That items were left in graves, especially the graves of children, bears witness to the fact that the Algonquians loved each other, treasured their children, and prepared for an eternity that resembled their life on earth.

The funerary objects also reveal that these American Indians were quite pragmatic. Depositing the deceased's finest belongings into his grave meant there was no great need for lawyers and probate courts in Native society. American Indians had socioreligious systems that managed estate distribution, and those systems took precedence over civil wrangling. The planks the Algonquians left uncovered at grave sites were grave markers or grave houses and were put there so that spirits could orient themselves to their altered state of being. Fledgling spirits could see the planks, recognize their "new homes," and have a reference point for their travels. The boards further suggest that graves were marked so that they could be revisited. Marking burial sites indicates that Algonquians did not fear properly buried bodies and respected the memories of the departed.

A twenty-first-century rationalist reading the accounts related above— an animal trap, the caches of corn, and the discovery of a house and graves—would not conclude that there was anything esoteric or particularly significant about such findings. Men reconnoitering an inhabited new continent are likely to find burial plots, homes, trapping equipment, and foodstuffs. It is only natural to examine unfamiliar articles, and falling into snares is an occupational hazard for a true discoverer. From an American Indian point of view, however, there was much amiss with Pilgrim activities on November 15, 16, and 17. During the inspection of their new surroundings, the men from the *Mayflower* inadvertently offended their hosts. They stole Algonquian winter food supplies from several separate caches, and they dishonored the Algonquian dead.

Mourt's passage is significant not only because it details the extent of the English grave desecrations and thefts, the acts that contribute to the attack later known as the First Encounter, but also because it symbolically depicts the descent of the explorers into the Indian spirit world. The men from the *Mayflower* touched holy relics and taboo items. They moved into sacred spaces, the dwelling places of the dead—places Indians rarely, if ever, speak about and almost certainly never visit except to place memorial stones. When the English opened these funerary texts, they entered a subterranean American Indian text.

The *Mayflower* explorers encountered an Algonquian ethos and ontological order when they opened Algonquian graves. As Bradford, Winslow, and the others looked into these burial places, they saw skeletons drawn into the fetal position lying on their sides. In *Cautantowwit's House*, William S. Simmons reports that the Algonquians usually buried their dead positioned toward the southwest since that is the direction many Algonquian souls are believed to take in their journey to the spirit world. Algonquian dead were interred in the fetal position because they "considered death a reenactment of birth."[4] Simmons, quoting archaeologist Wendell Hadlock, goes on to explain that the red ochre found with the bodies "may have been intended to resemble 'the blood or placenta which accompanies birth.'"[5] Simmons further notes that anthropological studies of Algonquian social customs indicate that birth rituals and taboos were echoed by similar death rituals and taboos. Postpartum women refrained from sexual intercourse for one year and mourners grieved for the same period of time. Newborns were covered with grease and soot, while mourners blackened their faces. Newborns were not immediately named, just as the names of the dead were rarely spoken, because the proper observation of name taboos at times of birth and death ensured infant health and the immediate departure of spirits.[6]

Customs marking the beginning of life and the end of life with ritual replication indicate that the Algonquians had a well-developed worldview that appreciated parallelism, or proportion, in deed as well as word. They were not savages acting out random, superstitious exercises haphazardly, but were people with ordered customs indicative of discerning conceptualizations of human existence that pointed to a meaningful teleology.

In Algonquian metaphysics, even objects have souls,[7] so when the Plymoutheans handled the bones and funerary objects of the Wampanoags, they established, at least tenuously, contact with the spirit world of the Algonquians, and in a Native worldview, the spirit world informs the physical.[8] Plymoutheans touched Algonquians in the earth, the mother text, the place where life and death converge, and they later transferred that touch to their friends, wives, children, possessions, writings, and daily rituals. Metaphorically, they had put their hands on Algonquian souls. Figuratively, they had come into contact with Algonquian spiritual understanding and wisdom. Perhaps this encounter was as significant as any other in terms of American letters. The Newcomers had gone to the source of Algonquian religious and literary life, the earth and its people. The Algonquian people and the earth would continue instructing the Newcomers for years.

ꞪꝄ

ꞪꝄRꝄꝊꝎ

The earth, of course, was not the only agent of Indianization transforming the Newcomers. Medicine people, or DhꝄꝅꝎꝄꝊꝄꝅꝘ, were another major force compelling them to mutate. Passaconaway, ꞪꝄRꝄꝊꝎ, was one such medicine person. Bradford tells us that before the Indians "came to yᵉ English to make freindship, they gott all the *Powachs* of yᵉ cuntrie, for 3. days togeather, in a horid and divellish maner to curse & execrate them with their cunjurations, which asembly & service they held in a darke & dismale swampe."

Passaconaway, a Penacook medicine man, was one of the "Powachs" taking part in this action. When he became aware that his country had been invaded by a small group of foreigners, he and his colleagues made an effort to drive them out. To precipitate their flight, he used his most powerful weapon: medicine. The most renowned of all the Eastern Algonquian medicine men, this ꝅꝎꝄꝊꝄꝅꝘ could "make the water burn, the rocks move, the trees dance, [and] metamorphise himself into a flaming man. . . . In winter, when there is no green leaves to be got, he will burn an old one to ashes, and putting those into the water produce a new green leaf which you shall not only see but substantially handle and carry away, and make of a dead snake's skin a living snake."[9]

ꞪꝄ

In *Return to Creation* (1991), Manitonquat, a present-day Assonet Wampanoag Lore Keeper, relates that the Penacook medicine man saw the European invasion as an occasion for "great trouble for [Indian] people and for the earth. So he went through a series of ceremonies to banish the whites from these shores. When at last none of his rituals [effected] the removal of the offensive intruders, Passaconaway decided that Creator intended for them to come here to be taught the ways of Creation."[10]

Teaching Europeans the "ways of Creation," or, in other words, instructing Europeans in American Indian thought and behavior, has been a long, subtle, and continuous process that has created distinct features in the political systems, food choices, lifestyles, and literatures that evolved in the Americas. This Indianization began at Contact, took hold, and has had several interesting outcomes, two of which are the presence of Native texts embedded in European American canonical works and traces of American Indian literary poetics in the national literature.

In their several histories, both Bradford and Mourt recount an unmistakable example of American Indian influence at work in Plymouth Colony when they relate events surrounding the disappearance of a little boy who once strayed from the settlement. In late July or early August 1621, young John Billington "lost him selfe in yᵉ woods, & wandered up & downe some 5. days, living on beries & what he could find."[11] Finally he came to Manamet, a village twenty miles south of Plymouth. The people of Manamet took John to Nauset for the probable reason that the Nausets had been enraged in 1614 when some Englishmen captured seven Nauset males and sold them into slavery; furthermore, it was the Nausets' corn the Plymoutheans had stolen in November 1620, when they made their initial exploration. In an American Indian view, the Nausets deserved compensation. Delivering John to them would partially satisfy Algonquian requirements for justice since he could symbolically replace the lost seven or partially make up for the stolen corn.

For historical and cultural accuracy it should be pointed out, however, that the naïve Manamets did not realize that young John Billington, scion of one of Plymouth's most dysfunctional families, was what we might term a "problem child" and was not exactly the symbolic catch they thought they had. With characteristic good nature nonetheless, the Manamets persevered with what Fate had sent them and attempted to even the socio-political score. Bradford, perhaps seeing that this was a good time to test the articles of a nonaggression pact signed earlier with the Massasoit, sent word to Sowams that the boy was missing. "At length Massassoyt sent word wher he was, and yᵉ Gover sent a shalop for him, & had him delivered."

Mourt, too, relates John's rescue, but he remembers several details that Bradford neglects. The omission is understandable since it was Mourt, Tisquantum, and another Algonquian resident of Plymouth, Tokamahamon, who went to collect the boy. Mourt writes that the rescue party stopped for the first night near the village of Cummaquid. The following morning, the Plymoutheans met a company of Cummaquidean women catching lobsters. The women took them to their sachem, Iyanough (Innemo or Janemo), who was "very personable, gentle, courteous, and fair conditioned. . . . [and] his entertainment was answerable to his parts." After providing the travelers the midday meal, Iyanough led the Plymoutheans to Nauset. After a preliminary conference with Tisquantum, who had been sent ahead to explain to Aspinet, the Nauset sachem, the reasons for the Plymouthean visit, Aspinet came to the place where the Pilgrims were waiting "with a great train, and brought the boy with him, one bearing him through the water." Mourt continues that "there he delivered us the boy, *behung with beads,* and made peace with us" (emphasis mine).

Mourt's diegetic text reports that when Aspinet returned John, he brought a hundred warriors with him. *Mourt's Relation* thus presents us with several questions. Why does a principal chief take a hundred warriors to convey one small boy to a peaceful rescue party? Why is John decorated with beads when he is reinstated with his fellows?

The fact that John was returned wearing beads is evidence that the Nausets were attempting to Indianize him. By prolonging John's stay with them, and by putting the beads around his neck, the Nausets were creating an opportunity to make a lasting impression upon John, and they were altering his clothing in order to make him look like them. Changing a captive's appearance was generally one of the first actions an adoptive tribe took.[12] Although John was not actually a candidate for adoption, his having been beaded is, among other things, evidence of the Native predisposition to Indianize outsiders who came among them.

On the trip back to Plymouth, Mourt describes Native "women joined hand in hand, singing and dancing before the shallop, the men also showing all the kindness they could, [and] Iyanough himself taking a bracelet from about his neck and hanging it upon one of [them]." The dancing and singing suggest that some kind of adoption or friendship ritual is taking place. Iyanough's presentation of a bracelet was an offering that could well have had American Indian contractual and literary significance if the bracelet were made of wampum. Even though we do not know the bracelet's composition, that it was given not to John but to an older, more responsible person suggests that the bracelet was an official record of a transaction, not a simple gift.

The rescue party sent to retrieve John consisted of a shallop of men, or approximately ten or twelve persons. Even if Aspinet had feared an attack, he hardly needed one hundred men to confront twelve. Could Aspinet have been using his one hundred warriors to make a statement? If he were using this occasion "to speak" to the Plymoutheans, he may have been saying, *There are more of us than there are of you. We are strong, well ordered, and impressively arrayed. You are few, plainly dressed, and a little ragtag. Join us and learn our ways. At present you are frightened by every moving shadow. Your children are easily disoriented and lose themselves in the forest. Give us a chance, and we will teach you useful things. With the proper instruction, you and your children can be appropriately garbed, strong, prosperous, and at ease with your new environment. It is time you learned to fit in.*

The gracious people at Cummaquid had just served the Newcomers a lobster dinner to which the Plymoutheans had neglected to bring champagne; the Nausets had preserved young John and returned him more attractively clothed than when they found him, yet the Plymoutheans, who by this time had been in the area for well over a year, still seemed not to understand that the Algonquians were offering to bring them into another, and possibly better, way of life.

What is significant about this passage from my standpoint is that the Billington narrative, one of the several captivity narratives contained in the Bradford history, indicates clearly that the newly beaded, partially Indianized John has become a body of European literature marked by Algonquians. More important, he has become a new American text, a text with an American Indian narrative. He has been "sung" over. New words and novel experiences have been given to him. He now has an Indian story to tell, and he can create new metaphors in an evolving English-American language.[13] John's captivity, his modification, his new narrative powers, and his release constitute an American Indian literary transaction even though the Plymoutheans probably did not understand it as such. Additionally, John's sojourn with the Algonquians was placed into Native legal history and into memory. The American Indian changes wrought upon John had been officially recorded by the mnemonic beads and the bracelet. John, the young American, had become a legal written document filed in an Algonquian courthouse.[14] What is significant for American letters is that a copy of the transaction was sent to Plymouth and recorded in the Governor's history.

Passaconaway's initial efforts to deal with the Colonists centered on the repetition of weighty formulaic codes that had been transmitted by means of the American Indian oral tradition for centuries. These codes had been devised to effect change. The codes probably did not work as quickly as Passaconaway had intended; neither did they effectuate the precise outcome he visualized. The codes' apparent "failure," however, initiated a change in approach and anticipated outcomes. These sacred formulae, together with their accompanying rituals, did engender a process of Indianization that eventually bore fruit. The Colonists stayed, but they were very much changed, and so was their writing.

In a manner of speaking, Passaconaway succeeded. His ritual words set into motion a chain of literary and non-literary events that quietly prevailed. His actions open Bradford's second book and his name closes it, or very nearly closes it. Bradford's Passaconaway narrative echoes book 1's Puritan theme, the travail of the Saints against the sons of hell, just as it prefigures one of the principal metaphors unifying the action in book 2, the tension between American Indians and the Colonists. ⍵⍺Ɽ⍥ɵ℧.

2 THE EARTH AS NARRATIVE SOURCE

The most important stratum of narrative in a medicine text is its land narrative, which, among other things, sets spatial boundaries and prescribes the work's major themes. *Of Plimoth Plantation* has a land narrative that assumes ritual form and demonstrates spatial and thematic content similar in essence to Native medicine texts. Bradford's land narrative establishes an über objective correlative by which the text's other constituent narratives can be read. Here elements of terrain, geographical formations, bodies of water, rocks, winds, storms, and precipitation fashion a minor narrative that runs parallel to the principal account.

Medicine texts include land narratives because the creative essence empowering a medicine text resides in the earth and transfers its sovereignty to the spoken word when evoked. Something like a sacred chant's power supply, this essence directs, shapes, and contains the narrative flow. As the interpretative center of the work, the land narrative reflects the truth of the story. Characters lie. Narrators are forgetful and sometimes suspect. The land is constant and is the most reliable of all narrators. For example, Paula Gunn Allen's novel, *The Woman Who Owned the Shadows* (1983), contains a pronounced land narrative that moves the action in and out of sacred space and time, replicates the psyche of the protagonist, and thematically underlines the plot. In this novel, notable features of landscape operate as characters with which the protagonist interacts; furthermore, the Laguna novelist directs her protagonist's steps in conformity with the sun's movements across the earth's quadrants. Ephanie's life moves in a ritual way beginning in the east, completing a full circle, then transforming ultimately in the west, the Laguna place of death.

Many traditional American Indians believe that the essence of a particular spirit either is embedded in a certain landform or is somehow intimately connected to a certain feature of the landscape such as a mountain, a river, or a rock formation. Because American Indian holy spirits, such as the Algonquian Glooskap, or the Navajo's Ever Changing Woman, or the Cherokee's spirit people, the ᏄᏁᎯ, are associated with specific locations, the places where pivotal events take place in American Indian narratives are always crucial to the interpretation of a text. In American Indian epistemology the earth is First Text, and the study of its features constitutes textual exegesis.

Susan Scarberry-Garcia's explanation for embedded spiritual essences can be found in *Landmarks of Healing: A Study of House Made of Dawn* (1990). Although Scarberry-Garcia delineates Navajo conceptualizations, the principles she puts forward apply to other American Indian Nations as well:

> Story emerges from the land. For the Navajos, each landform contains an inner form. This concept of inner forms is very specific and originates at the time of the creation of the world. . . . The inner forms. . . . possess the 'power of life and movement,' shape the character of the outer forms, . . . and bring strength. Although the inner and outer forms of plants, animals, and mountains are inseparable, the inner forms or spirit essences remain the same, while the outer forms may change or transform.[1]

Eastern Algonquians, like many other Native people, have landforms that call up primordial events and historical figures. After the Massasoit Osamequin died, it is said that "there appeared in the forest of the Assonets a rock formation . . . much in the image of the great Sachem."[2] Many of the original place names of Massachusetts are Algonquian words that indicate the importance of rocks or rock formations to the Natives. For instance, Assonet means "at the place of stones"; Assawompsett is "place of the white stones."[3] That these particular stone groupings are named suggests that rock formations had some cultural significance to the early Algonquian residents.

Charles Leland's work with Wabanakis suggests that at least some Algonquians held to the belief in inner forms: "Over all the Land of the Wabanaki there is no place which was not marked by the hand of the Master [Glooskap]. And it is to be seen on hills and rivers and great roads, as well

as mighty rocks, which were in their day living monsters."[4] Further sub-
stantiating the hypothesis that Algonquians accepted the notion of inner
forms is this observation from Evan T. Pritchard (Micmac):

> Each thing we encounter on our journey is either the embodiment of
> one spirit or soul, *otchitchahaumitch(oh)*, such as a person or moose or
> beaver, or it is imbued with a greater spirit or soul which can also be
> embodied elsewhere. A single blade of . . . sweetgrass, *umptseegooabee*,
> puts you in touch with the spirit of sweetgrass everywhere. [5]

Bradford's land narrative, powered by inner forms, serves as the core
narrative for his history. *Of Plimoth Plantation* is a palimpsest in the sense
that it has several layers of narrative strata, none of which has been completely erased. Traces of the land narrative surface momentarily then recede only to emerge again, often transformed but always recognizable.
Before *Of Plimoth Plantation* terminates, the land narrative is reconfigured
into a narrative of Native people just as the stone in Massachusetts is re-
cast as a representation of the Massasoit in order to leave a long-lasting
record of his being. This transformative process has a dual function in
Bradford's text. It forges a nexus of land and people for Natives and for
non-Natives alike. As the land narrative merges with Algonquian history,
it begins to assume the properties of the Pilgrim story, which, to complete
the circle, replicates the Native narrative in major outline. The Plymouth
landscape, the Newcomers, and the Old Patuxets mirror each other. *Of
Plimoth Plantation* is unique in European American letters. It is at once
a place and text; fully Indian and fully Plymouthean. It is a ceremony of
conjoined narratives.

Of Plimoth Plantation's land narrative is pronounced. It opens the work,
and it does so in American Indian ceremonial fashion with a metaphorical
mention of the seven cardinal directions beginning with the east. Ritually, Wampanoags move "clockwise to thank the good spirits and counterclockwise to pay respect to the evil spirits."[6] Bradford moves his text
counterclockwise in an effort to keep evil spirits, or perhaps calumnious
misrepresentations, away from his name, his life's work, his sacred vision,
and his inscription of that vision. This counterclockwise movement also
indicates that the work is meant to be a power text, or a very significant
narrative, because it replicates the movement and energy of tornadoes or
hurricanes north of the equator. These storms are two of the strongest
forces of nature; therefore, rituals that move counterclockwise duplicate

this energy.[7] The major directional thrust of Bradford's work moves from east to north then west to south to center in keeping with a counterclockwise movement. *Of Plimoth Plantation's* opening sentence in Chapter One orients us to the land and direction:

> It is well knowne unto y[e] godly and judicious, how ever since y[e] *first breaking out of y[e] lighte* of y[e] *gospell* in our Honourable Nation of *England*, (which was y[e] first of nations whom y[e] Lord adorned ther with, affter y[t] *grosse darknes of popery* which had covered & overspred y[e] Christian *worled*,) what warrs & opposissions ever since, Satan hath raised, maintained, and continued against the Sainicts, *from time to time*, in one sorte or other. (3, emphasis mine)

Metaphorical references to sun/son rise and mention of the Gospel indicate that this sacred narrative begins with an orientation toward the east (sunrise) and the eastern part of the earth, i.e. the Middle East, the originating place of the Gospel. Reference to the "grosse darknes of popery" emblematically moves the narrative west toward "darknes" or blackness. Transitioning the narrative from the Middle East to England through Rome puts the text on an east-west course via the north. Invoking the "worled" incorporates the European four cardinal directions while mention of "Lord" and "Satan" emblematically moves the narrative up and down in a Christian sense. Center is the location, either actual or metaphorical, of the speaker or writer. The use of phrases like "ever" and "from time to time" gives the passage a sense of movement from prehistory into recorded time. This portion of text creates a genesis. Thus, in one sentence using Christian events connected to European reference points, Bradford sets his land narrative on its unchanging directional course of east, north, west, south, up, down, and center, the seven American Indian cardinal directions. This pattern will be observed in both books of his history.

Plymouth can be designated center since this is the location of the writer for most of the time covered in the narrative. Bradford's history begins in the east with his description of affairs in Holland and England. When he finishes the information relative to the Pilgrims' sea journey to the New World and the organization of the Colony, Bradford directs our attention to the American north. As Bradford moves his narrative north, he relates the history of Weston's men at Wessagusset, the incident at Mare Mount with Thomas Morton, the establishment of a trading post at Kennebeck, and the arrival of a patent for this outpost. The American part of the history stays on its northerly course through the recitation of the various salt production attempts and the establishment of a church at Salem.

The narrative turns west with Bradford's account of Roger Williams and events in Rhode Island. It continues west through the relation of the establishment of the Windsor trading post in the Narragansett territory and with the epidemic there that killed many of the Natives. Bradford moves his chronicle south with his recollection of the events leading to what Francis Jennings calls the First Puritan Conquest, usually referred to as the Pequot War. Bradford describes the massacre at Mystic and documents the execution of Sassacus. With the election of Thomas Prence as Plymouth's governor in 1638, the narrative returns to east and center.

When participating in rituals, American Indians often use colors to designate the four directions.[8] It is interesting to see that the colors implied in Bradford's opening passage closely correspond to Wampanoag color symbols. In Wampanoag ritual, east is designated by white for the "blanching" light of daybreak; north by black, the place of cold and eternal sleep. West is represented by red, the long road of life; and south by yellow, emblematic of serenity and warmth.[9] If we use possible Christian emblematic meaning to read Bradford's color symbols, we could understand white as his representation of the Gospel's purity; yellow to stand for daybreak, black to denote Satan's evil; and cardinal red to signify popery. We can perhaps see a replication in Bradford's passage of the Wampanoag ritual colors—although not necessarily in their prescribed order.

Of Plimoth Plantation's land narrative, begun in the opening lines by orienting the reader first to geographical direction both visually and metaphorically, is embellished with frequent references to the ocean storms and stills, the winds, the temperature, and the frequent changes in weather during the ocean voyage:

> After they had injoyed faire winds and weather for a season, they were incountred many times with crosse winds, and mette with many feirce stormes, with which ye shipe was shroudly shaken.... In sundrie of these stormes the winds were so feirce, & ye seas so high, as they could not beare a knote of saile, but were forced to hull, for diverce days together. (91–92)

After anchoring first in Provincetown Harbor and later touching ground at Patuxet, the land narrative announces itself more prominently in a ritual-like passage. Like traditional Indians, the Pilgrims mark their setting foot on terra firma with a ceremony:

> Being thus arived in a good harbor and brought safe to *land*, they fell upon their knees & blessed yᵉ God of heaven, who had brought them over yᵉ vast & furious ocean, and delivered them from all yᵉ periles & miseries thereof, againe to set their feete on yᵉ firme and stable *earth*, their proper elemente. (94, emphasis mine)

This passage is ceremonial in tone. Bradford's word usage gives the reader a sense of ritual directional movement. The narrative setting moves from east to west following a northerly course. Pilgrims fall to their knees and rise to their feet like the rise and fall of ocean tides. Directing our attention to heaven and earth, the selection creates a metaphorical up and down motion that duplicates the tides, the rise and fall of people, and the motion of the heavenly bodies.

The passage quoted above is written in prose, but like English epic poetry it employs iambs counterweighted with spondees to give dignity and solemnity to its measures. The passage's verbal ritual movements, stately rhythm, and majestic tone combine to give the impression that this is a work to take seriously. The selection's poetic presentation indicates to an American Indian reader that a sacred story is in progress. The textual movement, which brings people, earth, and heaven together in one swirling entity, eventually comes to rest upon the earth—humanity's proper element—and center. Bradford's narrative progresses from the more common use of the word *land* as in **S V .Ꝺ** to the more poetic *earth*, **R Ꮹ.Ꝺ**, when he associates it with people and designates it "their proper element."

From an American Indian perspective, connecting people with land is important. Many American Indians associate themselves closely with the earth. For instance, the name *Oklahoma* is two Choctaw words joined together and usually translated as *home of the red man*. According to Betty Jacob, Choctaw Native speaker of Broken Bow, Oklahoma, *Okla* means "people" and *homa* means "red." It is not necessary to add a word to the agglutinate meaning "land" because "Choctaws feel that wherever they set foot makes them part of land beneath them."[10] The connection between people and earth is emotional and verbal as well as physical.

Bradford's land narrative becomes more obvious in the ninth chapter of his history. Stronger and more powerful than in its earlier metaphorical presentation, the later land narrative sets up a paradox that continues throughout the history. The land is a desolate wilderness, but at the same time it is a welcoming refuge. Similarly, the pattern is repeated with the land's original inhabitants. The Natives are "savage barbarians," yet they save the Newcomers from starvation. The savages eventually become "speciall instrument[s] sent of God." Throughout the history the reader will notice a continuation of this particular contradiction.

In Bradford's chapter 10, the land takes control of much of the action. Here the land begins to initiate and instruct the Newcomers in the ways of America. "Foule weather" and a shallop in disrepair prompt the Newcomers to make their foray into the new land on foot. Afraid but "resolute," they begin their exploration November 15. After going about a mile by "ye sea side, they espied 5. or 6. persons with a dogg coming towards them." The Natives, however, flee. They run into the woods, and the English give chase. Desiring to speak to the Natives and to find out if more are "lying in ambush," the Pilgrims race after them. Perceiving that they are being pursued, the Indians "forsooke the woods, & rane away on ye sands." The English follow, but the Indians evade them.

This cross-country pursuit is punctuated by frequent allusions to the sands and the woods, thickets, ponds, and creeks. Bradford carefully details the natural characteristics of the area. In this section of the history he personifies the land and its features as he describes both its benevolent and its hostile aspects:

> The next morning [they] followed their tracte till they had headed a great creake, & so left the sands, & turned an other way into ye woods. But they still followed them by geuss, hoping to find their dwellings; but they soone lost both them & them selves, falling in shuch thickets as were ready to tear their cloaths & armore in peeces, but were most distresed for wante of drinke. But at length they found water & refreshed them selves, being ye first New-England water they drunke of, and was now in thir great thirste as pleasante unto them as wine or bear had been in for-times. (98–99)

Although the trees tear at their clothes, the land offers the thirsty travelers refreshing waters. They are at once attacked and refreshed.

After the travelers cross a "necke" of land, they arrive at the seaside, where they find a "pond of clear fresh water, and shortly after a good quantitie of clear ground wher yᵉ Indeans had formerly set corne, and some of their graves." It appears by this passage that the land is becoming less frightening. It offers even more water and shows signs of human habitation. The pond, the cleared fields, and the graves indicate that the land is not a wilderness but an inhabited area. Here the New World is somewhat welcoming:

> And proceeding furder they saw new-stuble wher corne had been set yᵉ same year, also they found wher latly a house had been, wher some planks and a great ketle was remaining, and heaps of sand newly padled with their hands, which they, digging up, found in them diverce faire Indean baskets filled with corne, and some in eares, faire and good, of diverce collours, which seemed to them a very goodly sight. (99)

This passage reveals much about the Native civilization. The pond gives testimony to American Indian water conservation practices and land management. American Natives were acquainted with the principles of hydraulic engineering and frequently built dams, weirs, ponds, and irrigation systems. They built earthworks in order to preserve swamps and wetlands for places of refuge. They maintained fields for wildlife fodder and for fiber crops. By skillful engineering, the Natives were even able to build islands within the swamps for places of sanctuary in time of war.[11]

Algonquians in southern New England regularly practiced forest management by ritual burning, a practice that "not only caused a measurable change in global climate over the last 40,000 years but also played a significant ... role in accelerating the warming during the last glacial retreat."[12] Indians burned the forests to clear out the hunting areas, kill venomous snakes, balance the soil, and purify the water that ran over the burn. Burning also controlled forest and brush fires. In fact, "while Europeans talked about the weather, the rituals that related Indians to their environment enabled them to alter the weather [and environment] in their favor."[13] Bradford's land narrative provides information pertinent to a modern understanding of the New World the Newcomers had entered.

New England was not the isolated wasteland that has often been described. The kettle that the land revealed to the Pilgrims is evidence of established trade routes that extended from the Algonquians to the Iroquois, who were, in turn, trading with French explorers and trappers and subsequently bringing merchandise back to the Algonquians. It speaks to the fact that Natives traveled and had contact with other people, both Native and non-Native. That the fields contained "new-stuble" is testimony that the area was not abandoned, but in fact inhabited and "manured." *Mourt's Relation* confirms that assertion and fills in other interesting details about that section of Massachusetts the Newcomers were exploring. In describing this area, Mourt writes they descended into a valley and "found much plain ground, about fifty acres, fit for the plow, and some signs where Indians had formerly planted their corn. . . . We went on further and found new stubble . . . and many walnut trees full of nuts, and [a] great store of strawberries, and some vines."

This region is more welcoming than other sites the Colonists had visited previously, and Bradford's pages reiterate the land's capabilities for succor and protection:

> This was near yᵉ place of that supposed river they came to seeck; unto which they wente and found it to open it *selfe* into 2. *armes* with a *high cliffe of sand* in yᵉ enterance . . . [and] ther was good harborige for their shalope. . . . So their time . . . being expired, they returned to yᵉ ship, . . . and so like yᵉ men from Eshcoll carried with them of yᵉ fruits of yᵉ land, & showed their breethren; of which, & their returne, they were marvelusly glad, and their harts incouraged. (99–100, emphasis mine)

In this passage, the land displays human qualities. The river has arms and a soft breast of sand. It produces walnut trees and strawberries, plants the Pilgrims find familiar. It also offers a hoard of seed corn, unfamiliar but nourishing and interesting nonetheless. The corn has "diverce collours" and its "eares" are "faire and good."

As the tenth chapter continues, Bradford relates more Providential gifts from the earth and Native people. Continued exploration reveals additional houses, implements, corn, and beans, all evidence of occupied living quarters and salvific "gifts" from Algonquians. At this point in their explorations, the Colonists have picked up two of the three essential American Indian agricultural products—corn, beans, and squash—usually referred to as the Three Sisters. In most Native societies, corn in some form, either corn pollen or corn meal, is a sacramental. Some tribes, like the Cherokees, have a corn deity, 4M, and their principal festival is the Green Corn

Dance. Similarly, the high holiday of the Mvskogee Creeks is the Green Corn Busk or *boosketah*. The Iroquois have a Corn Husk Mask society that concerns itself with planting and healing. Joseph Nicolar, Penobscot elder writing in the nineteenth century, records a story in which a sacred woman's body becomes corn and tobacco.[14] The Wampanoags also have a corn mother, and they hold dances for the Three Sisters.[15] We can safely conclude that Eastern Algonquians were Nations that also venerated corn.

Corn is used in many Native ceremonies in a way that is similar to the use of incense or holy water in the Roman Catholic tradition. Although the Pilgrims are picking up what they presume is only a Native food, they are actually handling ritual goods that they will later ingest. The sacred corn will be the Plymoutheans' dietary and economic mainstay for the next several years, and it is noteworthy that they immediately transfer this American Indian sacramental to the realm of "spetiall providence." Their assigning divine significance to American Indian holy grains suggests that they are learning the earth's lessons, albeit unknowingly. In this instance again, the Pilgrims are quick studies. By the second trip off the *Mayflower,* they are sipping Native holy water and dipping into the Indians' Eucharist basket. Their lives in the New World are beginning in an American Indian ceremonial way.

The Newcomers, furthermore, are discovering that the Algonquians are knowledgeable agriculturists, fishermen, and woodsmen who order their lives, to some extent, around food production operations. They move from vegetable gardens to fishing areas to hunting grounds on a seasonal sched-ule. Laurie Weinstein-Farson, in *The Wampanoag* (1989), reports that the Wampanoags had been farming since 1060. Their principal crops were corn, several varieties of squash, beans, pumpkins, Jerusalem artichokes, and tobacco.[16] Women cultivated all the crops except tobacco, which was grown by men.[17] Bradford's land narrative, together with *Mourt's Relation*, confirms the fact that the Newcomers did find seasonal dwellings, crops, and signs of agricultural and land management during their initial explora-tions, and this information registers with the 1620 settlers in a significant way. The Plymoutheans never reached the conclusion that Massachusetts was the "Lord's Wast" as John Winthrop reiterated in a letter to Bradford written in 1635. When they needed land, they always "bought" it in some fashion because they recognized and respected the Native "ownership."[18]

Bradford's history reveals that the land continued to offer instruction in the customs of its inhabitants and in basic survival. On December 6, the

Newcomers venture out again. "The weather was very could, & it frose so hard as y⁵ sprea of y⁵ sea lighting on their coats, they were as if they had been glased." Here it seems as if the New World, which Bradford personifies in his text, again takes a hand in the Pilgrims' introduction to the land and to the traditions of the Native inhabitants. The baptismal conceit in the passage above models actual parturition rituals observed by the Reverend Mr. Samuel Kirkland, a Protestant missionary to the Oneidas. "After their children are born, and if they are males, although the weather be ever so cold and freezing, they [the mothers] immerse them some time in the water, which, they say, makes them strong brave men and hardy hunters."[19]

Immediately following their American Indian baptism, the Colonists are started on a course of survival training. That evening they see "some 10. or 12. Indeans very busie aboute some thing." The next morning, the English proceed to the site of the activity and find that the Natives "had been cuting up a great fish like a grampus, being some 2. inches thike of fate like a hogg." Further exploration reveals that more of these fish have washed up and are available for food. Since it will be nearly a year before crops can be planted and harvested, that food source, unappetizing as it sounds, could possibly be the difference between life and death. Here the land teaches the explorers a basic subsistence lesson, one that the Plymoutheans put to good use three years later when the starving Colonists find that they must rely totally upon the sea:

> They were in a very low condition, many were ragged in aparell, & some litle beter then halfe naked; though some yᵗ were well stord before, were well enough in this regard. But for food they were all alike, save some yᵗ had got a few pease of yᵉ ship yᵗ was last hear. The best dish they could presente their freinds with was a lobster, or a peece of fish, without bread or any thing els but a cupp of fair spring water. (175)

As Bradford recounts the Colonists' explorations, he conflates references to the Natives and to the new land. As he does this, he emphasizes the welcoming yet hostile aspects of each. For example, he writes that "they ranged up and doune all yᵗ day, but found no people, nor any place they liked." The next morning, December 8, they are attacked by Indians, and though they repulse the attack and none of their party is injured, they are shaken by the event. The weather seems to replicate the human attack by following suit. Later that day, "after some houres sailing, it begane to snow

& raine, & about ye midle of ye afternoone, ye wind increased, and ye sea became very rough."

In these rough seas, the shallop breaks her rudder and later her mast. When the explorers are finally able to regain control of the shallop and strike for the harbor, they find that their "pillott was deceived in ye place" and they are again lost and in treacherous waters. Thanks to the efforts of a brave seaman who steers and exhorts them to row "lustly," they are able to land safely. "And though it was *very darke*, and rained sore, yet in ye end they gott under ye lee of a smalle iland, and remained ther all y^t night in saftie." Despite blowing wind and the hard freeze, "God gave them a *morning* of comforte & refreshing . . . for ye next day was a faire sunshinig day, and they found them sellvs to be on a iland secure from ye Indeans."

Because the next day is Sunday, the Pilgrims observe the Sabbath. Further exploration on Monday reveals a good harbor on the mainland leading to a spot with "diverse cornfeilds, & litle runing brooks, a place . . . fitt for situation."

> On ye 15. *of Desem*^{r}: they wayed anchor to goe to ye place they had discovered, & came within 2. leagues of it, but were faine to bear up againe; but ye 16. *day* ye winde came faire, and they arrived safe in this harbor. And after wards tooke better view of ye place, and resolved wher to pitch their dwelling. (107)

On December 25, the Colonists begin building their common house. Although the land is cold and seemingly inhospitable, it nevertheless offers the Newcomers asylum and sustenance.

Plymouth's settling in is "hard & difficulte." In the first three months "halfe of their company dyed, espetialy in Jan: & February, being ye depth of winter." The Natives do not visit, and the Plymoutheans remain in isolation like dormant seed, but with the coming of spring and the Indians, conditions improve. Osamequin signs a nonaggression pact with Plymouth, and Tisquantum teaches the Pilgrims how to live off the land.

Because Tisquantum teaches them a variety of fishing techniques, the Plymoutheans are able to harvest shellfish and eels, which at low tide they dig out of the beaches. In addition to shellfish and eels, the Newcomers learn to catch bass and cod. Because the English seeds they brought with them do not germinate, they learn to eat groundnuts as the Natives do. Necessity improves their hunting skills, and eventually they are able to kill water "foule" and "dear," which they divide amongst themselves. To maintain them further, "ther was a great store of wild Turkies, of which they tooke many, besids venison, &c."

Natives and the land continue to sustain the Plymoutheans for the duration of the Colony's existence. Even though they have signed a non-aggression treaty with the Massasoit that requires each to come to the other's aid in case of enemy attack, Osamequin is never obliged to defend Plymouth. In fact, many of the other Native leaders also sign nonaggression pacts with them. Even the recalcitrant Corbitant capitulates. "They had many gratulations from diverce sachims, and much firmer peace; yea, those of yᵉ Iles of Capawack sent to make frendship; and . . . Corbitant." The peace agreement with Corbitant is a substantial gain since Corbitant was "never any good freind to yᵉ English to this day." When the 1623 harvest comes, instead of famine, the land gives them "plentie." Now it seems that Native people and geographical attributes have united to accommodate the Plymoutheans. No American Indians have attacked the Colony since its inception, and the land has given them succor. The Native text has admitted the Newcomers to its pages peacefully and copiously.

As the land narrative continues, the reader learns that, by 1623, Bradford is convinced that the "common course" is not working. The Plymouthean experiment with communal ownership of property and shared land use is not serving the Colony's immediate needs, so, in an effort to increase productivity, land is parceled out to individual owners so that "they should set corne every man for his owne perticuler." This first division of the land sets a precedent for many further divisions. Because the 1623 setting corn for their "perticuler" turns out to be successful, in 1624 the land is once again divided into individual, one-acre plots that will be the owner's to keep in continuance, not apportioned by yearly lot as had been done previously. As the land is severed into parcels, the people separate. Plymouthean and Algonquian communities alike are set adrift when they "sell" and "purchase" the land; conversely, as they share land, or sacred space, their texts merge. One of the results of the Plymoutheans' buying into the American Indian basal reader is that these purchases caused complications in Native texts. As the American Indians left their land to move to other places, they abandoned their original texts and much was forgotten.

By 1627, Plymouth Colony begins to acquire small amounts of land outside her immediate environs for the establishment of a trading post and small settlement on the Kennebec River. In 1630, another trading company with a contingent settlement is established at Penobscot. Matianuck on the Connecticut River is the site of one more trading post, Windsor house, constructed in 1633. The Colony purchases these lands from the Algonquians at a "fair price," but with these acquisitions comes a mixed blessing. The trading posts enable Plymouth to pay her debts to the Adventurers, but they also bring the Colony trouble with other settlers, particularly with the French, the Dutch, and Massachusetts Bay. Events concerning affairs at these trading companies are the generating points for much of Bradford's text, but the Plymouthean greed for more pasturage and farmland results in the scattering of the Colony. The land, which initiates much of the plot for *Of Plimoth Plantation*, seems to give with one hand and to take away with the other.

Bradford's land narrative, which eventually transforms into a narrative of people, concludes with several momentous upheavals—swarms of insects, a hurricane, an eclipse of the moon, and an earthquake. Each natural cataclysm presages momentous events both for Native people and for Plymoutheans who are by now, like the Indians, locals. In the spring of 1633

> ther was . . . a quantitie of a great sorte of flies, like (for bignes) to wasps, or bumble-bees, which came out of holes in y⁰ ground, and replenished all y⁰ woods, and eate y⁰ green-things, and made such a constante yelling noyes, as made all y⁰ woods ring of them, and ready to deafe y⁰ hearers. They have not by y⁰ English been heard or seen before or since. But y⁰ Indeans tould them y' sicknes would follow, and so it did in June, July, August, and y⁰ cheefe heat of somer. (374–75)

As predicted, a great sickness hit all the people of the area. More than twenty English settlers died of an infectious fever, and "this disease allso swept away many of y⁰ Indeans from all y⁰ places near adjoyning."

More analogous occurrences transpire as the pathetic fallacy becomes reality. In the final pages of Bradford's history, the land narrative is punctuated by the hurricane, the eclipse, and the earthquake—all portents of disturbed, displaced Natives and uncertain settlers. As more and more land is surveyed or marked by artificial boundaries, divided, sold, and parceled out, societal and atmospheric distress intensifies for Plymoutheans and Algonquians alike. For instance, Winslow journeys to London in 1635 and petitions the Commissioners for Plantations in England to allow Plymouth to defend her trading companies against the French and

Dutch who are attacking these outposts, seizing goods, and killing people. Winslow tells the Commissioners that the Dutch have "made entrie upon [the]Conigtecute River, within ye limits of his Maj^{ts} . . . patent, where they have raised a forte, and threaten to expell your petitioners thence, who are also planted upon ye same river." Winslow's actions annoy Ferdinando Gorges and the Archbishop of Canterbury, who manage to turn the Colonists' political arguments into religious issues, and consequently, they have Winslow jailed for heresy. Bradford writes that his friend was "comited to ye Fleete, and lay ther 17. weeks. . . . But ye charge fell heavie on them hear, not only in Mr Winslows expences, . . . but by ye hinderance of their bussines."

Plymouthean fortunes continue to fall with the Peach affair, in which one Arthur Peach murdered a Narragansett and was executed for the crime, a punishment that caused "some of ye rude & ignorante sorte [to murmur] that any English should be put to death for ye Indeans." In fairly rapid succession following the Peach affair come William Brewster's death, John Billington's execution for murder, Thomas Granger's capital punishment for sodomy, and the slaughter of his "defiled" animals. The loss of Elder Brewster, Plymouth's foremost spiritual advisor, and the turmoil caused by the criminal cases are mirrored by the slow dissolve of Plymouth's mother church and official moral center as parishioners move into the newly developing outlying communities.

As Bradford's history nears its finish, the Principal Patriarch remarks in his 1638 section that the earthquake has disrupted the growing seasons for "divers years togeather." The summers are "not so hotte & seasonable for ye ripning of corne & other fruits as formerly." In a later account he details the Pequot War and a threatened uprising of the Narragansetts. The Algonquians, like the weather and the Plymoutheans, are at variance with their normal patterns of behavior. As the land narrative dissolves into a Native narrative, we see that the fortunes of the Algonquians have plummeted with the Plymoutheans.' The two histories merge in misery. As early as 1637 the Pequots have been able to read the writing on the wall or, in their case, the writing on the land:

The Pequents . . . sought to make peace with ye Narigansets, and used very pernicious arguments to move them therunto: as that ye English were strangers and begane to overspred their countrie, and would deprive them therof in time, if they were suffered to grow & increse; and if yᵉ Narigansets did assist yᵉ English to subdue them, they did but make way for their owne overthrow, for if they were rooted out, the English would soone take occasion to subjugate them. (423)

The Narragansetts, for vengeful reasons, do not heed the Pequots' advice, and eventually both Nations are severely diminished. At least three hundred Pequot women, children, and old men were massacred at Mystic. Most of the Pequot's surviving warriors were killed later, while those who escaped were sold into slavery and taken to the West Indies.

The treaty finalizing the conflict with the Pequots obliterates their name from usage. Item four of the *Articles between yᵉ Inglish in Connecticut and the Indian Sachems* in 1638 reads, in part, that "the Peaquots shall be divided as abovesd, [and] shall no more be called Peaquots but Narragansetts and Mohegans."[20] As the Pequots are divested of their names and rendered powerless by the machinations of Massachusetts Bay, Bradford's land text does something interesting. Contrary to Myra Jehlen's assertion that there is an "explicit erasure of Native Americans" in the Bradford text, *Of Plimoth Plantation* perpetuates their presence.[21] It preserves something of their power, and it does so by naming them. From an American Indian point of view, Bradford's replication of so many Native names, both for people and for places, is important for his history, because names "contain the power of the beings named."[22] Bradford's employment of Native appellations thus infuses his text with the energy and vitality of the persons and places cited. In his chronicle, we find the names of many Pequot, Narragansett, Wampanoag, Micmac, and Mohegan leaders, shamans, warriors, and headmen. There are Canonicus, Sassacus, Uncas, Miantonomo, Weetowish, Pampiamett, Chinough, Pummunish, Pessecuss, Innemo, Mixano, Awasequen, Pumham, Sokanoke, Cutshamakin, Shoanan, Passaconaway, Weequashcooke, Tassaquanowite, Awashawe, Ewangsos, Wipetok, Pumanise, and others.

Names of places as well as humans empower the Bradford history. More often than not, Plymouth's second governor refers to geographical places by their original American Indian designations even though English names have supplanted most of the Native ones by the time he begins writing his history. Nauset, Patuxet, Kikimuit, Manamoyick, Manonscussett, Scituate, Seekonk, Piscataqua, Pokanoket, Naumkeag, Nantasket, Wessagusset, Shawmut, and Kennebec became points on the map in his heart and geographical references in his narrative. The inclusion of so many American Indian names in his text helps make the work American. It also gives his work invincibility, substance, identification, definition, and much deeper meaning. For instance, Pokanoket designates the "land of the bitter water bays and coves." Kikimuit reminds us that there was "the path where the otter passes."[23] These names anchor the work in terms of living entities, place and time, memory, and sacred events. When Eastern Algonquians hear these words, they remember many things. A small part of their history, their language, and their ethos is preserved.

Despite the risk of over simplification and generalization, the following information is useful in understanding how many American Indian languages work:

American Indian languages can . . . express a complex of ideas in a single word. This agglutinative . . . characteristic, which emphasizes word and form, is dominant and fundamental. . . . In Native American languages several ideas retain their separate identity even though fused in one word. . . . To the European, subject, object, and verb are separate entities and are perceived as independent. When [one] says, for example, "he sits on the rock," [one] visualizes the subject, the action of sitting, and the rock as having no relationship other than that which is directly expressed. The Indian can express the same concept with one word and convey with that word that the person, the rock, and the sitting are equal parts of the natural world.[24]

For example, the word **ᏗᏓᏍᎪ**, meaning automobile in Cherokee, is an old coinage that came into use with the invention of the Model T Ford. Literally the word means "that bug-eyed thing that goes down the road." Here description merges with form and function. The word describes the headlights on the Model T, draws an analogy between the artificial construct and something in the natural world, and indicates that the machine is used for traveling. By extension, the place names for geographical formations, petroglyphs, marked stones, and the rock edifices that cover the New England landscape serve as vehicles for expressing thought. As American Indian words designate certain sites, they preserve form and function. They speak, and they prod memory. Bradford's land narrative, by insisting upon the retention of the old words, preserves the ideas and histories associated with the words. The Principal Patriarch's linguistic proclivities perpetuate Algonquia.

As Bradford's history nears its conclusion, we see that its land/Native text and the Colony's text merge. We can also see that the end is in the beginning, and the Bradford text has come full circle. The land text shows us that, from the beginning, the Plymoutheans' experiences in the New World duplicate the Natives.' Given the intercourse between the two groups, boundaries blurred and realities began to mirror the other.

Immediately upon their arrival at Patuxet in 1620, the Plymoutheans began to die just as the Patuxets before them had recently died. Like the Old Patuxets, the New Patuxets found themselves wasted by disease and hardly able to bury their dead within days of disembarkation. It is as if immediately at Contact, Plymouthean bones began to mingle with Native bones in the text of the earth. Experiences crisscrossed. Burial grounds commingled. Here is the beginning of the new American text. **SG A ʃ'T**.

Aboveground, the Newcomers resided in the location of former Algonquian houses and gardens. They took on a Native diet. They drank where Algonquians had drunk. The Patuxet Tisquantum arrived and ministered to a starving Plymouth. Months later Winslow resuscitated a dying Osamequin. The New Patuxets began to plant corn in the same fields the Natives once tilled. The English learned Native words and used them in their literary creations and official documents. Plymouth contended with troubling gossip and internal betrayals just as the Native communities did when indigenous opinion divided over the immigration problem. Uncas sold out Algonquia. Allerton betrayed Plymouth.

Other Englishmen began to put the Plymoutheans into the same category as Indians. For instance, John Winthrop of Massachusetts Bay regarded the Plymoutheans' land in the same sense that he defined the Indians' in his "Reasons for the Plantation in New England." In this document he rhetorically asks, "Why then should one strive here [England] for places of habitation . . . and at the same time suffer a whole continent as fruitful and convenient for the use of man to lie waste without any improvement?"[25] In 1635, settlers from Massachusetts Bay attempted to take over the Plymoutheans' trading post on the Connecticut River. When Plymouth objected, Winthrop wrote that "we at first judged yᵉ place so free yᵗ we might with Gods good leave take & use it, without just offence to any man, it being the Lords wast." Plymouth's reply to this outrage was "You cast rather a partiall, if not a covetous eye, upon that wᶜʰ is your neighbours, and not yours. . . . Looke yᵗ you abuse not Gods providence."

The Algonquians were having similar internal difficulties. Corbitant could never muster a majority to challenge Plymouth because his supporters such as Iyanough and Aspinet, who intimated they would back him, gave way, ostensibly under pressure from the Massasoit. Inability to unite against the English eventually caused the Algonquians to lose their land and their political control of the area. Plymouth's fortunes followed suit when the First Colony was eventually overshadowed by Massachusetts Bay.

For all intents and purposes, the history of the Pequots and Narragansetts takes up most of Bradford's final chapters. He records the Narragansetts' dealings with Massachusetts Bay and the sad results. Bradford chronicles Uncas' execution of Miantonomo, the nephew of Canonicus. He duly describes the Narragansetts' retributive attack on the Mohegans and the apprehension these Native skirmishes cause the English, but when the Narragansett history stops, Bradford's diegetic narrative stops.

It is, I think, significant to note that throughout his text, Bradford spells the word *Indian* "Indean," but when he finishes the passage on the "troubles with the Narigansetts," which is one of his final entries, he spells the word "Endeans" in a copy of an agreement made among the United Colonies, the Niantics, and the Narragansetts. His spelling foretells the fate of New England's tribal people, who were almost obliterated from history and from the printed page. American Indian history in New England effectively "ends" twenty-nine years after Bradford's journal breaks off. It is as if Bradford's closing orthography predicts this outcome.

Of Plimoth Plantation breaks off before the war with Metacomet erupts and before the Colony dissolves. As the history terminates, Bradford's land text transforms into a narrative of Native people who were losing their autonomy, their homes, their land, their people, their lives, their fortunes, and their sacred honor. Their losses, perhaps inexorably, prefigured those of Plymouth. The Plymoutheans, like the "Endeans," vanished.

The good news is, however, that the Indians did not really end or vanish, but they did diminish and recede into the shadows of American reality. According to tribal administrators, presently there are approximately 1,099 Gay Head Wampanoags; 2,300 Wampanoags; 2,600 Narragansetts; and 500 Mashantucket Pequots residing in New England today, just as there are descendants of the *Mayflower's* passengers now living in the United States. Plymouth Colony, as Bradford conceived it, ended too, but in the terminus that Bradford shows us, the original settlers and the English came together, historically and metaphorically.

Bradford's land narrative is many things. In literary terms it is a cautionary tale. *Of Plimoth Plantation* is a sacred history and a prophecy, an ecology and a paradigm for an ecology. When a land is divided, people divide and consequently perish. Just as important, Bradford's land narrative is the prototype of countless other land narratives that will eventually characterize American literature. As Richard Slotkin observes in *Regeneration Through Violence* (1973), "by 1784 . . . landscape description [in American literature] was a major interest, and nature was functioning in literature as a godlike agent for the regeneration of man."[26]

3 THE RITUAL MEETING
OF TWO CULTURES
ᎥSᏢET

The *Mayflower* had touched American shores in November 1620. After exploring their new homeland for several weeks, the Newcomers finally located a place "fitt for situation; at least it was yᵉ best they could find, and yᵉ season, & their presente necessitie, made them glad to accepte of it." On December 16 a fair wind brings them into Plymouth Harbor, and "after wards [they] tooke better view of yᵉ place, . . . and yᵉ 25. *day* begane to erecte yᵉ first house for commone use to receive them and their goods." It was near the time of the winter solstice when the Plymoutheans arrived in the deserted village of Patuxet, but their relations with the Algonquians would not formalize until the vernal equinox. That both the arrival and the official greeting took place at ceremonial times could perhaps be described as Providential. If not Providential, the timing of these pivotal events was certainly ceremonially significant.

The Algonquians had been watching the Newcomers' building project for several months but had kept their distance. Each group was aware of the other's movements and activities, yet there was no formal meeting until spring when the Indianization of the Newcomers officially, or perhaps humanly, began. On Friday, March 16, 1620 (NS 1621), Samoset walked into the fledgling village and announced the impending arrival of Tisquantum and the Massasoit. Mourt relates that he "saluted [the Newcomers] in English, and bade [them] welcome." A headman, or minor chief among the Abenakis, Samoset was from Pemaquid. Even though he was not native to the area, he had lived in the region for eight months and was familiar with it. According to Mourt, Samoset had learned "broken English among the

Englishmen that came to fish at Monchiggon." The headman had, in fact, been introduced to English customs and foods in his visits with many of the fishing crews that navigated the Atlantic coast prior to 1620, and he knew most of the ships' captains by name.

Mourt notices that Samoset carries with him a bow and two arrows, one "headed" and the other "unheaded." The arrows, which the emissary presents to the Newcomers, symbolically ask a question: Do the New Patuxets want war or peace?[1] After this query is answered satisfactorily, Samoset begins taking questions. Before he discloses much pertinent information about neighboring tribes and populations, Samoset gives the English some instructions in local customs. He asks for some beer. The Newcomers have none, so they give him some strong water, bread and butter, cheese, pudding, and a piece of mallard. Samoset's request for food was his first lesson to the English in Native hospitality: Always serve a guest food before asking him questions.

Mourt continues that after refreshments Samoset told the English they were now living in a place called Patuxet, meaning Little Bay, and four years earlier the village had been devastated by a terrible plague. Only Tisquantum, a former inhabitant of that village, was left alive.[2] Samoset reported that the closest Massasoit to them was Osamequin and that he had only sixty warriors remaining after the plague struck his village. He elaborated further that the Nausets lived southeast of the Massasoit's people, and they were a hundred warriors strong. The headman then revealed that some of the Massasoit's band would soon come to Plymouth to meet the Newcomers. In Mourt's account of this momentous meeting with Samoset, the Diplomatic Pilgrim recalls that "all the afternoon we spent in communication with him; we would gladly have been rid of him at night, but he was not willing to go." It was not until morning and after the English had presented him with a few gifts that Samoset left.

The Newcomers had spent an uneasy night. After much prodding and safety-guaranteeing by the Pilgrim Fathers, Stephen Hopkins reluctantly agreed to share his house with the Abenaki. Why did Samoset not leave after his message was delivered? There are several reasons. First, Native observations from afar had revealed that the English were socially inept in terms of New World codes of gracious behavior. They disturbed the peace with their noisy firearms and killed animals without first asking the animal's permission. Never once had they made a proper kill offering. And not only that, they even beat their children. It was time to step in. The

New Patuxets needed a lesson in basic etiquette if they were to be brought into the local cultural milieu, and American hospitality required offering one's quests lodgings for the night. Second, it was forty miles—more than a day's journey—to Sowams, the Massasoit's home, and it was a six-hour trip to Nemasket, the first stopping place on the way. Had Samoset begun his journey in the late afternoon, he would have found himself in the forest at nightfall with no lodgings for the evening.

A third possible reason that Samoset stayed the night in the Colony could have been a fear of Patuxet and the surrounding area, since in those days some Native people believed that spirits walked after dark. Because disease had recently destroyed the Native village, it is likely that many bodies had not been properly buried. In the Algonquian world, souls of the unburied linger.[3] Neither Bradford nor Mourt reports skeletal remains above ground at Patuxet, but omissions of unpleasant material are noticeable in Bradford's text. Bradford does, however, when reporting Winslow's trip to Sowams, mention that the Massasoit had only a few followers at the time because of the "late great mortalitie which fell in all these parts aboute *three years* before yᵉ coming of yᵉ English, wherin thousands of them dyed, they not being able to burie one another; ther sculs and bones were found in many places lying still above ground, where their houses & dwellings had been; a very sad spectakle to behould."

Thomas Morton, writing in *The New English Canaan* (1637), describes the Patuxet area as a "new-found Golgotha" since the "bones and skulls upon the severall places of their [the Wampanoags'] habitations made such a spectacle." Morton comments further that it is customary for "Indian people to bury their dead ceremoniously, and carefully, and then . . . abandon that place, because they have no desire the place should put them in the minde of mortality."[4] Being in a place at night where so many people had miserably died would unnerve almost anyone, and Samoset, mindful of Native tradition, probably found the idea of being outside alone near Patuxet at night unappealing.

A fourth, and certainly the most likely reason Samoset stayed the night, is that he was ritually preparing the place for the Massasoit's impending arrival. In order to assure harmonious deliberations, meeting grounds must be cleansed with smoke, usually tobacco, cedar, or sage. Ritual smokings sometimes occur either late at night or early in the morning. The People of the Eastern Light, the Wampanoags, would probably favor a morning ceremony.

For whatever reason, Samoset remained at Patuxet and left on Saturday morning. He returned the next day with five men, who came into the village on the pretext of trading, but they had brought with them only three or four skins to barter. Mourt remembers that these men were painted and dressed in ceremonial regalia. "The principal of them had a wild cat's skin, or such like on one arm. . . . [and] they sang and danced after their manner, like antics. . . . They brought with them . . . a little of their corn pounded to powder, which, put to a little water, they eat" (53).

After eating with the New Patuxets, the men smoked tobacco, used corn ritually, sang, danced, and left. In American Indian cultures, tobacco can be smoked to lift words or prayers to the heavens; it can be used as an offering to the earth, the fire, or the water; and it is also a purification agent. Corn pollen or meal is usually sprinkled like holy water, but small amounts can be placed on the tongue. It is an offering as well as a blessing. Tobacco and corn ceremonies, along with singing and dancing, are elements of Native liturgical rites, so it is apparent that these men were participating in a ritual preparation of the area for the impending ceremonial occasion, the meeting of the Massasoit with the Pilgrims. Literally, they were preparing the earth for a new narrative. These emissaries were not song and dance men come to entertain the New Arrivals with "antic" or clownish, grotesque motions. Neither were they naïve savages doing whatever savages do. They were men with a sacred purpose. The ceremony performed openly in daylight suggests that the Wampanoags were hoping for peaceful, mutually fruitful negotiations and good will. They wanted a meeting that would successfully introduce the Newcomers to their ways.

Samoset remained until Wednesday, when the impatient, ceremonially naïve Newcomers sent him to bring in the Massasoit even though it was not yet the appropriate time. On Thursday, March 22, Samoset returned with Tisquantum and said that the Massasoit, the Massasoit's brother Quadequina, and sixty warriors were hard by. For the Wampanoags, the date is important. Thursday was either the vernal equinox or one day after, and for agricultural people, the equinoxes and solstices are the high holidays of the ecclesiastical year. These times are important because they divide the year into seasons of planting and of harvest; thus they are times for important rituals celebrating sowing, the arrival of the first green plants, and the garnering of mature crops. In addition to the food production rituals common at such times, rites for tribal conciliation and unity are also observed.[5]

Alvin Weeks, in *Massasoit of the Wampanoags* (1919), suggests that Osamequin arranged the meeting either "to inquire the purpose of this unbidden camping upon the grounds of which he was still the rightful owner ... [or to form] a league ... to assist him in case of further encroachments by ... Canonicus."[6]

Although the Massasoit's reasons for meeting his uninvited neighbors are not definitively known, we do know that at this first meeting the Plymoutheans purchased land from him. This transaction is omitted in Bradford's history but noted in the *Records of the Colony of New Plymouth in New England* (1855-61).[7] At this meeting the Wampanoags and the Pilgrims also signed a nonaggression treaty stating that they would not hurt each other and would come to each other's aid if either were attacked. The agreement further stipulated that when the Massasoit's people, the Pokanokets, came to Plymouth they would be unarmed. The English, however, were exempt from that requirement. The meeting concluded the following day, Friday, March 23, when the Newcomers were invited to join the Massasoit's camp for groundnuts and a tobacco ceremony.

From Bradford's and Mourt's accounts of the meeting, it is unmistakable that the Wampanoags were greeting the Pilgrims ritually. The conference, with its attendant preparations, covered a seven-day period beginning March 16 and ending March 23, and seven is an American Indian sacred number.[8] According to Evan T. Pritchard (Micmac), seven is an important number for Algonquians. He reports that from Glooskap's first council fire seven sparks flew out and those sparks became seven tribes. From the tribes' seven council fires, seven more ignited. He goes on to say that Algonquians conceive of seven "inner planets," seven types of creatures, and seven races of humans.[9] The repetition of this number in the Micmac creation account indicates that seven is a potent signifier to some Algonquian cultures; therefore, the seven-day time frame of Osamequin's first meeting with the New Patuxets almost certainly indicates that he was attaching ceremonial significance to the conference.

In addition to planning for a seven-day meeting, the Algonquians accompanying Osamequin were also ritually attired. Mourt remembers that the Massasoit was painted. "All of his followers likewise, were in their faces, in part or in whole painted, some black, some red, some yellow, and some white, some with crosses and other antic works; some had skins on them, and some naked, all strong, tall, all men in appearance."

The fact that in attendance were Samoset, a chief, and Tisquantum, a *pniese*, emphasizes the notion that the Massasoit intended this meeting to be ceremonial. The presence of high-ranking tribal officials, the timing of the event to coincide with the vernal equinox, the seven-day time frame, the ritual preparation by chiefs and medicine men, the singing, the dancing, the corn and tobacco use before and after the actual meeting, and leaving a man to live in the Colony suggest that this parley was something much more than a "let's get acquainted" affair. These details suggest an all-encompassing effort to modify the actions of the Plymouthean band. This coming together constituted a very evident acceleration of the metaphysical Indianization program previously begun; it was a significant exchange designed to bring the Newcomers into the American Indian ethos. What is important for American literary studies is that bringing the Plymoutheans into the "ways of Creation" also brought them into the Algonquian literary tradition.

The Newcomers themselves recognized the ceremonial aspects of the First Meeting, and they, perhaps subconsciously, responded accordingly. As the Massasoit entered the compound, Mourt confides that the Pilgrims placed before him

> a green rug and three or four cushions. Then instantly came [the] governor with drum and trumpet after him, and some few musketeers. After salutations, [the] governor kissing his hand, the king kissed him, and so they sat down. The governor called for some strong water, and drunk to him, and he drunk a great draught that made him sweat all the while after; he called for a little fresh meat, which the king did eat willingly, and did give his followers. Then they treated of peace. (56)

For people who prefer Plain Style, who detest ritual, pomp, and circumstance, this protocol seems something of a departure from normal Brownist operations. Hand kissing? Cushions? Sitting on the ground? Toasting? Separatists? Ir Ʊ Ꮪ Ꮐ.Ʌ Ꮕ . The Indians appear to be modifying Pilgrim behavior, but the Pilgrims seem unaware of the denaturing.

The Massasoit and his informants had been watching the Pilgrims from a distance since their arrival, so the actual First Meeting gave them a closer look at the New Patuxets and a better understanding of their social order. The Pokanokets could now ascertain who among the New Patuxets was responsible for various civic obligations. Distant reconnaissance had revealed clearly that Miles Standish was their military commander, or war chief. He had been observed bearing arms and directing military exercises. Closer contact with the Plymoutheans will disclose that the short, waspish Standish, called "Captain Shrimp" by Thomas Morton and "Little Chimney" by others, is bellicose to the extent that even the English acknowledge that he must be controlled. After the murder of Wituwamat, the Reverend Mr. John Robinson will insist upon restricting the Captain, saying that Standish "may be wanting y^t tendernes of ye life of man . . . which is meete."

John Carver was the governor, head diplomat, or peace chief, but only for the moment. Moribund, he will be replaced by Bradford the following month. Neither Carver nor Bradford seemed militaristic unless provoked or badly frightened. Inclined toward peaceful, verbal deliberations, both men, however, quickly realized that they must develop a pragmatic way of conducting affairs that was compatible with their new surroundings. As George Willison observes, they were facing many situations not addressed by the Holy Discipline; furthermore, their perspectives were changing.[10] Survival was supplanting points of order. More important, the Plymoutheans were finding new books to read. Like their old ones, the new texts were leather bound but were not filled with the familiar English-speaking talking leaves. These volumes were the buckskin-clad Wampanoags, and the new talking leaves were human tongues and quite difficult to decipher.

It seems clear that by the First Meeting, the Wampanoags had discovered that Plymouth, in actuality, was governed by at least two leaders. In their view, the Colony had a war chief and peace chief in much the same way their Iroquoian neighbors did. There is no definitive evidence that the Algonquians used the two-chief plan, but Bragdon reports that "early descriptions of the Narragansett refer to a dual sachemship, wherein a community was led by two men, related by blood or marriage."[11] The two-chief plan was common to many tribes all over the United States, so it is conceivable that the Algonquians were using a similar system, particularly since the Massasoit was accompanied by his brother when he arrived for the First Meeting. Even if the Algonquians did not rely on a two-chief plan, they did, nevertheless, have a group of leaders who served the Massasoit in an advisory capacity.

To ensure cultural adaptation and to keep serene the social order, the Wampanoags installed tribal members in the new village as a means of influencing Plymouthean actions. It appears that Tisquantum, possibly acting as a peace chief, was assigned to Carver and later to Bradford. Hobomok, generally thought to have military prowess, arrived in late July or early August and was delegated to Standish, probably as a war chief or consultant. In this way the two *pnieses*, by modifying the political pro-clivities of the principal Plymouthean leaders, could ensure balance and harmony between the two extremes and effect subtle changes at the same time. Whether speculations about their presumed war and peace func-tions are valid or not, it can be said without hesitation that whatever their actual societal functions were, the two *pnieses* did represent a feature of tribal life that Paula Gunn Allen refers to as "complementariness," a bipo-larity that demonstrates wholeness, not "opposition."[12] The two men could have been representatives of Summer and Winter people, Sky and Earth people, or any one of a number of dichotomous pairings. Representatives from differing moieties can create a balanced society in a way that one man alone cannot. It is unlikely that the Massasoit would have sent two *pnieses*, counselors and much-needed warriors, to interpret and run er-rands for the Pilgrims unless he had some specific purpose in mind, a pur-pose that would best serve the interests of the Native community. What is important about Tisquantum's and Hobomok's residence in Plymouth is that they were sent to operate as a coordinated entity to regulate the Colony's activities, and they were attached to what the Wampanoags prob-ably considered to be dichotomous governing entities similar to their own. The nineteenth-century historian Benjamin Thatcher, in *Indian Biography* (1832), agrees that Tisquantum and Hobomok were sent to Plymouth at the Massasoit's direction:

> It was probably at his [the Massasoit's] secret and delicate sugges-tion,—and it could scarcely have been without his permission, . . . that his own subjects took up their residence among the colonists, with the view of guiding, piloting, interpreting for them, and teach-ing them their own useful knowledge. Winslow speaks of his *ap-pointing another* to fill the place of Squanto at Plymouth, while the latter should be sent out among the Pokanokets, under *his* orders, "to procure truck [in furs] for the English."[13]

Winslow seems to be under the impression that Tisquantum had been designated a trade negotiator, and that is partly true. Native tribes were anxious to get European trade goods, but given their population losses, they were also concerned with making the Newcomers an integral part of tribal society. They needed hunters, warriors, wives, and agriculturists as much as they needed foreign imports.

George Willison notes that after the death of Carver and the election of Bradford, there was a significant change manifested in Plymouth's government. Willison attributes the modifications simply to altered circumstances, but it is worth noting that these changes also coincided with the arrival of Tisquantum and Hobomok following the ritual meeting of Plymoutheans and Wampanoags in March:

> Up to this time [the death of Carver in April 1621] affairs had rested largely in the hands of Elder Brewster, Pastor Robinson, Deacon Cushman, and Deacon Carver, all of whom were getting on in years. Now this group was scattered—one was dead, another was in London, a third was in Leyden, and only Brewster was here at Plymouth. When these men spoke, they still commanded great respect and spoke with unchallenged authority. But their function increasingly became that of elder statesmen. The actual conduct of affairs, the day-by-day direction of operations, ... fell ... to an able and diversely talented group of much younger men, to Governor Bradford, ... Allerton, ... Standish, ... and to ... Winslow.[14]

The Mayflower Compact, which earlier had bound the signers together in a "civill body politick," did not provide for the mechanics of government, so whether deliberately or coincidentally, the Plymoutheans early began to govern themselves like Algonquians.

Pilgrims and Pokanokets, in many respects, were as alike as they were different.[15] Their principal leaders were relatively young men. Bradford was thirty-two when he was appointed governor. Osamequin, as depicted by Mourt, was in his prime:

> In his person he is a very lusty man, in his best years, an able body, grave of countenance, and spare of speech. In his attire little or nothing differing from the rest of his followers, only in a great chain of white bone beads about his neck, and at it behind his neck hangs a little bag of tobacco, which he drank and gave us to drink; his face was painted with a sad red like murry, and oiled both head and face.
> (57)

The Plymouthean governor, like the Massasoit, did not have supreme authority. The Massasoit maintained his position, which some early settlers took to be hereditary, by a kind of judicious juggling of political interests, but he did not have the power to act arbitrarily on important matters. He was constrained by a group of advisors and by popular opinion.[16] Similarly, the Plymouthean governor was surrounded by an advisory council. Only with the approval of his council could either leader transact important business. Both Osamequin and Bradford had militias that could be called up for active duty, but in reality these military groups spent most of their time engaged in tasks involving the community and the home. The Pilgrim militia cleared fields, built stockades, hunted, fished, and went on trading expeditions. The Wampanoag warriors cleared fields, manufactured weapons, hunted, fished, trapped, and traded.

The Plymouthean governor and the Massasoit had holy men who served as spiritual advisors and visibly participated in ceremonial functions. William Brewster directed religious services in the Colony until a reliable pastor for the Plymouth congregation was finally located several years after the founding of the Colony. Brewster walked by Bradford's side, along with Miles Standish, during the weekly processions to worship, and the Algonquians viewed this formation as a regularly occurring ceremonial procedure involving persons of power who represented the worlds of war, peace, and spirits. Osamequin's religious advisors or medicine men were unnamed, but they attended him in time of illness and they presided with him over all ceremonies.

The Massasoit's decision to Indianize the Newcomers exemplifies a predominant Native view regarding immigration in the seventeenth century. In the years immediately following Contact, Indianization and taking Europeans captive seemed the most practical means of ensuring domestic tranquility and stabilizing population numbers. American Indians sometimes took Europeans captive as a way of replacing tribal members who had died. In many cases, the Indianization process was quite successful and some captives voluntarily stayed with the Natives rather than be redeemed. Other immigrants, like several of Weston's men and Plymouth's Edward Ashley, initially chose to live with the Natives of their own accord, so there was a commingling of people from America's earliest days.[17]

By the eighteenth century, however, the American Indian intellectual position regarding the influx of Europeans on this continent had changed. From the eighteenth century onward, American Indian policy has generally been either to resist the foreigners with all strength or to pretend to accept European manners while maintaining the ancient ways covertly. Before the influx of Europeans became so great, and before the American

Indians were wasted by war, land loss, and disease, the option of Indianizing the foreigners seemed a better plan, and it seems evident that is the course the Algonquians pursued.[18]

ᎣᏏᏲ. From an American Indian perspective, William Bradford was a good candidate for Indianization because in certain ways he was like Indians. A protégé of William Brewster, a Separatist teaching elder, Bradford was a devout man who came to the New World well versed in scriptural knowledge and Brownist doctrine. Like Indians, both the Separatists and the Puritans who followed them were steeped in precepts perceived to be sacred. Religion infused every aspect of their lives. It dictated their laws, their governments, their attitudes toward marriage, women, children, recreation, and land tenure. It influenced their attitudes toward illness, prosperity, impoverishment, and death. In Massachusetts, Puritans established theocracies that ordered their lives. From cradle to grave, the Separatist/Puritans were surrounded by religious observances and scriptural admonitions.

In Bradford's day, American Indian society, likewise, did not separate the religious from the secular. Joseph Epes Brown explains this aspect of American Indian life:

> The presence of the sacred . . . permeates[s] all lifeways to such a degree that what we call religion is . . . integrated into the totality of life and into all of life's activities. Religion . . . is so pervasive . . . that there is probably no Native American language in which there is a term which could be translated as "religion" in the way we understand it.[19]

With the meeting of the Plymoutheans and the Indians, two reverent groups came together. Bradford and his Algonquian neighbors had a mutual regard for words, for miraculous Providential interventions, and for visions.

Archaeological findings published in 1989 report the presence of ancient stone vision chairs in New England, and this discovery clearly demonstrates that vision quests were part of Algonquian ritual life in the seventeenth century.[20] Seventeenth-century Protestantism had visionary aspects ranging from tasks of personal meditation and self-examination to an anticipation of the millennium. Separatist/Puritans accepted scriptural accounts of miraculous events such as the Annunciation, the Virgin Birth, the Resurrection, the Ascension, Pentecost, and other improbable events without reservation. American Indians had similar visionary components to their cultures, and the American Indian oral tradition abounds with miraculous occurrences, mighty deeds, and remarkable transformations.

Respect for the power of the word is central to Indian belief systems, and this respect for words is analogous to the Puritans' reverence for the Holy Scripture and its verbal, creative power. Bradford's meticulous attention to words in *Of Plimoth Plantation* suggests that he seriously ascribed to logos theology, a belief based on the generative power of the Word as set forth in the Gospel of John. In *The Presence of the Word* (1967), Walter Ong remarks that early adherents to the Hebrew-Christian tradition regarded the Word not as an "inert record but a living something, like sound, something going on."[21] Bradford's adherence to logos theology is evident in one of his verses, entitled "On the Various Heresies":

> The Word was God, as scriptures tell,
> And was made flesh did with us dwell.
> And His glory, then, men did see,
> The Father's only begotten Son to be.
>
> John 1.1, 9, 11, 14[22]

Ong explains further that the Old Testament suggests that the Hebrews regarded the Word as an agent that could act upon a human being, but the New Testament moves the Word into other dimensions. It announces that "the Word was made flesh and dwelt, a Person, among us," while John 16:13 promises that "if you ask the Father anything in my name, he will give it to you." Thus for Christians, the Word is God, and the Word used ritually has a kind of magical efficacy, particularly in celebrations such as the Eucharist.[23]

Word magic is something Indians have always known. In his article "The Native Voice" published in the *Columbia Literary History of the United States* (1988), the Kiowa/Cherokee N. Scott Momaday reminds us that for Indians "words are intrinsically powerful."[24] Carrying that point further, Margot Astrov points out in *The Winged Serpent* (1946) that American Indians understand the word as an "independent entity, superior even to the gods."[25] Joseph Epes Brown summarizes American Indian attitudes about words best: "In Native languages the understanding is that the meaning *is* in the sound, it *is* in the word; the word is not a symbol for meaning which has been abstracted out, word and meaning are together in one experience."[26]

Traditional American Indians believe that having the right words in the right order, and coupling those words with appropriate rituals, produces change. Like traditional American Indians, Bradford was a believer in the world of spirits, specifically God and angels, and he was the possessor of a holy vision that he related and lived. Bradford's reverence for words is obvious through all his writings.

In the prefatory material to his history, Bradford scribbled Hebrew scriptural verse citations, verb conjugations, and word definitions on a flyleaf. On the verso of the flyleaf he inscribed a wish written in the shape of what is generally considered to be a chalice reminiscent of the concrete verse formations of George Herbert:

Though I am growne aged, yet I have had a long-
ing desire, to see with my own eyes, something of
that most ancient language, and holy tongue,
in which the Law, and oracles of God were
write; and in which God, and angles, spake to
the holy patriarks, of old time; and what
names were given to things, from the
creation. And though I canot attaine
to much herein, yet I am refreshed,
to have seen some glimpse here-
of; (as Moses saw the Land
of canan afarr of) my aime
and desire is, to see how
the words, and phrases
lye in the holy texte;
and to dicerne some-
what of the same
for my owne
content

J

Bradford's word choice here is significant. He does not say he wants to learn an ancient language, though he was diligent in his study of Hebrew.[27]

Instead he asks to see the language as it manifests itself in visible form. He seems interested in the word as object, not the word as signifier.

The printed and the spoken word fascinated Bradford. *Of Plimoth Plantation* indicates he respected and venerated words. The history is a repository for words. It is a recollection of words given, words rumored, words honored, and words dishonored. For the most part, *Of Plimoth Plantation's* tone is serious. Rarely does Bradford use words lightly, and only an exceptional scholar can find humor in his writings. Bradford's narratives, like his verse, frequently take on a heavy religious tone. His writings are much more dogmatic and doctrinal that those of several of his contemporaries—men such as Edward Winslow, William Wood, or John Winthrop. Infusing his history with scriptural quotations and Biblical allusions, Bradford seems to insist upon scriptural references to emphasize the truth of his observations and to add shades of meaning to his text. Bradford is also prone to draw parallels between the Pilgrims and biblical characters. He likens the Plymouth settlers both to the wandering children of Israel and to early Christians who struggled with adversities. Conflating metaphors of Old and New Testaments, Bradford fashioned his history into an American bible.

Of Plimoth Plantation abounds with covenants, contracts, laws, genealogies, apothegms, prophecies, and epistles. It sermonizes. It deplores sin as it reveals it. It extols human virtue and condemns frailty. The Bradfordean history contains a pantheon of saints and sinners. Among the former the greatest are the teaching elder William Brewster and the clergyman John Robinson. John Billington, the first Plymouthean murderer, and Thomas Granger, the Colony's first sodomite, do the honors for the latter. Isaac Allerton becomes the Iscariot who betrays the Colony, and James Sherley serves as the Pilate who washes his hands of it. *Of Plimoth Plantation's* Patriarch-Apostles are Bradford, Standish, and Winslow, while the Indians are the Philistine-Samaritans, enemies but help-givers; barbarians but kind strangers outside the pale.

For purposes of American Indian exegesis, it is significant to note that one of the first major works produced in this country is something like a holy book. With its solemnity, *Of Plimoth Plantation* conveys a serious intent as it claims to "manefest . . . ye simple trueth in all things." In Bradford's mind, words are the vehicles of truth. They are actual objects of veracity. In his history the spoken word receives scrupulous attention. Conversations ranging from the trivial to the momentous are sometimes quoted verbatim while others are summarized. The spoken words of American Indians as well as the words of European Americans are faithfully recorded. The written word is also meticulously preserved. Bradford carefully includes accounts of the words of others by inserting copies of their letters into his text. This preoccupation with words is also evidenced by his eloquent rhetoric from time to time. Several of the Governor's passages qualify as sacred oratory. In generations past, American schoolchildren learned by heart:

> Being thus arived in a good harbor and brought safe to land, they fell upon their knees & blessed ye God of heaven, who had brought them over ye vast & furious ocean, and delivered them from all ye periles & miseries therof, againe to set their feete on ye firme and stable earth, their proper elemente. (94)

In addition to eloquently worded oratorical passages, *Of Plimoth Plantation* reveals something of the Pilgrims' dreams for themselves in the New World. In a sense, they had articulated a holy purpose while still in Holland, and their settlement in Massachusetts was their first enactment of that vision. Bradford himself relates and explains the endeavor. "Lastly, . . . a great hope & inward zeall they had of laying some good foundation, . . . for ye propagating & advancing ye gospell of ye kingdom of Christ in those remote parts of ye world; yea, though they should be but even as stepping-stones unto others for ye performing of so great a work."

Many American Indian tribes have long understood the importance of visions and have observed the tradition of the vision quest, which is time a person spends in isolation waiting for a dream or revelation that will give direction to his life or penetrate some enigma of existence. Relating the quest to the greater community allows the community to "integrate the new knowledge with the [older traditions.]"[28]

American Indian poetics are also present in quest recitations. An example can be found in Black Elk's vision as dictated to John Neihardt in the 1930s. Black Elk was nine years old at the time of the vision and he relates that the major characters of his dream were animals (horses) and gods (the Grandfather spirits). The horses later transform into "all kinds of animals and fowls"; directions are personified; colors are brilliant; symbols are Siouan and must be correctly read; action is continuous and takes in the entire universe. The spirits give Black Elk special songs and word combinations to assist him in life. The vision begins and ends at the center of the earth, which in this case is Black Elk's teepee. Human beings are minor participants in the visionary events.[29]

Like many of his American Indian contemporaries, Bradford was a spiritual person, a man with a sacred vision. Like many American Indians, he felt a commitment to honor that vision, meaning that he had to explain his vision for Plymouth Colony to the greater community when the time was right, and he had to live out that vision. The dream must be given form. Centuries later, in an American literary continuum and in a temporal reference much like seventeenth-century Old Algonquia, the Lakota medicine man Black Elk will recount and paint his sacred vision. These conscious, artful acts will fix the vision in time and space, but in order for Bradford to render his vision permanent and intelligible, he must write it, since it was unlikely that his vision would pass into the European American oral tradition intact. For that reason, a portion of the history's opening chapters delineates the undertaking he envisioned for himself and Plymouth Colony.

By 1644, Bradford's vision was weakening when it became clear that the Colony was spreading out for reasons of private economic gain. Instead of advancing the Gospel in the New World, the Plymoutheans had begun to advance their own various economic agenda. As the Plymouth congregation lost parishioners upon the removal of its citizens to the more recently organized churches in neighboring villages, Bradford was greatly saddened. At this point, much as Black Elk will centuries later, Bradford laments the people's loss of purpose or vision. In tone and sentiment there is little difference between Bradford's "And thus was this poore church left, like an anciente mother; growne olde, and forsaken of her children," and Black Elk's "Here at the center of the world, where you took me when I was young and taught me; here, old, I stand, and the tree is withered, Grandfather, my Grandfather!"[30] With kindred voices, the Lakota medicine man and William Bradford articulate their broken visions in metaphors of blood relations, aging, and the ineluctable transitions of all living things. Both are sorrowful yet reconciled to the Great Mystery that seems unfathomable.

Pilgrim and Algonquian, outwardly disparate but similarly sensitive to language and spiritual experiences, shared, borrowed, stole, appropriated, learned, corrupted, and used each other's words. They brought words like Manitou and Jesus into their literatures and into their sacred rituals, and sometimes they discovered that these exchanges had been made centuries earlier.[31] In their day-to-day living, the Newcomers came into contact with facets of Algonquian theology. Boundaries began to blur. Pilgrims began to edge their fields with Algonquian holy stones. They stored their winter vegetables in vision pits, Algonquian sacred sites. Unknowingly the English were approaching, invading, and incorporating the building blocks of Algonquian literature. Ever so slowly bridges were built, and things crossed over. Both ways. For seven generations. And longer. ᎣᏗᏓ. ᏍᎩᏫᏲ ᎯᏛᎣᏛᏗᏢᏎᏴᎬ.

4 CORN AND WAMPUM
ᒐᏕᎾᏓ

Running through Bradford's chronicle is a narrative of corn, which at midpoint transforms into a narrative of wampum. This lustrous, gold-changing-to-white-then-purple strand of Bradford's text replicates mottled kernels of Indian corn while it illuminates a work grounded in the dark colors of New England's winter aspect. This transformative, thematic thread serves both as trope and history. Giving light and stateliness to Bradford's somber prose, the corn-wampum stratum of narrative documents the Colony's actual agricultural and economic practices just as it illustrates an American Indian literary process informing Bradford's text.

Corn was so prominent in American Indian diets and religious thought that social customs, poetic creations, and ceremonial life revolved around its planting and harvest. Corn was tribal tribute and charity; corn pollen was blessing and protection. Corn was the worldly manifestation of a benevolent guardian, the Corn Mother. The Penobscots tell of First Mother of the People, who sacrificed her blood, which became corn so that her seven hungry children could eat.[1] Cherokee tradition relates that from the blood of ᏐᎻ sprang up corn.[2] For American Indians, corn is both food and sacramental; it is also a constituent part of American Indian sacred oral traditions. Corn is central to many creation accounts. Traditional Navajos believe that 'Altsé Hastiin (First Man) and 'Altsé 'Asdzáá (First Woman) were created from ears of corn. Some tribes pay homage to corn mothers and hold corn festivals; others retain corn clans. Nearly all tribes use either corn meal or corn pollen as a sacramental. Since corn is considered a holy substance, it is not unusual to find American Indians named for this venerable grain in an effort to keep people constantly aware of the staple's importance for humans and to reinforce the close ties between man and the divine. There are Hopi surnames that honor corn. *Siwingyawma* means "Corn That Has Been Rooted"; *Sakhongva* means "Green Corn Standing."[3] The Senecas have Cornplanter. Various Cherokee families call themselves *Corn Tassel, Corn Silk, Gritts, or Roasting Ear* in memory of 4M, the Corn Mother. In American Indian oral traditions, corn goddesses are featured in creation accounts and sacred narratives. In modern American Indian novels one can occasionally still find a corn narrative running through the work. Forrest Carter's *Education of Little Tree* is a prominent example.[4]

In *Earth Is My Mother, Sky Is My Father: Space, Time, and Astronomy in Navajo Sandpainting* (1992), Trudy Griffin-Pierce explains that the essence of corn, the pollen, is a ritual symbol that bridges action and belief in Navajo sandpainting traditions. Strewing pollen is an act that blesses a sandpainting, which is an intricate drawing made of colored sand created upon the earth. Sandpaintings are drawn for healing purposes. A patient is placed upon a sandpainting while holy words are sung over him, and "the pollen itself animate[s] the sandpainting with life."[5] Corn transforms art into therapeutic power. Quoting Navajo Community College Museum director Harry Walters, Griffin-Pierce explains further that, in a Navajo teleology, corn is a metaphor for life because people go through the same stages corn does. We sprout and grow, tassel out, burst forth with fruit, and eventually wither. Just as corn diffuses its pollen, every time a thoughtful person "talks, thinks, or acts, he does so in radiance, or in a state of wisdom and harmony."[6] The multi-layered connotations of corn as creatrix, sustenance, and sacramental cannot be overstated. As the Laguna writer Paula Gunn Allen lay dying, she asked only that corn songs be sung for her.[7]

In most Native societies, corn is also closely associated with creative and procreative observances. Cherokee brides give their husbands ears of corn signifying their vows to be industrious helpmeets. Puberty rites for Navajo girls as well as wedding ceremonies for traditional Hopis emphasize corn's affinity with the feminine and the generative. At their *kinaaldas*, or becoming-a-woman ceremonies, Navajo girls grind enough corn to make a cake sufficient for all invited guests. Hopi brides grind corn for three days as part of their nuptial rites; furthermore, their wedding garments replicate an ear of corn. When Hopi babies are born, they are kept in a darkened room for nineteen days. On the twentieth day, they are presented to the sun, named, and corn mush is put in their mouths and they are told that corn is their primary sustenance for the remainder of their lives. Corn gives and sustains life to man just as corn pollen animates verbal and visual art. It follows then that corn is essential to American literary creation. Corn is generated in the earth, First Text, and it is closely associated with the divine. Like the earth, corn operates as substance as well as metaphor, and it has empowering and transformational qualities. Given the importance of this grain to Native societies, it is reasonable to believe that the Wampanoags also venerated corn, and their attitudes and customs must have touched Bradford in some way.

It was in April, during the corn planting season, that John Carver died and a new governor was chosen. Here Plymouthean history seems to correspond to Algonquian ceremonial timing. Carver was planted in the earth like corn, and a young stalk, Governor Bradford, subsequently grew, tasseled out, flourished, and disseminated his verbal pollen just as his corn narrative engendered his history and informed its plot. Corn eventually withers, and so did the corn trade, Bradford, and Plymouth Colony; thus the Principal Patriarch's corn narrative, historically and metaphorically, duplicates both the historian's life and the Colony's. Equally important, however, is the recognition that Bradford's corn narrative eventually transforms into a wampum narrative and finally into a narrative of the Algonquians themselves. These transformations mirror the events of the initial explorations when the Newcomers first find caches of corn, then graves containing wampum strings, and finally encounter the Natives themselves.

As the Plymoutheans settle into their village, corn quickly becomes important to them as a primary food source, as a commodity for trade, and as a substance for commercialization. Bradford notes its significance in many passages beginning in book 1 and continuing through book 2. Although it is unlikely that Bradford ever consciously regarded corn as a holy substance, it is obvious that his unintentional text does. Bradford's diegetic text shows corn used only as food and currency. His hypodiegetic text, however, assigns it its feminine attributes and its holy office.

The Plymoutheans discover corn on the second day of their second foray into the land, November 16, 1620. They find a field where corn had recently been grown, and they uncover a store of it, which they describe as "faire and good, of diverce collours . . . a very goodly sight." Bradford's language here assigns corn feminine and beneficent qualities. It is both "faire and good." Taking this Native grain back to the ship, Bradford refers to it as a "spetiall providence of God and a great mercie to this poore people." Although the relevance of his determinations probably does not penetrate his consciousness, he has, nevertheless, connected corn both with the feminine and the divine. He has underscored its importance to humanity. More important, the Principal Patriarch has entered these associations into American letters.

Unfortunately, Plymoutheans never consciously recognized the sacred aspect of corn. It was for them primarily a food and a substitute for money. After Tisquantum taught the New Patuxets to plant and till it, corn became their chief support. Their first harvest was so good that "they had aboute a peck a meale a weeke to a person, or now since harvest, Indean corne to yᵉ proportion. Which made many afterwards write so largly of their plenty hear to their freinds in England, which were not fained, but true reports."

At the same time that the Plymoutheans were learning to grow corn, they were also trading extensively for it and with it. Their expanding corn trade resulted in boatbuilding, which increased Plymouthean exposure to Algonquians and their territories. Success in the corn trade also occasioned additional construction in the Colony since storehouses had to be erected to accommodate the grain. Utilizing every acre of available ground, the Plymoutheans planted corn even around their trading posts as soon as they constructed them. Wherever they went, they took the grain with them. They set great store by this commodity.

Corn's value as currency was always apparent to the Plymoutheans. As early as 1624, corn becomes "more pretious than silver," and it assumes the function of the gold standard. "Those that had some [corn] to spare, begane to trade one with another for smale things, by yᵉ quarte, potle, & peck, &c.; for money they had none, and if any had, corne was prefered before it."

Although the Plymoutheans never understand corn's holy office, the grain does eventually acquire metaphorical and political status in the Colony. Corn becomes a measure for telling time, maintaining peace, and waging war. During difficult occasions, the Plymoutheans make "shift till corne was ripe." In legal documents, such as the Niantic-Narragansett Treaty with the United Colonists, all parties agree that "no hostile acts should be comitted upon Uncass . . . until after yᵉ next planting of corne." Weston's men spread the rumor among the Natives that Bradford was going to "take their corne by force," and that prevarication becomes the provocation for an Algonquian "conspiracie against yᵉ English," which ultimately leads to the murders of Wituwamat, Pecksuot, and the others, an event that results in a serious reprimand for Plymouth's second governor. Plymouthean issues of morality and legality often center on corn, so much so in fact that criminal offenses involving corn became part of the Colony's legal code. In Plymouth's dark days, when starvation stalks the settlement, stealing corn constitutes an offense punished by whipping even "for a few ears."

As the Plymoutheans became adept at cultivating corn, their trade with the Algonquians increased and so did the jealousy of neighboring colonies. "But now they begane to be envied, and others wente and fild ye Indeans with corne, and beat downe ye prise, giveing them [the Indians] twise as much as they [the Plymoutheans] had done, and under traded them in other comodities allso."

Within the Colony, corn was instrumental in initiating Plymouthean social change. It was one of the reasons Plymouth switched from communism to capitalism, and it was the impetus for allotting land to individual families or to households of which single men were a part:

> So they begane to thinke how they might raise as much corne as they could, and obtaine a beter crope then they had done, that they might not still thus languish in miserie. At length . . . the Govr ··· gave way that they should set corne every man for his owne perticuler, and in that regard trust to them selves. . . . And so assigned to every family a parcell of land. (162)

It is interesting on several counts that here Bradford substitutes the term *family* for *man* when referring to a household. The use of *family* could perhaps indicate a move away from the constraints of patriarchy for which the Separatist/Puritans were noted. Linking corn and families aligns Plymouthean families with various American Indian families for whom the Corn Mother provided. Ꭴ The Cherokee Corn Mother, 4M, appeared on the earth in human form and instructed her sons to kill her and drag her body over the ground. 4M then caused her blood to sprout corn for her family's sustenance and for all Cherokees. DhBᎾᏆ. Ꭴ Algonquians, too, tell that story. Their First Mother of the People, a woman "fair" and ageless, convinced her loving husband to kill her and drag her body across the earth so that her blood and bones would provide corn and tobacco for her children.[8] Bradford's renderings are not as vivid as the Native accounts, but they nevertheless advance themes of feminine action and maternal involvement with familial subsistence.

Among the Algonquians in the seventeenth century, only women cultivated corn, and by 1623 the Plymouthean women were doing the same because the men were needed for other tasks. Bradford writes that "the women now wente willingly into yᵉ feild, and tooke their litle-ons with them to set corne." It seems as though the women were becoming Indianized and corn cultivation was becoming a family enterprise, but more important, the Plymoutheans were also understanding intuitively the feminine connection to the life-giving corn. Men were no longer tilling it. Women were. Of course, the Plymouthean women should have planted their corn at night while singing the appropriate songs, but that small fault can be overlooked since they were just learning and did not have a Native woman to instruct them properly.

It is humorous and thought-provoking that the generative attribute of corn was not completely lost on Bradford. The linking of corn and procreation is perhaps subconsciously evidenced in the passage below. In 1627, an English ship bound for Virginia had trouble, got lost, and its passengers and crew eventually were forced to spend the winter at Plymouth. The wealthy passengers asked the Plymoutheans for land so that their servants might clear and plant in order to be kept busy during the winter and spring months instead of remaining idle. Bradford mentions that these visitors were duly appointed ground, and one Passenger Fells put in a crop:

> Fells & some other of them raised a great deall of corne, which they sould at their departure. This Fells, amongst his other servants, had a maid servante which kept his house & did his household affairs, and by the intimation of some that belonged unto him, he was suspected to keep her, as his concubine; and both of them were examined ther upon, but nothing could be proved, and they stood upon their justification; so with admonition they were dismiste. But afterward it appeard she was with child, so he gott a small boat, & ran away with her, for fear of punishmente. (265)

In keeping with his theme of the godly, put-upon Saints, Bradford rarely misses an opportunity to expose the moral failures of Plymouthean visitors, and the Fells interpolation is essentially an adultery narrative, or an DꞮⱠⱣⱭⰬ 0ⱫꝒꝰ ⱺⱨ, that emphasizes the ethical watchfulness of the elect. Then why the mention of corn? In this passage at least two points are clear: One is that First Mother is whispering in William's ear, telling him what corn is all about—creation and people. The other is that, like a knowledgeable Indian, Fells apparently planted his corn at night.

Bradford's corn narrative continues through more than five hundred pages of his history. Corn generates plot and historical realities just as it nourishes the Colony. We see that the first taxes levied in Plymouth were to be paid in corn. "Towards ye maintenance of Gov^rt, & publick officers of ye said collony, every male above ye age of 16. years shall pay a bushell of Indean wheat, or ye worth of it, into ye commone store." In Bradford's bible, corn functioning as legal tender frequently occasions betrayal. The Principal Patriarch shows us how Allerton betrayed the Colony and tried, like Weston's men, to cut into the corn trade. "Mr Allerton plaid his owne game, and rane a course not only to ^ye great wrong & detrimente of ye plantation, who imployed & trusted him, but abused them in England also."

We find out that after the Algonquians are supplied with English hoes, their corn production increases, and yet for reasons not stated some Algonquians near the Colony stop cultivating it. At this juncture, the Plymoutheans reverse the process begun at Contact, and they begin supplying the Natives with corn, an act that advances the Plymouthean mirroring of the Algonquians. This strange twist also suggests that Plymouth is, probably unknowingly, becoming a part of the Algonquian cultural system. It is not inconceivable that the local Algonquian women recognized a good thing when they saw it. They may have been thinking, *Let those Pilgrim women work for a while, and we will get caught up with the mending. . . . In fact, we could even go fishing or take a trip up the coast.*

Prosperity finally prevails in Plymouth, and appetite for land increases. By 1627, Plymoutheans are demanding twenty acres per family in addition to the one-acre plots they already possess. Dividing the land into twenty-acre parcels will cause an expansion of the Colony and move citizens apart. Bradford and his council attempt to keep the community intact:

> But yet seekeing to keepe ye people togither . . . they allso agreed upon this order, . . . before any lots were cast: that whose lotts so-ever should fall next ye towne, or most conveninte for nearnes, they should take to them a neigboure or tow, whom they best liked; and should suffer them to plant corne with them for 4. years; and afterwards they might use as much of theirs for as long time, if they would. (260)

Bradford and his Deputy Patriarchs, Brewster and Winslow, earnestly desired that Old Plymouth continue to be the moral, social, and legal center of the Colony. They knew that as the Plymoutheans dispersed to acquire additional land, the center could not hold. The passage above indicates that Plymouth's chief administrators used corn as a way of keeping the community tightly bound. Here Bradford's diegetic and hypodiegetic narratives converge as they insist upon the notion that there is both a familial and a civil connection to corn, a belief that American Indians have long respected.

As interest in corn increases and its status changes from "necessity" to surplus, "the planters [find] their corne . . . to be a comoditie," which the Governor manages and confines to the "generall good." In Plymouth, corn is never traded on the "perticuler." The practice of not allowing corn to be traded for individual profit attests to the Pilgrims' liminal acknowledgment of its sacred nature. Corn was given to profit all humanity, not just the mercantile few. In this respect, Plymouth does not abuse First Mother's intrinsic nature.

Learning to cultivate corn brought the Plymoutheans peace and prosperity. Although they never assigned corn a sacred status, they did acknowledge its beneficent power. Their ability to cultivate a new crop successfully and sustain themselves with it in the New World became a source of self-satisfaction for the Plymoutheans. Bradford's words, which emphasize ideas of community and happiness conjoined with corn, summarize the Plymoutheans' regard for this precious commodity. With pride the Principal Patriarch notes that his colleagues suffer hardships in order to protect it:

> It pleased ye Lord to give ye plantation peace and health and contented minds, and so to blese ther labours, as they had corne sufficient, (and some to spare to others). . . . After harvest . . . they sende out a boats load of corne 40. or 50. leagues to ye east-ward, up a river called Kenibeck. . . . They had laid a litle deck over her midships to keepe ye corne drie, but the men were faine to stand it out all weathers without shelter. . . . But God preserved them, and gave them good success, for they brought home 700.[pounds] of beaver, besids some other furrs, having litle or nothing els but this corne, which them selves had raised out of ye earth. (246–47)

Bradford's corn narrative is highlighted by his relation of the 1623 drought in which "ye corne begane to wither away, though it was set with fishe." In the face of such disaster, Bradford orders a day of humiliation. After much prayer, rain falls, and the corn revives. The dying corn and other fruits "did so apparently revive & quicken . . . as was wonderfull to see, and made ye Indeans astonished to behold." At this point in the history, Bradford's hypodiegetic text connects corn to the divine and to the miraculous.

When Bradford's corn narrative transforms into a wampum narrative, the same nexus is continued. His corn and wampum tropes show us that the Plymoutheans initially found both substances in the earth, or in the First Text. They touched them and literally ingested them, but what is important in an American Indian worldview is that the Native symbolic attributes of the corn and wampum, perhaps expressed in western European thought as muse and word, or as literary inspiration and the artifact, are never rendered powerless by European innocence. The essential nature of the wampum, the metaphors of corn, together with Indian words and characters, exist and signify in many European American works in much the same way that they are presented in the Bradford text.

Wampum, or "wampampeak," is first mentioned in Bradford's text in the *Articles of Agreement Between Plymouth and the Adventurers* in 1627. "Secondly, ye above-said parties are to have and freely injoye ye pinass latly builte, the boat at Manamett, and . . . all other implements to them belonging, that is in ye store of ye said company; with all ye whole stock of furrs, fells, beads, corne, wampampeak, hatchets, knives, &c."

That the usage of the word *wampampeak* occurs in a contract is altogether fitting and highly significant. Bradford's hypodiegetic text has discovered the true function of ceremonial wampum, which was to seal a verbal agreement mnemonically. Ceremonial wampum was an incipient writing system used to document the articles of contracts, social compacts, or treaties.[9] Wampum belts were also used to send messages and call meetings. Small strings of wampum sent to women were marriage proposals. Before it acquired an archival function, however, it is possible that wampum had been used simply for ornamentation, but with the passage of time wampum took on more than one employment.[10]

Ceremonial wampum was a drilled tubular bead either purple or white. White wampum was made from a fairly common seashell, *Pyrula carica*, and purple or black wampum was made from the clamshell, *Venus mercenaria*. In order to be read and preserved, the wampum was usually woven into chains or belts. According to Frank Speck in *The Functions of Wampum among the Eastern Algonkian* (1919), wampum was developed first by the Iroquois and was designed for use in ceremonies such as the Iroquois

Rite of Condolence.[11] Special keepers were designated to preserve the wampum and to read the belts. Perhaps the most famous of the wampum belts are those commemorating the Great Law of Peace of the Iroquois League. Coastal Algonquians, noting the demand for wampum, began to manufacture great quantities of it to supply the Iroquois, and they also began using it for recording their own contracts, treaties, and other important transactions.

Colonization caused a permutation of wampum's true function. Since the beads changed hands when agreements were made, Europeans probably assumed it was Native currency. They began to acquire it first as a trade item and then began using it as legal tender. As Richard Slotkin observes, "The European concept of 'intrinsic value' currency (with its concomitant ideas of the methods for economic success) was antithetical to the Indian concept of currency as a mask for 'spiritual and supernatural interplay.'"[12]

Wampum has its own origin accounts. The Penobscots tell of a bird that can shake wampum from his feathers. The bird has the power of prophesy, and when he shakes out white wampum, good news is forthcoming. When he drops black wampum, the news is unfortunate.[13] There are several other Algonquian accounts declaring that wampum is a gift from birds, but a Wabanaki narrative recalls that wampum derives from the tobacco smoke of sorcerers. White wampum is produced by the strongest sorcerer; black, or actually purple wampum, is brought forward by the weakest.[14] Tobacco is also an American Indian sacramental, so its connection to wampum underscores the sacred nature of the bead. Sorcerers are medicine men, persons who specialize in ritual words, so in both accounts the relationship of beads to words is evident.

It is pertinent to this discussion to note that a significant number of American Indian languages employ classifiers to designate nouns as either animate or inanimate. In a paper read before the American Anthropological Association at Philadelphia in 1915, Speck notes that among the Wabanakis "the ceremonial wampum is figuratively termed *gelusewa'ngan*, [or] speech," and in *Functions of Wampum* he marvels that the Algonquian language tends to use animate substantive endings for the plural forms of the various Algonquian words referring to wampum beads."[15] Although Speck dismisses this tendency as linguistic carelessness, I and other scholars like Jerry Martien see the significance of these classifiers.[16] Wampum represents the spoken word, and the spoken word is animated or alive.

William Weeden in *Indian Money as a Factor in New England Civilization* (1884) likewise notes that the "facts [of tribal life have] been 'talked into' the beads, literally. A mystic power animate[s] the beads, thus quickened by the acts and deeds of this simple but intense savage life."[17]

Probably Bradford's first exposure to wampum was in its original form as ornament or gift. When the Plymoutheans opened the Native grave containing a small child, they found upon its skeleton "strings and bracelets of fine white beads." It is true that some wampum pieces, often discoidal, were intended for gift giving and personal decoration, but either as gift or ornamentation, the wampum serves as a *remembrance* just as a ring today can symbolize a friendship, an engagement, a marriage, an anniversary, a birthday, or one's sense of aesthetics.[18]

Symbolic function aside, Bradford's diegetic concern with wampum is with the beads as commodity. He asserts that what "turned most to their profite, in time, was an entrance into the trade of Wampampeake." By 1628, wampum was replacing corn as the Colony's principal asset. As it did, Bradford's tropes, noting the changes that the permutation of wampum makes upon the Natives, followed suit. For a brief time, wampum renders the Algonquians very strong:

> And strange it was to see the great allteration [wampum] made in a few years amonge yᵉ Indeans them selves; for all the Indeans of these parts, & yᵉ Massachusetts, had none or very litle of it, but yᵉ sachems & some spetiall persons that wore a litle of it for ornamente. Only it was made & kepte amonge yᵉ Nariganssets, & Pequents, which grew rich & potent by it, and these people were poore & begerly. (282)

As wampum transformed into currency, American Indians were able to purchase guns and powder, thus temporarily brokering military power in their favor and consequently making the English uneasy. The political unrest generated by Native ascendancy resulted eventually in the Indians' undoing.

Wampum's literary significance was translated into economic potential for Colonist and Native alike. A Native literary critic could conclude that it was actually the vitality of the word, or the Native literature, that made Plymoutheans and the Algonquians momentarily rich. For one brief bibliophilic moment, Algonquians and Plymoutheans alike were cranking out best sellers, but as the ideogram became coin the Algonquians flooded the

market with penny dreadfuls, and that which could have been a literary renaissance for all became a debacle for the Indians and contributed to their
political ruin. What is important to understand about this metamorphosis
of wampum in early American history is that American Indian literature,
whether oral or written in wampum, is essentially power, and that power
can be manifested in many different ways. Bradford's text underscores
the wampum's strength when released from its intended purpose and set
adrift.

In 1634, Bradford was advised via a letter from John Winthrop that
the Pequots had come to Boston offering wampum and beaver if the Bay
would ally with them against the Narragansetts. With Winthop's letter
to Bradford in which he describes the Pequot offer, Bradford includes another note from Winthrop saying that when the Bay sent a pinass to the
Pequots to pick up their promised tributes, "they put of but litle comoditie,
and [we] found them a very false people." I believe that this information
means that the Pequots did not come forward with the wampum because
no satisfactory agreement had been reached. The Bay had demanded that
the Pequots deliver up the men who had killed one John Stone, an English
trader with an unsavory reputation. They also wanted the Pequots to cede
their lands in Connecticut to them, and they ordered the Pequots to make
peace with the Narragansetts. The wampum would have been an official
record of the mutually agreed upon accord. If there were no agreement to
this rather tall order, there could be no confirmation. Rather than being
"false," the Pequots were probably being astute businesspeople and quite
honest. It is fair to hypothesize that the Pequot Council could not and
would not agree to the Bay's stipulations that the Pequot diplomats had
reported to them. They did not deliver the expected wampum because
there was no agreement to draw up. In other words, they took their paper
and ink off the table.

The Pequots' overture in Boston, with its attendant outcomes, eventu-
ated in their massacre at Mystic, an atrocity that in turn created a precari-
ous state of affairs between colonists and Natives. Bradford relates that
the general uneasiness was increased in 1638, when Arthur Peach, Thomas
Jackson, Richard Stinnings, and Daniel Crose killed a Narragansett for
five fathoms of wampum and three cloth coats. This crime resulted in
three executions and intensified colonial animosity toward the Algonquians. The Peach affair, and several similar incidents perpetrated by both

Indians and non-Indians, resulted in widespread unrest, which culminated in the Second Puritan Conquest known as King Philip's War of 1675, a war Bradford did not live to see.[19]

In the period between the 1637 massacre and 1645, Bradford reports "sundrie insolencies and outrages [committed] upon severall plantations of yᵉ English." He further notes that the Natives "have combined them selves against [the English]." In order to protect themselves, the plantations of Massachusetts Bay, Plymouth, Connecticut, and New Haven form a Confederation of United Colonies for "mutuall help & strength . . ." against the Algonquians, and they draw up articles of confederation to define their purpose and provide guidelines for their actions. It is interesting to note the similarities between their articles and Native practice. Their articles call for peace chiefs and war chiefs and decree that decisions be made by consensus. They prohibit any one commissioner from having absolute authority. They also designate that annual meetings will be "yᵉ first Thursday in September," a time that closely corresponds to many American Indian new year celebrations, and they prescribe a ritual order for those meetings, beginning and ending in Boston, or in this case, center.

It appears that in addition to modeling its articles on European models such as the Articles of Utrecht 1579, the Confederation is also emulating American Indian paradigms to some extent. Native cultural practices and European political applications quickly fuse in the New World.[20]

The Confederation began to concern itself with Algonquian affairs in an effort to maintain a Native equilibrium that favorably accommodated the colonies. Thrown off guard by so many new players in Old Algonquia, American Indian Nations became fraught with internal strife and they inadvertently played into the colonists' hands. When the Confederation of United Colonies convinced Uncas to execute the Narragansett Miantonomo, the Narragansetts and the Niantics, who apparently had not paid his ransom in wampum, revolted.[21] The country was then brought to the brink of civil war. Bradford writes that the Narragansetts "gathered a great power, and fell upon Uncass, and slew many of his men." Because this attack abrogated an agreement made between the Narragansetts and the Confederation the previous year, the Confederation began to raise troops to defend Uncas as they had promised. "Yᵉ Narigansets, hearing therof, tooke the advantage, and came suddanly upon him [Uncas], and gave him another blow, to his further loss."

When the Confederation tried to convince the Narragansetts and Niantics to leave Uncas alone, they were treated with "scorne & contempt." The Indians

> resolved to have no peace without Uncass his head; also they gave them this further answer: that it mattered not who begane yᵉ warr, they were resolved to follow it, and that yᵉ English should withdraw their garison from Uncass, or they would procure yᵉ Mowakes against them; [moreover], . . . they would lay yᵉ English catle on heaps, as high as their houses, and yᵗ no English-man should sturr out of his dore to pisse, but he should be kild. (516–17)

Winthrop's return of their proffered wampum gift-offer, however, did open the way for new negotiations. The Narragansett sachems, Pessecuss, Mixano, and Witowash, with the Niantic Awasequen, met with the Confederation to arrange a cessation of hostilities that resulted in the following agreement:

> 1. It was agreed . . . that yᵉ said Narigansets & Niantick sagamores should pay or cause to be payed at Boston, to yᵉ Massachusets comis-sioners, yᵉ full sume of 2000. fathome of good white wampame, or a third parte of black wampampeage, in 4. payments. . . .
> 2. The foresaid sagamors . . . [shall] restore unto Uncass . . . captives, . . . canowes, [and] . . . such corne as they . . . have spoyled. . . .
> 5. The said . . . sagamores . . . will pay . . . a yearly tribute, a month before harvest, . . . for all such Pequents as live amongst them, . . . namly, one fathome of white wampum for every Pequent man, & half a fathume for each Pequent youth, and one hand length for each mal-child. (521–23)

These tributes amount to an immense quantity of beads, or in my view, a copious outpouring of powerful native words; moreover, four Narragansett and Niantic children were to be held hostage until these tributes were paid.[22] In an American Indian hermeneutic, there is a blurring of distinction here between word and blood. American Indian boys and wampum were the surety for the ascendance of European American letters. Native contractual language was sacrificed to secure human life.

The Narragansetts and Niantics received nothing from this agreement. Essentially, they paid a very high price for having committed some random acts of violence against the English and Uncas who had profited by supporting the English against the Pequots at Mystic. As Bradford's hypodiegetic text notes, it is the end for the "Endeans."

Bradford's wampum narrative depicts the transformation from wampum as remembrance to wampum as currency. *Of Plimoth Plantation* demonstrates how ceremonial art was cut into pieces to maintain the Native social order, to ransom (or not) Indian lives, and to pay taxes on Indian land then occupied by Europeans. This desperate trend culminated years later in the quartering of Metacomet's wampum-clad body and in the bestowal of his sacred belts to Benjamin Church. Reputedly, Church presented the wampum records to Josiah Winslow, then governor of Plymouth, as a war trophy, and Winslow in turn sent them to England as a gift to Charles II. The belts were carried to England by Winslow's brother-in-law, Major Waldegrave Pelham, but it is unclear whether the British ever received them or not. Metacomet's ceremonial belts are, for the present, lost to history.[23]

As wampum degenerated from American Indian letters to European currency and conquest souvenirs, it nevertheless preserved its close connection to American Indian lives and fortunes. As the Christian Word became Corban, so did the American Indian's. It was severed and scattered but not obliterated. Transfigured, it entered American letters to become a rarely noticed but vibrant trope at the moment the Pequots brought it to Winthrop as a pledge and a sacrifice.

5 ANIMALS AND TRICKSTERS
SᴲWᴶP

RᴛT. Human characters, or characters understood to be human, play minor roles in American Indian medicine texts. There is, however, a blurring between entities described as human and those described as animal. A Micmac storyteller explains the concept like this: "In the beginning of things, men were as animals and animals as men. . . ."[1] The concept pertinent to this volume is the understanding that in most sacred narratives, many of the major characters appear primarily in animal form. Because these narratives are set in primordial time, man is relatively inconsequential to the series of events. Holy People, animals, birds, reptiles, insects, plants, and minerals are the beings that assist in forming the earth and in making the world safe for human life.

In one Wampanoag tradition, 4WᴕᴔⅡ, or Muskrat, brings up mud from the ocean floor and creates earth.[2] In Native sacred narratives there are animal benefactors who enhance human existence, and there are animal tricksters who remind man of his intellectual and physical limitations and show him how to overcome them. Because animals normally precede man in the scheme of things and assist him in myriad ways, their hierarchical position is respected in Native sacred works. Their power is essential for physical and psychological healing.

Modern Native literature continues this tradition. Novels such as Linda Hogan's *Mean Spirit* and James Welch's *Winter in the Blood* are two examples of this widespread practice. In *Mean Spirit*, bees adumbrate the central action; the slaughter of eagles galvanizes a Nation to assess the present reality and reaffirm its values; bat medicine revives and sustains a threatened culture. In *Winter in the Blood*, deer understand the mood of the times; a wayward calf and a headstrong horse precipitate a fatal accident that shapes the plot; and a wise duck provides a symbolic narrative interpolation. These American Indian novels, and many like them, feature animals as catalysts for action. Animals are central to the plots, and often their status equals that of humans in terms of importance to the meaning of the works. European writers and critics center textual meaning on portraying and interpreting human action. Native writers often use animal action to substitute for human action and give symbolic weight to their works; therefore, critics must analyze any embedded animal narratives if they are to interpret Native works meaningfully.

Algonquian sacred texts existed at one time and probably still do. Charles Leland, who did extensive field work with Wabanakis in the latter part of the nineteenth century, collected many oral narratives and published them in a volume originally entitled *The Algonquin Legends of New England; or, Myths and Folk Lore of the Micmac, Passamaquoddy, and Penobscot* (1884). He acquired most of the accounts from living storytellers, and he came to the conclusion that "most of these Indian traditions were originally poems. It is probable that all were sung, while they still retained the character of serious mythical or sacred narrative. Now they are in the transition state of heroic tales. But they unquestionably still retain many passages of very great antiquity."[3]

Replicating the essence of the Native medicine texts swirling about them, both Winslow and Bradford include animal stories to give depth, animation, factual information, and allegorical substance to their works. *Mourt's Relation* and *Of Plimoth Plantation* have two distinct animal narratives. One features European animals while the other portrays Native creatures.

As Mourt describes the *Mayflower's* entry into American coastal waters, he mentions the abundance of cod, the presence of whales, mussels "full of sea-pearl[s]," and "the greatest store of fowl that ever we saw." Mourt's opening lines seem to correspond closely to the opening of Leland's version of a Wabanaki creation account. In order to regain his family, which an evil sorcerer had stolen and taken across a bay, Glooskap, the principal Eastern Algonquian culture hero, sings a whale song to summon a sea creature large enough to ferry him across the water. A large female whale responds and carries Glooskap on her back to the opposite shore, but during the crossing she is warned by clams to stay out of the shoals. Glooskap overrides her objections to swimming in shallow water, and when she safely beaches him, he pushes her back out to sea and gives her tobacco and a short pipe, which she still smokes.[4] Mourt must have seen her smoke plume. Just as whales and bivalves are players in an Eastern Algonquian creation account, they likewise open Mourt's.

Once on land, Mourt is quick to mention that the hungry explorers shoot ducks and geese for their supper, and to some extent they live out another Wabanaki story—that of Lox's unseemly slaughter of waterfowl for his winter stores, an account in which he and a small boy lure a large number of birds into a wigwam so that Lox can easily kill them.[5] Granted, the Pilgrim Fathers do not deceive the birds, they just kill them; however, in Mourt's text, Native animals represent bounty just as they do in the Native tale. They also call up the sacred Algonquian narrative the Newcomers have entered.

It is Mourt's European animal narrative, however, that moves his plot and adds color, beastie characters, and symbolic content to his text. This stratum of narrative begins when Mourt relates that John Goodman, a *Mayflower* passenger, had apparently brought with him two dogs, a female mastiff and a spaniel. Here John is strangely reminiscent of Glooskap, who also owned two dogs, one white and the other black, and both wolves. On January 12, John Goodman and another passenger, Peter Brown, together with the spaniel and mastiff went out looking for a pleasant place to enjoy lunch after a morning of cutting thatch, but in the evening they did not return. Search parties were organized to look for the men, but they yielded nothing. After nearly two days, the two men reappeared much the worse for wear but still alive. Goodman suffered frostbite and both were famished. They reported that, as they had sat near a lake having their noon meal, the dogs spotted a "great deer" and chased it into the forest. The men ran after the dogs and finally caught them, but soon realized they had become lost. They had no weapons, insufficient clothing, and little food; the weather was freezing and snowing. As they tried to sleep on the cold ground, they became aware that three "lions" were stalking them. As one lion crept close, "the bitch they were fain to hold by the neck, for she would have been gone to the lion; but it pleased God so to dispose, that the wild beasts came not." It is interesting to note here that one of the Massasoit's first official greeters to the Plymoutheans came wearing a lion's skin. Continuity and transformation are basic to American Indian literature.

Several days later, Goodman again decided to venture out in order to "use his lame feet," and he took his little spaniel with him. Again there is an animal adventure.

> A little way from the plantation two great wolves ran after the dog; the dog ran to him and betwixt his legs for succor. He had nothing in his hand but took up a stick, and threw at one of them and hit him, and they presently ran both away, but came again; he got a pale-board in his hand, and they sat both on their tails, grinning at him a good while, and went their way and left him. (47–48)

In Mourt's text, the Native animals evoke the area's Native original creatures; they are living representations of primordial characters and they communicate with the humans. They expose the Newcomers to a sacred narrative and are somewhat emblematic of the Native people surrounding Plymouth. Like the Algonquians, the animals watch the Plymoutheans, interact with them and even tease them, but offer no harm. Perhaps the wolves were Glooskap's.

Mourt's text also establishes that European animals and Native animals communicate with each other before European and Native humans do; thus the medicine text sequencing of animals existing before people is preserved in *Mourt's Relation*. Mourt's narrative also makes clear that the Saints and Strangers have entered a New World and are basically as innocent and alone as First Man and First Woman at the time of Creation. Like the First Humans, they also are actors in a new narrative, and they must depend upon animals for their existence and protection.

Of Plimoth Plantation's animal narrative, like Mourt's, also bifurcates into distinct European and Native strata. Neither narrative is happy, and each provides symbolic significance to the history. Bradford's Part I begins the Native animal story with the casual mention of seeing "5. or 6. persons with a dogg coming towards them" on November 15, 1620. The Newcomers follow the Natives, but the Indians disappear, almost ephemerally. They leave no track that the English can follow. In many Algonquian narratives, Glooskap wanders the area with his dogs, and this possible and unintended Algonquian allusion could bring Native creation accounts to mind. It is as if the settlers have met with something greater than themselves. Something they cannot quite touch but intensely want. Because interaction was impossible at this time, Bradford simply notes the incident and moves on. In his December 6 entry, he mentions seeing Indians cutting up a large fish that the Newcomers cannot recognize. He also relates that they come across deer, water "foule," and wild turkeys.

As the Plymoutheans settle in, they take shellfish for food and begin to recognize familiar species of fish, particularly bass and cod. During their first year at Patuxet, they live almost entirely off native animals, fish, deer, and turkeys. Seeing an abundance of fish, they immediately attempt to fish commercially in an effort to pay down their debt, but they have only limited success at that undertaking. In order to transport fish to Europe, they must have a large quantity of salt, and their salt-production efforts are sabotaged at every turn.

Plymouth's big financial breakthrough comes when the Newcomers see **Vꙮ**, Beaver, and **Irꙮ**, Otter, for the first time and learn that there is a demand for beaver pelts in Europe. Beaver finances the Colony and keeps it afloat for more than sixteen years; and he quickly becomes the linch-pin that holds the Adventurers to the Colony, because beaver pelts are a surer commodity for trade than fish. When beaver prices fall, the investors can hold pelts in warehouses until prices recover; thus Beaver offers both Plymouthean and Adventurer commercial stability and durability. Beaver is the product that eventually discharges the Colony's debt to the Adven-turers, and Beaver enters Plymouthean official written documents and be-comes part of the literature when Bradford records the pounds of pelts the Colony sends to England and creates a narrative concerning these sales.

Of Plimoth Plantation depicts Beaver as a hero. His narrative dominates the animal stratum and winds through most of the history. At least once, Beaver goes down with a storm-tossed ship while endeavoring to save the Colony from financial ruin, and like Winslow, who was once jailed in London while attempting to assist Plymouth, Beaver endures English warehouse captivity for the good of the Colony. Enterprising and faithful, Beaver labors diligently for Plymouth yet is forsaken for wampum when that commodity rises in value. Somewhat emblematic of Plymouth itself in terms of sacrifice and eventual outcome, Beaver is second only to corn as a Native nonhuman helpmeet for Plymouth. *Of Plimoth Plantation's* Bea-ver narrative works like the animal narratives in American Indian medicine texts. **Vꙮ** is the spirit being that assists the Newcomers.

Of Plimoth Plantation's European animal narrative documents causa-tion and evokes pity. It begins when Bradford reports that, in 1624, Win-slow brought back from England "3. heifers & a bull." Swine were later introduced. The animals multiply and by 1627 can be allotted to individual families. A family of six persons was entitled to one cow and two goats. Swine were similarly proportioned. Bradford's European animal narrative creates plot. As animal numbers increase, demand for land increases exponentially, and the need for additional land causes the Colony to break up and scatter. "And no man now thought he could live, except he had catle and a great deale of ground to keep them; all striving to increase their stocks. By which means they were scattered all over y bay, quickly, and y towne, in which they lived compactly till now, was left very thine, and in a short time allmost desolate."

For the most part, Bradford's European animal narrative simply records predictable, historical events. Domesticated animals were introduced to the Colony for its survival and eventually became the reason for its dispersal. The unhappy portion of the domestic animal narrative surfaces when Thomas Granger, a teenage servant "to an honest man of Duxbury," is indicted for sodomy with "a mare, a cowe, two goats, five sheep, 2. calves, and a[n assimilated] turkey." He was executed for his crime, and the animals he accosted were similarly proscribed. "A very sade spectakle it was; for first the mare, and then ye cowe, and ye rest of ye lesser catle, were kild before his face, according to ye law, Levit:20.15. and then he him selfe was executed. The catle were all cast into a great & large pitte that was digged of purpos for them, and no use made of any part of them."

Bradford's mandatory, moral, and justificatory commentary on this unhappy event is limited to the observation that "one wicked person may infecte many; and what care all ought to have what servants they bring into their families." He found the Granger interlude troubling yet thought-provoking. It led him to wonder why "so many wicked persons and profane people should so quickly come over into this land, . . . seeing it was religious men y^t begane ye work." The Principal Patriarch's animal narratives, which include themes of survival, generosity, endurance, and the problem of evil, deepen the hermeneutical overtones of his text. The inclusion of nonhuman characters in his central action widens its scope.

With the passage above, Bradford's two animal narratives meld and end, but the coming together of European livestock and one Native wild bird, **EΘ**, presents at least two Native interpretative options. One: The unfortunate turkey's horrifying death could be read as yet another cautionary tale since it is somewhat reminiscent of the fate of American Indians across the continent. Apparently a close association with Europeans results in miserable and premature Native deaths. Two: That all the animals, the

Europeans and the one Native, are buried in the same pit points to the disappearance of obvious and well-executed animal narratives in American literature, until Herman Melville revives the genre after he reportedly learns about a mysterious white whale from Gay Head Natives.

It is probably no coincidence that Mourt begins American literature with a whale sighting, and that Melville elaborates on the same theme centuries later. Various interpretative perspectives notwithstanding, there are animal narratives in our first documents, and apparently Glooskap started the tradition when he shaped the animals, named them, and interacted with them at First Dawn.

DhR W ᏬᎫᏬᎩ

Closely connected to the animal narratives in medicine texts are the popular and well-known trickster tales that feature an animal in the title role. The healing chants usually contain a pronounced stratum of text concerned with deception, betrayal, general foolishness, dearth of intellectual and spiritual insight, contrariness, braggadocio, sex, and death, all components of life as humans live it. These threads of sacred narratives speak directly to the human condition and are often referenced as trickster tales, since they feature a protagonist dedicated to mayhem. Trickster narratives are not about the magnificent deeds of heroes or the beneficence of an unblemished Creator. They are about efficient-but-not-compassionate man and less-than-honorable behavior. Trickster tales are about us and gods like us.

Trickster tales, whether part of a sacred chant or operating independently as an oft-told fable, are highly entertaining narratives used to teach cultural values to children. It is important to remember that American Indian works are equilibratory. They have feminine and masculine properties; they honor the directions, the earth, the sky, the underworld, the upper world, water, air, and minerals, to name only a few. They also contain elements that appeal to elders and to children.[6] They are balanced works that seek to create a balanced world. Like fables and parables, trickster tales convey tribally specific cultural values or coping strategies that hearers then contextualize within a particular *Weltansicht*. Collaterally, the tales set up ethical conundrums that the hearers can deliberate. Because the conundrums are resistant to eternal ethical verities, hermeneutics are in constant play.

Trickster tales feature a hero who moves his narrative's plot from inception to finish. Trickster is usually recognizable to his hearers, who immediately understand that he must be viewed with suspicion. Like a used-car salesman in today's world, he may give us a deal, but there is always a possibility that he will cheat us. Trickster is arguably American Indians' most complex literary creation, and, according to Alan Velie, he is "alternately an evil spirit and a benevolent deity, a mortal and a god, a creator and a destroyer, a culture hero and a villain. . . . . He is always a wanderer, always hungry, and usually oversexed."[7]

Eastern Algonquians employ more than one trickster: **EC**, Raccoon; **Ir∂S**, Rabbit; **Irⱳ**, Otter; and **JℙꞪΘ**, Lox (or Wolverine) are several of his manifestations.[8] Some Southeastern Nations also employ **Ir∂S** while **GⱳℲ**, Coyote, or **AWCʼ**, Raven, do trickster work for many Western Nations. Some tricksters are just that and nothing more; others like the Wabanaki Glooskap or the Kiowa Saynday are morally complex Trickster/Creators. Regardless of his name, what is important about this character is his ability to prepare humans for life's complexities, perplexities, deceptions, and betrayals.

Trickster speaks to the intellect. He is about survival. When our flawed judgments cause misfortune, we must resort to our wits to save ourselves. Ethical lapses cause our distress, but quick mental expediency can save the day. When faced with a life-threatening dilemma, we can behave like the Algonquians' fairy-water-wives-turned-weasels who sweetly convince Lox to get them out of their self-imposed predicament. When we are out of the tree and on firm ground, we can then desert him. Lox can find other victims, and we weasel girls can go our merry way. Or like **Ir∂S**, the Cherokee Rabbit, we can outwit **ꝺW**, Fox, with reverse psychology after our runaway emotions have entangled us with Tar Baby.[9] We can be safe and recover in the briar patch. It is Trickster who teaches us to get in there and out again. Trickster insists upon rationality and expediency. For example, the Navajo Coyote proposed death as a means for ending the Dine's overpopulation problem. Trickster does not traffic in compassion or condolence. He's a very efficient finisher.

Trickster tales comprise a significant stratum of narrative in Bradford's history. Opening his chronicle by recognizing the Great Deceiver and reminding his readers that Satan "hath raised, maintained, and continued against the Saincts," Bradford weaves themes of deception, lust, evil, and betrayal and the agents of same throughout the history. Tricksters are everywhere working against the Pilgrims, duping them, selling them out, injuring them, occasionally underestimating them, and constantly offending their sensibilities. Like American Indian tricksters, the confidence men confronting Plymouth are never what they at first seem. They are men on the move, often lusty, frequently rowdy, always quick-witted and strangely ambivalent. Rarely can they be characterized as evil, but they are certainly controversial and they wreak havoc wherever they go. They also provide modern readers comic relief from the Saints' travails.

Of Plimoth Plantation's myriad and varied tricksters fall into two general categories: civil and religious. All are **DhR W ⚬J⚬**. Arguably Isaac Allerton, or **S GΘ⚬J⚬AT**, is *Of Plimoth Plantation's* chief trickster among the civil variety. His antics are performed on both sides of the Atlantic, where he takes in Saint, Stranger, and Adventurer alike. Prototypical both of Rabbit and Lucifer, Allerton leads Plymouthean Fathers straight to the "briers, [and] . . . leaves them to gett out as they can." Like Lucifer, Allerton begins as a trusted high official whose "owne gaine and private ends led him a side." Once fallen, he operates like Rabbit, hopping from scheme to scheme with clear intent to defraud.

One of the Scrooby émigrés, Allerton had come over on the *Mayflower* with the original one hundred. He was a signer of the *Mayflower Compact* and later an Undertaker of the Colony's debt. His wife, Mary Norris, died shortly after childbirth while on board the ship as it lay at anchor in Plymouth Harbor, and five years later he married a woman much younger than he, Fear Brewster, the daughter of William, Plymouth's revered lay-clergyman. Because Bradford was still suffering the effects of a serious illness when he was elected governor following the death of John Carver, Allerton was chosen his assistant and "by renewed election every year, [they] continued sundry years togeather." From the beginning, Allerton was located in a position of trust and respect, and he used that position to advance his aims.

Allerton quickly became the principal negotiator for the Colony's financial affairs. On several occasions he was sent to England to deal with the Adventurers, and it was on one of these trips that he turned into Rabbit. Thus some of the cardinal rules of tricksterism are observed: Trickster walks among us. We know him. He is always on the move and up to something. When opportunities for mischief present themselves, Trickster makes the most of them. For Allerton, the door to mischief opened easily. The Pilgrims were not shrewd businessmen looking for profit but were religious idealists dependent upon venture capitalists for temporary subsistence. The discrepancy between their dreams and the Adventurers' anticipated profits created a situation ripe for thimblerigging.

By 1625, the contract with the Adventurers originally agreed upon had broken down because of unexpected financial "losses and crosses" occasioned by maritime disasters and infighting among the investors over theological differences and fiscal uncertainties. Of the initial investors, principally James Sherley, Richard Andrews, William Collier, Thomas Fletcher, Timothy Hatherley, and John Beauchamp were left to carry on the business with Plymouth.[10] In order to forestall more deterioration of their vital partnership with the investors, Plymouth dispatches Edward Winslow and Isaac Allerton to London to salvage as much as they can of the original agreement. At this time, Plymouth's debt amounts to approximately 1,400 pounds sterling, but the interest rate offered by the Adventurers to keep the Colony afloat is 70 percent. Because Plymouth is not in a position to bargain, there is no alternative but to accept this outrageous agreement. The debt increases when a ship bound for England with the Colony's shipments of beaver and fish is lost to pirates. Miles Standish is then dispatched to England to discuss new terms with the Adventurers, but a plague hits London and effectively stops negotiations because businessmen have fled the city; however, Standish does receive an additional 150 pounds sterling worth of trade goods at 50 percent interest. Reeling from the impact of increasing debt and extortionate interest rates, Plymouth, disappointed with Standish's performance, sends Allerton by himself to England to pay down the debt, renegotiate the interest and payment schedules, secure additional supplies, and generally handle financial affairs.

On his first unaccompanied visit to England, Allerton's shrewd entrepreneurial agility impresses Sherley and the remaining investors, who immediately realize he is one of them. On this trip, Allerton arranges for an additional four hundred pounds' worth of supplies, ostensibly for Plymouth, and he secures a patent for the Kennebec trading post. Even though the patent is poorly executed and will have to be done over at a later date, he succeeds in winning both Sherley's and the Colony's trust. From this moment on, Allerton's course changes from nonconforming religiosity to private profiteering. An additional reason that Allerton is able to swindle Plymouth successfully is that he is married to Fear Brewster and can charge goods to his father-in-law, knowing full well that the Colony will never demand payment from their beloved elder. Neither will they extract a precise explanation for Brewster's son-in-law's questionable behavior and financial judgments. As Plymouth's agent, Allerton "scrued up his poore old father in law's accounte to above 200. [pounds] and brought it on yᵉ generall accounte . . . at 50. per cent."

During the period from 1627 to 1630, Allerton begins bringing over a small amount of goods "on his owne perticuler" to sell for his personal benefit. A problem emerges, however, when his commodities are not separated from the general merchandise and he takes the expensive items for his own inventory and leaves the cheap articles for the Colony. Adding insult to injury, Allerton then sells his merchandise outside the Colony, leaving the Plymoutheans without basic necessities. Allerton repeats this practice, and worse, on his next voyage. He brings back personal goods at Plymouthean expense and this time transports another trickster to the Colony, one Mr. Rogers, a minister who Bradford reports was "crased in his braine" and had to be sent back to the mother country at significant expense to the Colony. Allerton's behavior on this particular trip arouses suspicion; therefore, before his 1629 trip to England, Allerton is explicitly admonished to return with only fifty pounds' worth of shoes, stockings, and linen cloth and not to combine Plymouth's orders with his own merchandise. Bradford writes that they sent him with "some fear & jeolocie; yet he gave them fair words and promises of well performing . . . and to mend his former errors."

Instead, and with Sherley's blessings, he fills the ship with all kinds of trade goods, borrows money in Bristol at 50 percent, charges it to Plymouth's account, and brings New England one more trickster, the infamous Thomas Morton, a Maypole round dancer and Native womanizer. At Sherley's further instigation, and with the assistance of Sherley's ship, the *White Angel,* he involves Plymouth in trading deals with Edward Ashley, a Morton impersonator, who becomes an additional thorn in the Colony's bleeding side when he reportedly enjoyed "uncleannes with Indean women." Allerton also draws William Collier and Timothy Hatherley into his nefarious schemes, and they assist him in diverting funds, padding Plymouth's account, and obfuscating the books by merging shipments and doubling and tripling charges. It is not long before Allerton's dealings are even more far-flung. He "cleared up 400. [pounds] and put it into a brew-house of M. Colliers in London, at first under M. Sherley's name." Although he later "bought up yᵉ beaver that sea-men . . . brought over to Bristoll, [for Plymouth], . . . and charged yᵉ bills to London, which Mr. Sherley payed," it is unlikely that Plymouth got full credit for her payments. Muddled books, ledger lines blotted out and written over so that "not a word could be perceived," effectively erased the full extent of his bilking.

Sherley and Allerton were equal partners in crime and they aided and abetted each other in keeping Plymouth's financial reports confused. "In these accounts of M. Sherley's some things were obscure, and some things twise charged, as a 100. of Bastable ruggs which came in y^e *Freindship*, & cost 75. [pounds], charged before by M. Allerton, and now by him againe."

Events continue in this vein until the Plymoutheans remove Allerton from his duties; but before they do, Allerton has "hoodwinckte" them badly. His balance sheets have been "so larg and intrecate, as they could not well understand them, much less examine & correcte them" even though a special accountant, Josiah Winslow, an apprentice trickster, was hired for that purpose. Under Allerton's management, Plymouth began with a debt not "much above 400.[pounds] . . . and now [it came] to . . . many thousands." Bradford relates that "M. Sherley said in his leter, if their bussines had been better managed, they might have been ye richest plantation of any English."

That remark seems highly ironic given that Sherley was part of the scheme to defraud, and it certainly qualifies him as a supplemental trickster in Bradford's pantheon of deceivers.

Allerton continued as Plymouth's London agent until 1637, but, seeing that he "rane a course not only to ye great wrong and detrimente of ye plantation . . . but abused them in England also," Plymouth officially discharged him in 1630. Even though he was dismissed as their agent, Allerton retained his house and property in Plymouth and remained in the area wheeling and dealing. He was elected Plymouth's assistant governor in 1633 and served for one year. With his aptly named son-in-law, Moses Maverick, Allerton started a fishing business in Marblehead. While there he became theologically involved with Roger Williams, and town officials invited him to leave the city. From there he moved to New Amsterdam, where he increased his fortunes, but Indian aggression against the Dutch prompted his relocation in 1646 to New Haven, where he built a fine home and apparently prospered. After his death in 1658, however, an audit of his books revealed that he was deeply in debt.

Plymouth's religious tricksters are as impressive as the civil ones. Perhaps the most prominent Praying Lox is John Lyford. Lyford appeared in Plymouth in 1624. Unknown to the Plymoutheans except as an Anglican clergyman, he had been harried out of Ireland for raping a parishioner and fathering an out-of-wedlock child. Pretending to be a Separatist, he was received into the church at Plymouth, but in the community he soon began pitting Saint against Stranger over theological exercises while simultaneously engaging in sexual exercises with his maidservant, who slept at the foot of his bed, while his hapless wife looked on. His undoing, however, was not in engaging the maid but was occasioned by letters "full of slanders, & false accusations" that he sent to England. These epistles—some twenty of them—were intercepted by Trickster Bradford before the ship carrying them left the harbor. Bradford copied the most damning of them and sent the copies on, but he retained the originals to be used against Lyford in court at a later date. Content to let matters "ripen," the Principal Patriarchs payed out enough rope for Lyford to hang himself. With the help of John Oldham, Trickster Number Seven, he did.

Oldham had come over on the *Anne* in 1623 on his own "perticuler," meaning that as a non-Brownist he was entitled to receive a plot of land but had to abide by Plymouth's laws, pay taxes, and do military service, primarily guard duty.[11] Finding that Plymouth was not the Eden advertising brochures had described, Oldham began associating with other immigrant malcontents of Puritan persuasion and looked for ways to make a living. Since theology was a perennial bone of Plymouthean contention, he found that with Lyford he could befriend other dissatisfied Puritan residents, make a "reformation in church and commone wealth, and . . . have the sacraments," which the Brownists forbade. Like Lyford, Oldham, too, had written complaining letters to London, though "his hand was scarce legible," and the Saints intended to hang him with Lyford. Unaware that the Principal Patriarchs knew he was "as deepe in ye mischeefe" as Lyford, he began to "pick quarells at everything." He angered Standish by refusing to stand watch and even "drew his knife at him," an act that resulted in short-term incarceration.

Matters came to a head when Lyford and Oldham attempted to establish their own religious services on the Sabbath. They were arraigned, tried, convicted, and expelled from the Colony. Neither trickster took the expulsion seriously. Lyford, who had been given a six-month grace period to find a new home, continued complaint writing, and again his letters were intercepted and he was asked to leave. Oldham did leave after his first expulsion but returned weeks later in a rage. He was incarcerated for a second time, then marched to a waiting boat between a row of musketeers who had been ordered to "thump [his] brich, with yᵉ but end" of their muskets. Pummeled to the water, Oldham was put on a boat and sent sailing away.

Because unceremonious exits never deter tricksters, both Oldham and Lyford continued their careers outside the boundaries of the Old Colony for some years. Their altercation with and treatment by the Pilgrim Fathers resulted in fracturing the relationship between the Colony and its original Adventurers, and the company "broake in peeces," thus forcing Plymouth to renegotiate the Venture with a different mixture of investors at higher interest rates. After leaving Plymouth, Oldham became an Indian trader, working in the immediate area until Indians killed him near Block Island. After preaching in other New England churches, Lyford eventually decamped to Virginia, where he died.

Allerton, Sherley, Ashley, Morton, Williams, Lyford, and Oldham are only a few of Bradford's tricksters. Plymouth was further troubled by a shipmaster who had been hired to operate the Colony's fishing station at Cape Ann. The man's name was Baker and he "proved [to be] a very drunken beast, and did nothing . . . but drink, & gusel, and consume away yᵉ time & his victails." In a sense, Baker paved the way for Lyford and Oldham, who later commandeered the fishing station after their expulsion from the Colony and literally took it away from Plymouth.

A visiting trickster was a nameless-to-history saltmaker sent over by the Adventurers to instruct the Saints in salt production. He turned out to be "an ignorante, foolish, self-willd fellow" who could never dig a well that would hold water even though he had ten men working. The salter accidentally burned down his own warehouse and destroyed his pans and thus ended that "chargable bussines."

Plymouth's most colorful trickster may have been a Mr. Girling, a self-styled soldier of fortune Plymouth hired to take their Penobscot trading post back from the French. In 1635, a Frenchman, "Monsier" de Aulnay, "tooke possession of yᵉ house in yᵉ name of yᵉ king of France." This was the second time the Penobscot house had been raided, and Plymouth decided to recover it. After conferring with Massachusetts Bay officials and obtaining their highly inefficacious approval, the Colony rented a three-hundred-ton ship, fitted it with ordnance, and commissioned Girling to attack their own trading post, now held by de Aulnay. If Girling succeeded he was to be paid seven hundred pounds of beaver pelts, but if he failed he was to receive nothing.

Prior to Operation Take Back, Plymouth sent Standish and twenty men in a separate bark to supervise the raid. To their dismay, the Pilgrims discovered that like most tricksters, Girling was "rash & heady." He would not take advice from Standish nor would he give Standish time to bring in additional forces. Standish and the twenty soldiers piloted Girling into the harbor fronting the trading post and pointed him toward it, but, lacking patience, Girling did not wait until he was in proper firing range, but "begane to shoot at a distance like a madd man, and did them no hurte at all." By the time the Plymoutheans maneuvered him into range, he "saw his owne folly, . . . and bestowed a few shott to good purpose. But now . . . his powder was goone." All the while the French had been lying "close under a worke of earth, & let him consume him selfe."

At day's end, Girling promised to borrow more powder from neighboring plantations and return to finish the job, but, of course, he did not. Plymouth retreated and asked for assistance from Massachusetts Bay, which they promised but never delivered. "And this was ye end of this bussines." Sadly, there are several times when Massachusetts Bay took on the trickster role and disappointed Plymouth as it did in the Penobscot instance. The Bay may have enjoyed this small triumph in the game of one-upmanship that it played with Plymouth, but the only winner in this particular debacle was **V ꙍ**, who was allowed to go back to Plymouth intact.

In Bradford's view, the characters described above, as well as the ones mentioned in passing, are tricksters. History, however, has judged some of them more kindly than the Principal Patriarch did. Modernists often write off Morton as a merry prankster and Lyford as a clergyman maligned only at Plymouth. Allerton is now America's first entrepreneur and the progenitor of two presidents, Zachary Taylor and Franklin Delano Roosevelt.[12]

Bradford's Indian Book, however, evaluates these figures in a way that is consonant with Bradford's presentation of them. In the Principal Patriarch's view they were tricksters, and I will leave it at that. Trickster's literary dimensions make him essential to medicine texts. Even good people usually do not have superhuman powers or benevolent protectors; they must rely on their wits to survive. Trickster's transformative power contributes to his adaptability, another human coping strategy, while his enigmatic charm makes him a great read as well as an irresistible model. He inspires fledgling confidence men as well as imaginative conjurers with a flair for entertainment. Trickster unbridled is an unethical individual we can easily despise, but when we combine him with likeable animals as Walt Disney did, we get American classics loved the world over.

D ᏉᏉᏉ. Ꮃ ᏣᏟᎢᏚᎢ, ᎧᎭᎥᏍᎩ

PART THE SECOND

THE PEOPLE AND AMERICAN LITERATURE

6 THE NATIVE HAGIOGRAPHY

RWJ

Written documents recounting the colonists' experiences with American Indians accumulated quickly in the early days of the new nation, and concurrently a European American oral tradition that further preserved accounts of American Indian agency in English affairs also developed. This newly formed oral tradition, based partly upon the European imagination, took root, flourished, and still exists.[1] Our present literature, in terms of an American Indian presence, reflects the merging of these written and nuncupative records.

Not only do early documents like Bradford's history and Winslow's several relations carefully detail Native actions, but the narratives also provide engaging insights into the lives of many Algonquian people. In addition to their contributions to the colonial historical record, these biographical sketches of Algonquian Natives, either in part or in whole, also supply archetypes for the American Indians depicted in later European American lore and writings. Usually the archetypes originated with an actual historical referent, but occasionally the later fictional Indians were drawn from the symbolic function of a particular Plymouthean Native, such as Tisquantum-the-Caregiver or Tisquantum-the-Turncoat. In other instances, the characters are conflations of several types.[2] From Cooper's noble savages to Twain's miserable Goshoots, post-Colonial images of America's Natives mirror many of the Algonquians described by the first Plymouthean writers. Since American Indian people were active participants in the colonization process begun at Contact, it follows naturally that they entered American letters as fractured parts of American reality, not as imaginative constructs originating in the European mind.

Before the discussion of the archetypal Algonquians depicted by Bradford and Winslow continues, three essential points about American Indian life and American Indian leaders should be reviewed. First, it is important to understand that in most American Indian worldviews there is no distinction between religion, literature, science, technology, and other aspects of daily life. Joseph Epes Brown in "Becoming Part of It" explains: "As Peter Nabokov tells us in his book, *Indian Running*, when you track down a seemingly isolated or minimal feature of Indian life, such as running, the whole system opens before your eyes; and this is true because of the interrelatedness of all the components of a genuine tradition."[3]

Like running, literature cannot be separated from science or religious ritual in an American Indian world. Brown explains further: "Religion . . . is so pervasive in life that there is probably no Native American language in which there is a term which could be translated as 'religion' in the way we understand it. . . . Obviously in such a system life cannot be fragmented, due to that binding and interconnecting thread of the presence of the sacred."[4]

In American Indian communities, creative verse can be interwoven with domestic tasks, nutritional utility, moral integrity, and spiritual well-being. Today in Arizona, it is not unusual for traditional Hopi women to sing a prayer song when they grind corn. Their songs pray that no impure thoughts enter their minds and contaminate the corn that their families will ingest. As the Hopi women sing, literature, music, religious practice, and household drudgery come together; thought, words, and action meld. Traditional Navajo girls and women still observe prayer rituals when they grind corn for certain ceremonies such as kinaaldas.[5] Entertainment is only one of the reasons why American Indians create and tell stories. As Margot Astrov has observed: "The singing of songs and the telling of tales, with the American Indian, is but seldom a means of mere spontaneous self-expression. More often than not, the singer aims with the chanted word to exert a strong influence and to bring about a change, either in himself or in nature or in his fellow beings."[6]

Second, an important observation must be made about early American Indian tribal leaders, people who were sometimes referred to as sachems, sagamores, chiefs, or principal chiefs. Such people had backgrounds and functions that did not have equivalents in European culture. More often than not, these leaders were simultaneously civic leaders, medicine men, military strategists, and literary critics. Because these ancient leaders were first and foremost astute literary critics, they were able to develop the skills necessary to function in political capacities.

The Reverend Mr. Randolph Jacob explained these attributes in a sermon given at the Coal Creek Cumberland Presbyterian Church near Atoka, Oklahoma, on February 23, 1991. As Mr. Jacob pointed out, the chiefs of long ago were people well versed in their oral traditions. They understood the ancient stories; consequently, their well-ordered minds and lives reflected that awareness. Chiefs were elected to office because of their finely honed interpretative skills, their mastery of general knowledge, their internalization of this learning, and their display of intellectual acumen. Chiefs were people who "had gotten something out of the stories."[7] Their power derived primarily from their literary discernment since much of their acquired knowledge was presented to them in the form of narratives. Their lives were, in scholarly language, their well-reviewed publications.

The sachems and *pnieses* the Plymoutheans knew were people with the power to engender. Concerned with life in all its dimensions, the *pnieses* mentioned by Bradford and Winslow were not errand runners for the Pilgrims; neither were they "braves" spoiling for self-aggrandizement or war. The Algonquian headmen engaging the Plymoutheans were spiritual leaders of their people. They were examples of right interpretation and right living. Perceptive and powerful, orally literate and astute, they existed primarily as DhꓔꓡꓳꙨꝏꙄ or persons-who-know-things. The American Indian headmen interacting with the colonists were basically Algonquian writers and literary critics, not politicians.

Unfortunately, the Algonquian leaders mentioned by Winslow and Bradford have traditionally been viewed through lenses fashioned with western European cribbing tools. For the most part, their actions have been contextualized in terms of European political, economic, or military understanding, that is, nations meet, clash, conquer, or lose. The Algonquian headmen who engaged the first settlers have long been regarded by American historians primarily as leaders of warring bands who formed alliances for political advantage and exacted tribute from weaker entities.

The third major aspect of American Indian life is that the Caesarean paradigm, *Veni, vidi, vici*, has rarely corresponded to American Indian political reality. In actuality, war was only one of a leader's duties and was waged more for reasons of ritual or gene pool enlargement than for exploration or profit.[8] To frightened, migrating Europeans, who understood Caesarean impulses all too well, any New World leader's war-waging potential was the quality most expected and dreaded. The Plymoutheans knew they were in a foreign land uninvited and, in their minds, perhaps unwanted. It is a mistake, however, to continue reading colonial history and literature in terms of Puritan anxiety. To understand our national history and literature more comprehensively, we must modify our views of American Indians. The war-mongering savage has been studied and depicted at length; the Native poet has been too long ignored. The nation's theoretical Other—or the Puritans' Acute Neurosis—is actually just a writer with a story.

The names and deeds of Algonquians essential to Plymouth Colony were first documented by Plymouthean settlers and historians. Unlike other period writers, William Bradford and Edward Winslow did not often refer to American Indians in general terms, but instead designated particular Algonquians by name and frequently supplied interesting anecdotal information about them. Winslow's detailed relations, published between 1622 and 1624, record a significant amount of Algonquian participation in Plymouthean affairs, and these accounts have long been available to the reading public on both sides of the Atlantic. Although *Of Plimoth Plantation* was not published until 1856, Bradford's manuscript circulated in early New England. The Governor's nephew by marriage, Nathaniel Morton, used the chronicle for his *New-Englands Memoriall* (1669), and the antiquarian William Hubbard consulted the holograph for his *General History of New England*, a volume completed around 1683 but not published until 1815. Thomas Prince also reviewed Bradford's unpublished manuscript for his *Chronological History of New-England* (1736).[9] Consequently, it is safe to speculate that Bradford's and Winslow's tales of individual American Indians were known to people of letters on the East Coast to some extent shortly after they were written. It is, furthermore, quite likely that vivid recollections of the Pilgrim Fathers' encounters with American Indians entered the European American oral tradition from people who had either heard about or were actually present at these encounters and had first- or second-hand knowledge that they passed along. Before the days of radio and television, it was common for people to amuse themselves by telling tales, and all good tales need conflict and antagonists. The American Indians engaging the Plymoutheans were complex people capable of exercising free will. In a sense, they were absorbing and arresting figures just waiting to be put into books.

The Records of Plymouth Colony reveals that in addition to the *pnieses* assigned to live in the compound, ordinary Algonquians also occupied the settlement. Representatives from both Native groups, that is, medicine people and laypersons, became models for subsequent literary replications. These Eastern Algonquians were complicated individuals living at a critical time in a critical space. Their motivations and actions not only prescribed the course of many Plymouthean events but also set into motion a series of partial and incomplete images that permuted into stereotypical American Indian literary figures for generations to come. It is important to understand that the Algonquians living at Plymouth were not individuals mindlessly subsisting in the Great White Shadow. They were a very vocal part of the Plymouth community and enjoyed close contact with the English settlers. Plymouth's Algonquians visited with their neighbors, dispensed information, gossiped, and passed judgments on daily events and village cranks. They lent cornmeal. They borrowed flour. They let their pigs ruin Newcomers' gardens. They complained about Newcomers' pigs rooting through their gardens and sued said Newcomers in court for damages. Often they won their cases. The Algonquians living in Plymouth were normal people going about their daily lives, and in the process they created and told stories. These stories interacted with Plymouthean narratives and went into print. Bradford's history has more than one "the Indeans said," so we know the Algonquians talked and the English listened.

As one might expect, the flesh and blood characters given most space in Bradford's and Winslow's narratives are not the ordinary Algonquians living in the Colony, but are the sachems and *pnieses* that dealt with the Colony on business of some sort. *Mourt's Relation* emphasizes biographical material about the Massasoit Osamequin and attaches some importance to the *pniese* Tokamahamon, about whom Mourt says little except that he was a "special friend" of Plymouth Colony. *Winslow's Relation* tells us Tokamahamon was "found faithful before and after upon all occasions." Although Winslow's several narratives suggest that Tokamahamon's primary functions were those of messenger and guide, it should be pointed out that Tokamahamon occasionally did diplomatic duty since he was willing to go places Tisquantum and Hobomok would not, and he dealt with Native leaders that the other *pnieses* avoided, particularly Corbitant.[10] It was the non-speaking Tokamahamon who accompanied Canonicus' messenger with the oft-debated bundle of snakeskins and arrows brought into

Plymouth, ostensibly as a "chaleng." Tokamahamon's appearance with the bundle suggests that he, like Hobomok and Tisquantum, had a priestly role in the Algonquian community.

For Americanists looking for sources of American literary types, Tokamahamon is the Native figure who moves in and out of plots like a shadow. He is an ephemeral, silent presence with no certain purpose. He, and his various adumbrations, could be the grantors of the land deed in *The House of the Seven Gables* (1851) by Nathaniel Hawthorne, the three Indian kings of Herman Melville's *Pierre* (1852), or the departed cliff-dwellers in Zane Grey's *Riders of the Purple Sage* (1912). In *The Town* (1957), Tokamahamon is William Faulkner's last departing Chickasaw. In Ken Kesey's *One Flew Over the Cuckoo's Nest* (1962), it is Tokamahamon acting as the mute Chief Bromden who flees the asylum. It should be pointed out, however, that at least once Tokamahamon is mentioned by name in American belles lettres. He appears in Henry Wadsworth Longfellow's "The Courtship of Miles Standish" (1859).

A much more vivid example of an Algonquian who instantly became a prototype for the American Indian villain extraordinaire is Wituwamat, a Massachuset *pniese* who anticipated disaster whenever he contemplated the English presence in America. Winslow writes that Wituwamat, who steadfastly opposed any initiative to get along with the Newcomers, once looked at Miles Standish sneeringly and boasted that he had at home a knife that previously had "killed both French and English and.... it should eat." No sooner were these words uttered than Wituwamat became the "bloodthirsty" savage of American letters and tradition. He was so threatening, in fact, that Standish killed him shortly after he had spoken those words. Once entered into letters, however, Wituwamat took on another life. Springing lightly from Winslow's prose to the Principal Patriarch's, he taunts Bradford's readers as the hostile Native who commits "insolencies and outrages" upon the virtuous English. Later he attacks innocent settlers as Mary Rowlandson's "murderous wretch" in *The Sovereignty and Goodness of God* (1682). Wituwamat is dramatically diabolical as Cooper's Magua in *The Last of the Mohicans* (1826); he lurks in Nathaniel Hawthorne's "Young Goodman Brown" (1846) as the "devilish Indian behind every tree," and he menacingly enlarges into Mark Twain's Injun Joe and terrorizes children in *The Adventures of Tom Sawyer* (1876). In the twentieth century, the *pniese* enjoys himself immensely as Byron Snope's

Apache children in Faulkner's *Town*, and he materializes again, magnified and vilified, as Larry McMurtry's infamous Blue Duck in *Lonesome Dove* (1985). He is at it again as Lame One in *The Last Ride* (1995) by Tom Eidson.

After becoming a permanent, self-perpetuating fixture in American literature, Wituwamat moved to the West Coast in the 1920s seeking employment in the film industry, where he spent years attacking wagon trains and carrying off fair-haired young women. Not content with such mundane labor and still availing himself of his new cinematic form, he headed back East, crossed the Atlantic, and invaded Agatha Christie's imagination, where he provided savage metaphor and sinister plot in English murder mysteries ranging from *The Secret of Chimneys* (1925) to *And Then There Were None* (1940). It seems that this poor man carved out an impressive career for himself merely by vigorously and metaphorically speaking his mind. His simple warrior's vehicle has cut through the centuries. Wituwamat's narrative illustrates how Native oral propensity, if not tradition, pierced European American literature, rendered it American, and took it abroad.

Except for the Massasoit, the two Algonquians receiving the most attention in Winslow's relations and Bradford's history are Hobomok and Tisquantum, two of the three *pnieses* in residence at Plymouth. The Bradford text marginalizes Hobomok's role in the development of early Plymouth while it privileges Tisquantum's. Both Tisquantum and Hobomok were proven warriors and shamans; both were major contributors to Plymouth's early history. Winslow and Bradford recognized the importance of these men to the Colony's survival, and each writer documented the *pnieses'* words and actions.

Tisquantum and Hobomok together symbolize word and deity. They have both literal and metaphorical functions in Bradford's history. Several times referred to as "the English tongue," Tisquantum is word; Hobomok, named for an Algonquian deity, is spirit.[11] Each man at once is signifier and signified, muse and metaphor. Interpreting, guiding, hunting, and planting were their practical contributions to the Colony's survival, but these kindnesses dim when compared to their more lasting bestowals. Shape-shifters and dreamers, Tisquantum and Hobomok had religious obligations and tribal agenda that changed Plymouth and modified the literature that grew out of it. They were an Algonquian shaping presence within the English community; their sociopolitical influence was far-reaching. More important, Tisquantum and Hobomok were literary forces molding the emergent literature.

Both Bradford and Winslow seemed intuitively to understand that Tisquantum and Hobomok, as well as the other headmen the Plymoutheans engaged, were important to the Colony and to the official record of their undertaking. Perhaps for those reasons, Winslow scrupulously recorded the utterances of the Algonquians he met, and he occasionally transliterated their words so that we get a limited, and possibly erroneous, understanding of Algonquian sounds. Bradford also appears to give us Tisquantum's actual words when he recalls Tisquantum's utterances in Plymouth.

Bradford's Tisquantum narrative, which functions in the text as an interpolated tale, begins with an encomium:

> *Squanto* continued with them, and was their interpreter, and was a spetiall instrument sent of God for their good beyond their expectation. He directed them how to set corne, wher to take fish, and to procure other comodities, and was also their pilott to bring them to unknowne places for their profitt, and never left them till he dyed. (116)

The encomium is followed by several pages of text recounting portions of Tisquantum's intriguing biography. The Patuxet was taken to England in 1605 by Captain George Weymouth, who had led an exploration to the New England area that year.[12] In England, Tisquantum met Captain John Smith, and he returned to the New World with him in 1614. Later that year, he was kidnapped by a Captain Thomas Hunt, who took him, nineteen other Patuxets, and seven Nausets to Spain to be sold as slaves. In Spain, Tisquantum and a few of his compatriots were redeemed by monks who possibly converted them. Somehow Tisquantum managed to flee Spain and find refuge in London with John Slany, treasurer of the Newfoundland Company. In 1618, the *pniese* traveled to Newfoundland; there he became acquainted with Captain Thomas Dermer, a former employee of John Smith. Dermer took him back to England and introduced him to Ferdinando Gorges, who was trying to develop New England and consequently needed Native guides.

By 1619, Tisquantum, having been returned to America by Dermer, found himself home again but discovered that his village had been destroyed by a pestilence that some modern researchers now believe to have been a hepatitis virus.[13] When Tisquantum found that his village had been decimated, he decided to take up residence with the Massasoit, because his few surviving relatives had gone to live with the Pokanokets. That Tisquantum could speak English and had some knowledge of Europeans and their customs are the probable reasons he was the Massasoit's choice for ambassador for social change in Plymouth. Tisquantum's spiritual powers as a *pniese*, that is, his status as a priest, and his ability to visualize the spirit Hobomok further empowered him as a change agent.

Bradford interrupts his interpolated Squanto tale with yet another interpolation—an insertion of a letter from Thomas Dermer that combines Tisquantum's history with Dermer's own. This section of Bradford's history, covered in Annos 1621–1623, contains several interesting literary devices and motifs that will be repeated in many works of American fiction years later. One of America's first captivity narratives, Dermer's letter—like Bradford's history—contains a narrative of the land and a commentary on American Natives. Dermer writes:

> The *Pocanawkits*, which live to y^e *west of Plimoth*, bear an inveterate malice to ye English, and are of more streingth then all ye savags from thence to Penobscote. Their desire of revenge was occasioned by an English man, who having many of them on bord, made a great slaughter with their murderers & smale shot, when as (they say) they offered no injurie on their parts. . . . For which cause *Squanto* canot deney but they would have kiled me when I was at *Namasket*, had he not entreated hard for me. The soyle of ye borders of this great bay, may be compared to most of ye plantations which I have seene in Virginia. The land is of diverce sorts; for *Patuxite* is a hardy but strong soyle, *Nawsel & Saughtughteet* are for ye most part a blakish & deep mould. (117)

The Dermer letter is a microcosm of Bradford's history since it presents Dermer's personal narrative interlaced with tales of the land, of Native people, and of the valor of Tisquantum. Besides being an incipient captivity narrative, the letter also anticipates a type of literature that will come much later to the American scene, a genre that features an Indian or Indian-like hero who renders assistance to a white man. Dermer and Squanto, and for that matter, Bradford and Squanto, could prefigure William Faulkner's Issac McCaslin and Sam Fathers or Jim Harrison's Ludlow and One Stab. They could be the forerunners of the comic strip characters the Lone Ranger and Tonto or Red Ryder and Little Beaver. In television they could presage Scully and Cloud Dancing of *Dr. Quinn, Medicine Woman*. The effect of the letter is to set up Tisquantum as a Pocahontas or rescuing type, but one not quite as threatening. It is one thing for a man to save a man; it is quite another for a woman to save a man. The controversial Pocahontas narrative, suspiciously representative of certain male fantasies, suggests possible romantic motivations that hint at miscegenation. On the other hand, the Dermer-Tisquantum narrative, for *pre*-postmodern sensibilities, is "safer," or sexually neutral. Without a sacral female figure, the archetype is acceptably Protestant and appropriately patriarchal. In the years to come, this model will lend itself to further use in American plot development when the savior of white men, Tisquantum, transforms into the Indian-like white frontiersman, Natty Bumppo.

The Bumppo character is allowable in American fiction because, as Richard Slotkin intimates, he has been sanitized for European American consumption. Bumppo has the forest survival skills of the Indian and the integrity of the noble savage, but he is a nonthreatening white man. The European-approved traits of American Indians are emphasized in this character, but their socially unacceptable characteristics are eliminated by changing the new hero's bloodlines. In the nineteenth and twentieth centuries, genealogical lines change again as notions of blood quantum become a federal race determinant. Tisquantum and his alter ego, Hobomok, metamorphose into mixed-blood characters that can interact more openly with European Americans. These mixed-blood characters, like the Cherokee/Irish Huck Finn, whose American Indian background is disguised, or Ahab, the Gayhead, or Ramona, a heroine whose American Indian blood is neutralized by her Scots heritage, achieve prominence in American letters. In the 1990s, the television figure Walker, Texas Ranger, a character part Cherokee, part closet Lakota, and part European American, exemplifies a diluted Tisquantum who renders protection to Dallas Colony and unswerving loyalty to Texas law enforcement agencies.

Whether he operates as a literary archetype or as a historical person, Tisquantum, the friend to Plymouth, is an enigma. The facts that we have about him suggest that he was no stranger to suffering, alienation, and mystery—conditions that serve the requirements of literature and the readability of history quite well.

Of Hobomok, who came to Plymouth in August 1621, Bradford says little except that he was "a proper lustie man, and a man of accounte for his vallour & parts amongst ye Indeans, and continued very faithfull and constant to ye English till he dyed." Hobomok remained with the Plymoutheans for many years. In fact, it is thought that he remained in Plymouth for the rest of his life. Bradford's Hobomok narrative, which only briefly comments on the *pniese* and his actions, does yield important information about Plymouthean and Algonquian politics, social behavior, and the position of women in the Colony and in Old Algonquia. It turns out that Hobomok's unnamed wife is as important as the *pniese* to American history and letters.

That Hobomok was named for a powerful Algonquian spirit suggests that he held a significant place in Algonquian society, but regrettably, the information currently accessible to scholars about the spirit's function in Algonquian religion is not complete. William Simmons, in *Cautantowwit's House*, reports that the deity Hobomok "was thought to be a principal cause of disease and suffering."[14] Bragdon asserts that Hobomok "was the being associated with death, night, the northeast wind, the dark, and the color black." She goes on to say that he appeared in many forms, but most often as "an eel, snake or other under (water) world dweller." Bragdon further finds that Hobomok was frequently called upon to heal the sick. He was the spirit to whom Algonquians applied for succor, yet he was also held accountable for misfortune. Shamans occasionally assumed his name.[15] It is possible that medicine men appropriated his appellation as a way of internalizing and actualizing his power.

In the early days of the Colony, Hobomok lived with Miles Standish inside the fortified village, but by September of 1623 he had moved outside Plymouth's palisades. Hobomok was married. In fact, he had several wives and more than ten persons in his household.[16] Emmanuel Altham, on a visit to Plymouth, describes Hobomok as "our friend and interpreter, and one whom we have found faithful and trustworthy."[17] Altham speaks with some authority since Hobomok once accompanied him on a trip to the area south of Plymouth; thus the men had an opportunity to become acquainted.

Winslow's writings indicate that Hobomok was the loyal *pniese* who always placed Plymouth's needs above any others. Hobomok upheld the Massasoit in all alleged intrigues and asseverated that Osamequin would never undertake any hostile action against Plymouth "without his privity." On one occasion, when Hobomok was informed incorrectly that the Massasoit was dead, he broke into a dirge "with such signs of lamentation and unfeigned sorrow, as it would have made the hardest heart relent."

Hobomok, once queried for advice by Canonicus, suggested that a certain *powah* be put to death, and Canonicus had the man killed. Such an action suggests that Hobomok either had great power or unhealthy braggart tendencies. Killing the shaman, who reportedly had murdered a man in a gambling game gone awry, could have had serious personal consequences. This rather dubious incident is reported by Winslow, who apparently heard it from Bradford, who, in turn, received it from Hobomok himself. Hobomok's decision seems to have been based on the questionable premise that the murdered man's band would wage war in order to avenge his death. Since American Indians rarely, if ever, went to full-scale war over personal injuries, Hobomok's tale is suspect. Granted, Bradford did see the *pniese* queried by Canonicus, but Bradford did not speak Algonquian and was at Hobomok's mercy for getting at the truth of the conversation. Hobomok's rendering certainly made himself look impressive and vital to the community, and at times, the *pniese* really was. For instance, Winslow relates that in a battle between Miles Standish and some Algonquians who were annoyed with Weston's men at Wessagusset, Hobomok "cast off his coat, and being a known pinese, . . . chased them . . . fast." There is no doubt that Hobomok was powerful, but his veracity is occasionally open to question.

That Hobomok was a master at diplomacy probably explains his lengthy residence at Plymouth. Winslow continues that when Standish and other Plymoutheans were killing Wituwamat and Pecksuot, Hobomok "stood by . . . as a spectator." After Pecksuot was dead, the *pniese* congratulated Standish by saying, "Yesterday Pecksuot . . . said . . . you were but a little man; but to-day I see you are big enough to lay him on the ground."

Hobomok was essential to Plymouth's well-being in the early days of settlement, but one of his wives also played a significant role in Plymouthean-Wampanoag relations. This woman's contribution to political affairs has received little scholarly attention, but her actions did cause grave consequences that should be noted because of what they tell us about Algonquian society and women's place in it. This unnamed wife of Hobomok, sent by Plymouth to spy out Osamequin's camp for reported or imagined signs of trouble in 1622, is the agent who told the Massasoit that Tisquantum was undermining the Wampanoag-Plymouthean alliance. It was she who precipitated a crisis in Wampanoag-Plymouthean affairs. Her report also occasioned a Plymouthean loss of trust in Tisquantum. Bradford reports that a relative of Tisquantum

> came runing in seeming great fear, and tould them that many of ye Narihgansets, with Corbytant, and he thought also Massasoyte, were coming against them;. . . . Hobamak was confidente for Massasoyt, and thought all was false; yet ye Govr caused him to send his wife privatly, to see what she could observe (pretening other occasions), but ther was nothing found, but all was quiet. After this they proseeded on their vioge to ye Massachusets, and had good trade, and returned in saftie, blessed be God. (136)

Winslow's *Relation* tells us more:

> But to the end things might be made more manifest, the Governor caused Hobbamock to send his wife with all privacy to Puckanokick, . . . (pretending other occasions), there to inform herself, and so us, of the right state of things. When she came thither, and saw all things quiet, and that no such matter was or had been intended, [she] told Massassowat what had happened at Plymouth, . . . which, when he understood, he was much offended at the carriage of Tisquantum, returning many thanks to the Governor for his good thoughts of him, and assuring him that, according to their first Articles of Peace, he would send word and give warning when any such business was towards. (288–89)

Tisquantum's supposed treachery, alleged by Hobomok's wife, angered Osamequin, and he subsequently demanded that Plymouth kill the *pniese* in keeping with the articles of their nonaggression pact. Winslow continues:

> [Massassowat] sent a messenger to the Governor, entreating him to give way to the death of Tisquantum, who had so much abused him. But the Governor answered, although he had deserved to die, both in respect of him and us, yet for our sakes he desired he would spare him. . . . [Then Bradford] sent for Tisquantum, who, though he knew

their intent, yet offered not to fly, but came and accused Hobbamock as the author and worker of his overthrow, yielding himself to the Governor to be sent or not according as he thought meet. (290–91)

When Bradford failed to comply with the stipulations of the nonaggression pact, Osamequin halted most Algonquian visits to Plymouth. In a legal sense, Bradford should have honored the articles of the treaty, but he did not. Winslow writes that after Bradford refused to kill Tisquantum, "Massassowat seemed to frown on us, and neither came or sent to us as formerly."

Hobomok's wife's decision to relate either suppositions or blatant untruths about Tisquantum to the Massasoit has interesting implications for history and for literary archetypes. Winslow's unintentional narrative informs us that this woman apparently had ready access to the Great Leader's ear, and her reports, given at Sowams and again in Plymouth, were not only believed but were acted upon by Wampanoags and Plymoutheans alike. This information says a great deal about the status of women in Algonquian society.[18]

Hobomok's wife's narrative vividly illustrates the Plymoutheans' dependence upon an Algonquian woman's actions; moreover, it confirms their reliance upon an Algonquian woman's pronouncements. Briefly, the Pilgrims suspended patriarchal privilege and literally placed their lives in a Native woman's hands. Because Hobomok's wife said there was no impending trouble with the Pokanokets, the Plymouthean men left the compound undefended to pursue their trading interests elsewhere. Had Hobomok's wife purposely misled them, Plymouth could easily have been destroyed. Momentarily, the Plymouthean Patriarchy acknowledged an American Indian woman as an authority figure and acted upon that determination.

In metaphorical terms, Hobomok's wife is a feminine Native text, and a self-generating one at that. Not only does she engender stories, but she also underlines new character types for the emerging European American literature. With a kind of Native authority she reinforces notions of the Indian hero and the Indian villain while she herself could be either. In American Indian literary terms, her exploits add a feminine component to the principally male narrative structures of Winslow's and Bradford's texts and help balance them. In Native life nearly all entities have gender. For example, there is male rain like a heavy summer downpour, and there is female rain, a winter mist. In Cherokee thought, the sun is feminine. The moon is male. The Navajos have a long account of the misery that occurs when the sexes are separated.[19] Narrative, like life, must display gender balance. [20]

Translated to European American literary theory, Hobomok's wife echoes the Pocahontas story in that she uses her personal power to influence political decisions, but instead of saving a man she condemns one. She prefigures the various squaw sachems discussed by other New England writers like John Winthrop, John Mason, and Lion Gardiner. She presages Weetamoo of Rowlandson fame, and she anticipates Charles Brockden Brown's Old Deb in *Edgar Huntly* (1799). Hobomok's wife, in the form of a powerful matriarch, materializes as Nakomis of Henry Wadsworth Longfellow's *Hiawatha* (1855) just as her essence informs the character Lila Littlewolf in the film *Frozen River* (2008).

Hobomok's wife's decision to relate Tisquantum's alleged plot to the Massasoit raises questions the intentional narrative does not answer. What are her reasons for divulging such volatile and possibly unsubstantiated information? There are several possible human motivations for her act: feelings of jealously, personal dislike for Tisquantum, or well-intentioned but misguided loyalty to her husband. On the other hand, her disclosure of carefully selected information could indicate simply that she felt free to evaluate the political situation and to impose her own will on the course of Native-colonial events. She may not have approved of the Plymouth-Osamequin alliance; thus she may have welcomed an opportunity to weaken it. Wampanoag negotiations with a foreign entity could have appeared to her to be politically unwise and religiously suspect. In a broader sense, Hobomok's wife may have set the precedent for later American isolationists.

Whatever her reasons for discrediting Tisquantum may have been, her report did serve one end. Hobomok emerged from the incident as the more "trustworthy" of the two *pnieses* in Bradford's and Winslow's opinions. Hobomok's wife's decision to injure Tisquantum is also representative both of a greater problem and a larger truth. That American Indians knew each other well and played games with the Europeans to further their own immediate ends at the expense of one another is a factor contributing to their many losses after Contact.

When Governor Bradford, desperate for Tisquantum's aid and reluctant to kill a friend, refused to honor the nonaggression pact's demands,

Plymouth's relations with the Wampanoags cooled noticeably. In fact, the Native waters become so unpleasant that Tisquantum avoided them for the remainder of his life. Bradford writes that after "yᵉ discovery of his practises, Massasoyt sought it [Tisquantum's death] both privatly and openly; which caused him [Tisquantum] to stick close to yᵉ English , & never durst goe from them till he dyed."

7 TISQUANTUM
DᛉP

Death came suddenly and unexpectedly to Tisquantum in the autumn of 1622. Although his sojourn among the Plymoutheans had been brief, his legacy to them was apocryphal, long-lived, and far-reaching. *Pniese,* poet, and shape-shifter, it is hardly remarkable that such an extraordinary man generated deep gratitude as well as considerable controversy for Bradford and subsequent historians.

Much of the debate surrounding this man, in Bradford's day and in ours, centers not on Tisquantum's many widely acknowledged contributions to the Colony, but on his failure with narrative. Bradford's and Winslow's respective accounts suggest that Tisquantum's consummate blunder was to overestimate his audience's powers of metaphorical discernment. The shaman's naïve listeners seemed to have taken his metaphors literally, and these verbal miscalculations cost him his life. It is sadly ironic that the American Indian Word became mired in exegetical obfuscations at the critical time it most needed to give light.

By all accounts, Tisquantum's relations with Plymouth proceeded relatively smoothly from the time of his arrival until the spring of 1622, when Hobomok "intimated . . . some jealocie of Squanto, by what he gathered from some private whisperings betweene him and other Indeans." After this disclosure, Bradford writes:

> They begane to see yᵗ Squanto sought his owne ends, and plaid his owne game, by putting yᵉ Indeans in fear, and drawing gifts from them to enrich him selfe; making them beleeve he could stur up warr against whom he would, & make peece for whom he would. Yea, he made them beleeve they kept yᵉ plague buried in yᵉ ground, and could

send it amongs whom they would, which did much terrifie the Indeans, and made them depend more on him, and seeke more to him
then to Massasoyte, which proucured him envie, and had like to have
cost him his life. For after ye discovery of his practises, Massasoyt
sought it both privatly and openly; which caused him to stick close
to ye English, & never durst goe from them till he dyed. (136–37)

Until recently, literary critics have given this passage scant attention, and
historians, hypothesizing that the Patuxet Tisquantum did indeed oppose
the Pokanokets, tend to take Bradford's comments as holy writ.[1] A significant number of historical theories concerning this incident rest on the
belief expressed by Bradford and Winslow that Tisquantum resented the
Massasoit and wanted to take over his position. A typical rationale for
Tisquantum's alleged power plays can be found in "Squanto: Last of the
Patuxets" (1981) by Neal Salisbury, who argues that Tisquantum "sought a
reconstituted Patuxet band under his own leadership."[2] If Bradford's observations were based upon accurate information, Salisbury and his fellows are correct, but, while not totally discounting the various domination
theories concerning Tisquantum, I call them into question.

My reading of Bradford's passage raises several very different issues
involving Tisquantum, and none of them includes power brokering. The
major uncertainty concerning the *pniese* derives from the unhappy result
of Tisquantum's use of figural language, or rather his failure at storytelling. Another perplexity hinges on conflicting cultural expectations held by
Algonquians and Plymoutheans respectively. Because it is virtually impossible to separate constituent elements in an American Indian world, it will
be necessary to designate these problems "religious issues," even though
that term is largely inadequate.

In the passage above, we see that Tisquantum metaphorically connects
English political strength to "plague buried in ye ground" in an effort to
explain the destructive potential of English gunpowder, which the Plymoutheans kept buried for dry storage and used to effect immediate security,
if not political ascendancy. In a Native worldview, power is based on words;
however, Tisquantum has observed that in the European system, power
does not seem to be verbal, but appears to be tied to gunpowder that is
concealed in the earth, the primal text. By using figurative language, a stylistic device with which American Indians are normally quite comfortable,

Tisquantum attempts to explain European military technology and political strength to the Algonquians in terms he thinks they can understand: pathologies and bad medicine. Certainly American Indians understood epidemics of wasting diseases and necromancy quite well, but it appears that the vehicle of Tisquantum's metaphor was misinterpreted by the Algonquians just as the tenor was misunderstood by the Plymoutheans. These misconstructions contributed to Tisquantum's later troubles since all his colleagues seem to have been reading him literally.

Bradford's text also indicates that cultural complexities had maneuvered Tisquantum into an unenviable, no-win position. His actions in the Algonquian-English community had become suspect in Plymouth and despised in Sowams. Osamequin had sent Tisquantum to Plymouth to effect cultural change. A member of the Algonquian clergy, he was expected to Indianize the Newcomers, yet he had made little progress after a year and a half of residency.

The Plymoutheans, on the other hand, expected Tisquantum to act primarily as an interpreter and to parrot what he was told. He was not expected to be an independent thinker who involved himself in Plymouthean and Greater Wampanoag civic affairs. Tisquantum was a savage, not a civilized person. He was "tongue," not "brain"; furthermore, it would never have occurred to the Pilgrims to look to Tisquantum, or any other American Indian, for religious instruction, since they already had dogma sufficient for this world and the next. In addition to theological surfeit, Puritan investigations of the New World's ecclesiastical infrastructure had disclosed an American Indian deficiency in exercises of organized faith; thus the Saints viewed Tisquantum as a candidate for Christianization. Under no circumstances could they ever have entertained the notion that they were presumptive Native converts. That Tisquantum evidenced ambivalence toward the Wampanoags' Indianization Initiative suggests that at some point in his life Tisquantum had indeed converted.

Tisquantum's likely conversion, an act about which the Wampanoags had not been told but probably sensed because the Indianization program was not advancing, skewed the domestic tranquility of both camps. His problematic status invited scrutiny, if not outright criticism. Tisquantum's biography indicates that he had once been rescued from slavery by monks who earlier had openly stated their intentions to convert stolen Natives.[3] He was later employed by Ferdinando Gorges for a time, and Gorges had issued a written policy statement mandating the conversion of Native people. That Tisquantum had indeed converted is plausible because, in an American Indian world, it is impossible to separate religion from lifestyle, literature, science, technology, and the like. When an American Indian, like Tisquantum, looked at Europe in the seventeenth century and saw all the magnificent trappings of "civilization," he would have considered those things the result of strong "medicine" or the after-effects of great religious/ verbal power. In Europe, Tisquantum was alone and had no familial or spousal support to keep him tied to the old traditions, which require trib- ally knowledgeable participants and specific ceremonial accoutrement for the proper enactment of rites. Even if Tisquantum had resisted European conversion attempts, it is doubtful that he could have withstood Brownist assaults on his soul.

The most convincing argument for Tisquantum's conversion is Brad- ford's recollection of the *pniese's* final utterances, which petitioned the Governor to "pray for him, that he might goe to ye Englishmens God in heaven."[4] Tisquantum, furthermore, "bequeathed sundrie of his things to sundry of his English freinds, as remembrances of his love." The request to leave his friends his worldly goods further indicates that Tisquantum intended to be buried as a Christian, not as an Indian who would have expected that his favorite possessions be interred with him.

While residing in Christian nations, becoming a Christian was per- haps a judicious determination. Being a Christian Wampanoag in the New World was an agonizing liability. Tisquantum's Christian status partially explains his wariness in regard to Pilgrim Indianization, but further inten- sifying his quandary was the fact that he knew more of the world outside America than his colleagues did. Tisquantum had seen enough of Europe to realize that his Native world was not necessarily the best of all possible worlds in terms of technology and luxuries, and that knowledge, too, may partially have contributed to his hesitancy to Indianize the Plymoutheans. People accustomed to the domestic comforts of Europe would not adapt easily to spartan Native lifestyles steeped in cultural practices antitheti- cal to Christian belief. Also important is the certainty that Tisquantum understood the Separatist mindset well enough to know that any effort to turn Brownists into Indians would not succeed. Better medicine men than he had failed. Overwhelmed by the futility of his mission, he must have cast about for a way to couch the acculturation problem in terms the increasingly impatient Algonquians could understand. Tragically, his figural, albeit desperate, explanation of the power Europeans derived from their technology and cultural belief systems, metaphorically equated with gunpowder and disease, was ill chosen. In an atmosphere of fear, the metaphor was misunderstood and misrepresented by all parties concerned.

By 1622, Tisquantum thus found himself entangled in perplexing circumstances that had repercussions ranging from the merely troubling to the profound. He had reached a point at which nearly all his efforts worked against him. If he openly admitted to retaining some Native beliefs and attempted to Indianize the Plymoutheans, it is conceivable that he would have been expelled from the Colony. If he continued to do nothing to bring the Colony into an American Indian ethos, he risked condemnation by his peers and isolation from the Algonquian community. He was a Christian *pniese*, an oxymoron, and a question.

It is important to observe, however, that when Tisquantum was called to account for his "treacheries," Winslow relates that he "offered not to fly, but came and accused Hobbamock as the author and worker of his overthrow, yielding himself to the Governor to be sent or not according as he thought meet." This passage, like so many others, lends itself to several readings. On one hand, the selection suggests that Tisquantum was open, forthright, fearless, and obedient to the Governor's judgment. On the other hand, it offers the possibility that Tisquantum was counterattacking and gambling on Bradford's affection to save him. Either way, the *pniese* is revealed to be politic and courageous.

It should be noted that both Bradford's history and Winslow's *Good Newes from New England* document Tisquantum's alleged infidelity to the Great Leader largely on Hobomok's testimony. What makes Hobomok the more reliable of the two is a question the diegetic texts raise. Hermeneutic implications present in the hypodiegetic texts provide clues. One factor possibly contributing to the Plymoutheans' distrust of Tisquantum may be the fact that, as far as we know, Tisquantum was not married. Hobomok was. Bradford and Winslow provide commentary on Hobomok's wife, but they never mention a wife for Tisquantum. The Pilgrims, who were rarely without wives for more than several weeks, may have felt that a married man with children was more settled and less inclined to stir up political intrigue than a man not reveling in connubial bliss. An unmarried man in Pilgrim society was considered an anomaly, and anomalies often raise social suspicion, as Elizabeth Bennet will remind us two hundred years later. From an Algonquian point of view, however, Tisquantum's unmarried status deserves a different consideration.

What the Plymoutheans did not realize is that it would have been difficult for an unmarried man with few if any relatives to make a successful power play in Native society because he would not have had the support of women. A man with no mother, aunts, sisters, wives, or daughters would have found it nearly impossible to build the communal support essential for power consolidation. Even if, as current ethnohistorians believe, women had no political power in Algonquian society, they did have enough social and sexual power to make their influence felt. Had Tisquantum really been seeking political primacy, he must first have married. Had he been unable to find a wife, he would then have asked a large family dominated by women to adopt him.[5] Tisquantum would not have practiced extortion on his fellows as a means of consolidating political ascendancy, because that technique would not effectuate the desired end.[6] In order to gather a political following in seventeenth-century Algonquia, an American Indian would have to foster admiration. He could not succeed by creating fear or making exhibitions of wealth and power. Hobomok, with his several wives and extended family, probably had established a stable matriarchal power base, which Tisquantum likely did not have, and despite Hobomok's innuendos, it is not at all certain that amassing power was Tisquantum's primary concern.

Representative of past, and insightful, academic thinking, Frank Shuffelton, in "Indian Devils and Pilgrim Fathers" (1976), posits that Tisquantum tried to amass shamanistic power in an effort to rival the Massasoit's political power:

> [Squanto's] experiences among and knowledge of the whites gave him an imaginative lever against his tribe's power structure which could be presented in shamanistic terms. His threats to loose the plague on the Indians and to bring war to them were . . . the claims of a would-be shaman. His demanding of tribute and gifts from the Indians was not merely to enrich himself—he was not an Indian equivalent of the Plymouth Colony's London backers, despite what Bradford seems to have thought. Giving gifts and tribute was for the Indians a token of respect paid to men of spiritual and political

power, and the giving affirmed both the respect and the power. It was not capitalist accumulation. Squanto, like many other New England Indians, was using the whites against his enemies, but he was using them in the mode of a shaman.[7]

Shuffelton does not tell us who these enemies are or how a man gone from Old Algonquia so many years could have had many enemies. The fact is, Tisquantum was a genuine shaman, not a "would-be shaman," and DhꓕLꞒⵔꞬ usually do not have enemies. Shamans, who enjoy a status similar to that of modern clergymen, are unlikely to offend except by failing to effect a remedy. Such failures are usually written off with a "We paid our money, we took our chances; let's see another medicine person" attitude. Few people are foolish enough to oppose or confront a medicine person. Shuffelton, however obliquely, does point out the central issue of the Tisquantum dilemma: religion. The *pniese* was attempting to walk two theological roads at once: one white, the other red. It is not unusual for American Indians to maintain many of their former customs and beliefs when they take on a new faith. Accretion, not deletion, is often the rule. The gifts Tisquantum received suggest that he was being paid for shamanistic services, but do not necessarily intimate that he was amassing power to be used against the Massasoit. Tisquantum was simply practicing his profession as he had done in years past. More important, he was attempting to protect his essential identity while negotiating another culture. He foreordained today's modern Indian.

ᏫᎪᎮᎯ.

That Tisquantum was straddling two worlds is made clear by his reaction to the infamous and controversial bundle of arrows wrapped in a rattlesnake skin mentioned in an earlier chapter. Bradford reports that "ye great people of ye Narigansets, . . . sente a messenger unto them with a bundl of arrows tyed aboute with a great sneak-skine; which their interpretours tould them was a threatening & a chaleng" (133). Winslow recollects that this bundle was intended for Tisquantum, and I submit that the bundle, which is usually interpreted by historians to be a declaration of war, was not.[8] It was a sacred text of indeterminate designation. It was either a notice of impending religious obligations, an invitation to a ceremony, or a sacred commission for Tisquantum. One thing, however, is indisputable. The bundle operates as a text within a text, an enigma to the Plymouthe-ans, and a mystery to this day.

The bundle sent by Canonicus arrived at Plymouth in November, which is hunting season. Only a crisis could have precipitated an Indian war then, since every able-bodied Algonquian male was finalizing his pro-curement of winter meat supplies and the women were preserving it. More to the point, the bundle of arrows wrapped in a rattlesnake skin has an unmistakable religious significance. The object in question is a bundle, not a war belt. The arrows point to the Thunder Beings and the skin to the highly venerated Grandfather Rattlesnake, a spirit powerful enough to move freely and with impunity between the land of the living and the land of the dead.

DBꞀꞘGₒꝹE DƟꞀƟⱵC

In ancient Algonquian legends, the Thunder Beings are two brothers who are friends to man. They strike and kill what is harmful to him.[9] With their lightning-quick movements, poisonous snakes have an affinity with the Thunder Beings. When snakes strike, their movements imitate the actions of the Thunder Beings, who bring rain, and rain is a blessing, but not with-out danger. In another Algonquian legend, the rattlesnake's rattles are mir-ror reflections of the terrapin-shell rattles used in American Indian sacred ceremonies, and the coiled rattlesnake's head moves about like a dancing Indian.[10] In Algonquian figurative language, the rattlesnake is a metaphor for a man engaged in a holy rite, not a warrior preparing for battle.

Winslow reports that the Algonquian god Hobomok sometimes appeared "most ordinarily [as] a snake" when he presented himself to vi-sion seekers in dreams. Since the snake has both human and divine attri-butes, symbolically speaking, it seems only reasonable to propose that the bundle text was either an invitation to prepare for an upcoming religious ceremony or a private message to the *pniese* urging him step up his Indi-anization efforts. The imperative for bringing the Plymoutheans into the Algonquian holy discipline was the fact that they had settled in the middle of a sacred place. It is as if the Plymoutheans had camped on the high altar of Canterbury Cathedral, and the Archbishop needed to say Christmas Mass.

At Contact, hundreds of stone rows, vision chairs, stone mounds, underground chambers, and anthropomorphic standing boulders constituted and marked sacred sites—places for vision quests, astronomical calculations, and ritual ceremonies. In the Northeast there were Algonquian ritual sites. Near Plymouth there were

at least three known donation boulders, called sacrifice rocks, on which branches were piled as donations, along the Old Sandwich Road south of New Plymouth opposite Telegraph Hill and Morey's Hole. In the region of Manomet Hill, there are large marked boulders, traditionally Indian sacred places, that signal alignments to solstice solar horizon events. Two miles east of Plymouth settlement, along Beaver Dam Brook, . . . there is an array of stone rows one boulder high connecting larger boulders on a hillside, some of which have stone mounds on top of them. This linear array stands in the midst of a group of stone mounds. . . . [and designates] Indian ritual landscape architecture.[11]

These stone configurations indicate that the Plymoutheans were indeed living in sacred space. Unknowingly they had invaded a ceremonial ground. The stone edifices surrounding them were not only places of religious devotion but were also ritually prepared locations for Algonquian literary performances. The ceremonies performed at these stone monuments had poetic functions as well as scientific and religious purposes. The problem was that the Plymoutheans had not only built a village near an altar but had also planted themselves in the midst of a planetarium and had interrupted regularly scheduled literary soirees. Their place of settlement was alive with Algonquian words, power formulae, and verbal performances occasioned by the movements of the earth and the celestial bodies. The Newcomers were living in an Algonquian consecrated literary space resonating with sacred oral expressions. Power language, or American Indian poetry, was all around them. That they did not understand the language or the significance of their dwelling place is beside the point. The power was in the Algonquian words, not in the English comprehension. And the words penetrated.

As the Algonquians viewed the diplomatically difficult situation of lingering guests, they decided that the Plymoutheans must either convert or leave. The presence of so many heretics, or less-than-genuine people, was discomfiting.[12]

It was impossible to worship or seek visions with the noise of fort building, children playing, hymn singing, militia drilling, and turkey shooting going on in the pew in front of one. Additional colonists moving into the sacred area underlined the need for bringing the interlopers into the way of Creation quickly. Even though the new citizens of the Wampanoag Nation were now eating right, they were still wearing strange clothing and behaving peculiarly. Sadly, they were not much into dancing and had no aptitude for face painting. Not only that, the Newcomers still insisted upon building their fires indoors and treating them casually, never giving them offerings and using them only for cooking and heating. More incredible, the New Patuxets had not exhibited any interest in learning the sacred stories pertinent to the area. They did not seek visions. They never took part in purification rites. Worse yet, the English did not properly mourn their dead, but behaved at funerals as if nothing had happened. Inept at language acquisition, the Newcomers seemed to lack motivation. Unless appropriate steps were taken, the neighborhood would deteriorate even further, and social mores would weaken. There was urgency. If the required rites were not properly carried out, the society at large would wither. The ceremony performed in the area around Plymouth at the winter solstice was the "most important Algonquin Indian festival of all, the Feast of Dreams."[13] It was about a month before the winter solstice that Canonicus sent the bundle.

Long before Canonicus sent the bundle, other Algonquian leaders had stressed the importance of Indianizing the new settlers and made several attempts to do so. Osamequin had planted Algonquian clergymen in the Colony, and by installing Tisquantum with Bradford and Hobomok with Standish, the Massasoit had ensured that Algonquian influence on the Plymouthean leaders would be brought to bear. Iyanough had treated the Plymoutheans to a clambake while Aspinet had adopted John Billington. Despite all this, the Newcomers did not seem to comprehend what was expected, but the Algonquians persevered. At this juncture Canonicus, undaunted by the communication failures of his fellows, decided to try his hand at converting the Plymoutheans. His course of action was to send the Plymoutheans the bundle of arrows wrapped in a snakeskin; it was their engraved invitation to join the circle. He thought that surely the Pilgrims could read and appropriately respond to a holy text.

But, of course, they could not. Bradford filled the skin with shot and returned it to the Narragansetts. The Governor relates that the sachem "would not receive it, but sent it back againe." Canonicus may have reissued the bundle on the remote chance that the Plymoutheans would reconsider the invitation to the holy observances. That the Plymoutheans would refuse such a sacred summons was unthinkable. When the bundle was returned a second time, the sachem destroyed it. John Pory, a visitor to Plymouth, writes in a letter to the Earl of Southampton that Canonicus finally threw the bundle "in a river," an act that clearly demonstrates that the holy item had been defiled. Pory recognized that Canonicus was so troubled by the desecrated bundle that he would not touch it. "The shot and powder he liked not, nor would meddle with it, but caused it to be cast into the river."[14] American Indian religious convention demands that a badly compromised medicine bundle be ritually destroyed; therefore, it was. Had the bundle been a declaration of war, the Narragansetts would have attacked when it was returned the first time.

The Wampanoag historian Milton Travers offers information that substantiates my assertion. Whenever the Wampanoags considered making war, the "great Sachem . . . would then send out his messengers carrying bundles of arrows dipped in blood which was the signal for all to hasten to his seat for a council of war.[15] This convocation was only deliberative and would be attended by elders, younger men and women, and warriors. Warriors of the participating bands who stepped into the circle and began a war dance signaled their willingness to fight. If enough agreed to an attack, the chief medicine man would retire into the forest to read the signs. If signs were favorable the war would proceed. If they were not, the project would be abandoned.[16] For purposes here, it is enough to know that arrows tipped with blood were invitations to a meeting to discuss possible military action, not a declaration of war. Bradford and Winslow report only that the arrows were wrapped in a rattlesnake skin, and that description reinforces my position that the bundle was an invitation to a sacred event.

It is Winslow who establishes the connection between the bundle and Tisquantum. In "Good Newes from America," he reports that

> at length came one of them to us, who was sent by Conanacus, their chief sachim or king, accompanied with one Tokamahamon, a friendly Indian. This messenger inquired for Tisquantum, our

interpreter, who not being at home, seemed rather to be glad than sorry, and leaving for him a bundle of new arrows, lapped in a rattle-snake's skin, desired to depart with all expedition. But our governors not knowing what to make of this strange carriage, and comparing it with [war rumors] we had formerly heard, committed him to the custody of Captain Standish, hoping now to know some certainty of that we so often heard. (281)

Standish turned the prisoner over to Winslow, but instead of asking the messenger the significance of the bundle, Winslow asked him about rumors intimating that Canonicus was planning war against the Colony. The messenger responded that Canonicus had been persuaded to wage war by an earlier courier sent to Plymouth to arrange a peace because gifts previously remitted to Canonicus from Plymouth were "mean" and not befitting his person. The same very nervous messenger then stated that this unnamed tribal member would be killed for "false carriage," as soon as he, the bundle messenger, arrived home. This second messenger would also make certain that the Narragansetts and the Plymoutheans were friends again. The obviously lying and badly frightened envoy was then released. Refusing food in an unforgivable display of bad manners, he rushed home amid a violent rainstorm despite protests from the Plymoutheans that he take shelter.

Here again is a case of the Plymoutheans reading Native movements experientially in terms of their own political unrest, unrest that encompassed their financial and contractual problems with the Merchant Adventurers, their larger ecclesiastical debates with the world as well as their internal squabbles with their new ministers, assorted visiting felons, and each other. Instead of being curious about the bundle's meaning, they simply grilled the messenger about Canonicus' military intentions.

When Tisquantum returned, he declared the bundle, which certainly looked intimidating to the uninitiated, to be a sign of "enmity." Since Tisquantum was a religious leader as well as a warrior, and since the bundle was apparently intended for him, I reiterate that American Indian ceremonial exigency was the genuine concern here, not war. The snakeskin and the arrows are religious symbols, and American Indians rarely mix metaphors. The words Tisquantum used to explain the bundle are, according to Bradford, "threatening," "chaleng," and "warre." According to Winslow, the bundle represents "enmity," but these words are out of context with the symbolic meaning of the bundle.

There are several reasons to believe that what was taking place around the time of the bundle's receipt was a ceremony involving the seasonal change of rule from war chief to peace chief. It is just as likely that the war societies, made up of *pnieses*, were responsible for overseeing this ritual change called the Feast of Dreams. The bundle for Tisquantum may have been a reminder or a "chaleng" for him to contribute his part to the Feast, meaning that he should assemble the new guests. After all, the Newcomers were residing on the site of the village that had always performed an essential function for the ceremony in days past; thus the New Patuxets should now assume their social responsibilities. It was only fitting that Tisquantum do this, because he was one of the few Old Patuxets remaining. For reasons known only to Tisquantum, however, he chose not to reveal the bundle's intended meaning. Anticipating Stanley Fish, the medicine man's subreption allowed the Plymoutheans to read into the text whatever they would, and he validated with his equivocal response their bellicose inference.

Unfortunately, Tisquantum's failure to explicate the bundle honestly hampered the penetration of European American letters by American Indian literary arts; nevertheless, the bundle succeeded in spite of its handlers. It survives, not as a complete text, but as an American Indian artifact resting comfortably in a European American literary dig where it inspires archaeologists, ethnohistorians, sociologists, and critics to entertain visions and set forth narratives. Apparently Canonicus acted rightly.

Tisquantum's reluctance to translate the actual meaning of the bundle stems from the dilemma in which he found himself. Had he imparted the bundle's true meaning, he would likely have faced unpleasant consequences; therefore, he encouraged the Plymoutheans to believe what they were inclined to believe—that war with Canonicus was imminent. Also contributing to Tisquantum's decision to obscure the meaning of the bundle is the possibility that he lacked the verbal ability to explain in English the political and philosophical complexities of what was ritually occurring at the time. The Feast of Dreams would present serious problems for Tisquantum in terms of theology and translation.

Little is known about this ritual. Mavor and Dix posit that this was a time "when communication with all the spirits [was] sought, including those of the stars."[17] Travers calls this ceremony the Nikommosachmi-awene, or the feast ordered by the sachem. At the Nikommosachmiawene, tribal history was recounted and wampum belts were read.[18] It is quite possible that this celebration was similar to the Iroquois Rite of Condolence. According to Daniel Richter in *The Ordeal of the Longhouse* (1992), not only the Iroquois, but also the tribes bordering the Iroquois, observed these rites. If the Feast of Dreams were anything like the Iroquois Rite, it would have been a war mourner's rite, which was a "requickening" ceremony in which a dead person's social role and name were passed to a living person, often a captive.[19] Hence the possible ambiguity with the word "warre" and Tisquantum's reluctance to explain a tenet of Algonquian theology suggestive of reincarnation to Brownists. It is not inconceivable that a dead Algonquian warrior's name was to be passed on either to Tisquantum himself or to a Plymouthean. In such a case, Tisquantum's interpretative expertise would be strained to the breaking point. How could he explain such a complicated and "heretical" belief system without calling his conversion into question or being forced to leave a post he enjoyed? The "warre" in question could have been in Tisquantum's mind.

The incident that leads me to think that Tisquantum somehow betrayed the command he was sent to effectuate is the manner of his death. In September 1622, Plymouth planned a corn trading expedition south to the Cape with Standish in command. At the last moment, Standish developed a high temperature, so Bradford went instead. Uncooperative winds forced the party to put into Manamoyack Bay. There "Squanto fell sick of an Indean feavor, bleeding much at yᵉ nose (which yᵉ Indeans take for a simptome of death)," and within a few days Tisquantum died.

This passage seems to indicate that there was something peculiarly Indian about Tisquantum's death. Both Standish and the Patuxet had fevers, but Tisquantum's was an "Indean feavor." How would the illnesses differ? What would make Tisquantum's fever particularly Indian? What does the nosebleed signify?

John Humins hypothesizes in "Squanto and the Massasoit: A Struggle for Power" (1987) that Tisquantum "may have died of witchcraft, since, according to Indian belief, there is profuse bleeding from the nose when an evil spirit exits its victim."[20] Modern pathologies aside, that observation has some merit. Even Bradford, a man unacquainted with American Indian occultism, noticed something unusual or "Indean" about Tisquantum's death. His illness was markedly different from the General's, and

Standish lived despite the illness. Bradford's observation that it was an "Indean feavor" obliquely points to a factor that may have played a part in Tisquantum's demise. The *pniese's* failure to carry out his religious obligations to the Wampanoags may have resulted in their witching him fatally.

In his discussion of American Indian customs, Francis Jennings reports that "although participation in rituals was expected, the punishment for withdrawal was limited to public obloquy; in extreme cases the offender might be bewitched or poisoned by the ritual powwow, but such acts were clandestine."[21] Although the cause of Tisquantum's death will never be known, it is probably fair to surmise that the Patuxet paid a high price for his sojourn at Plymouth.

Tisquantum was given Christian burial and has become part of American sacred legend. *Of Plimoth Plantation* gives only Brewster more biographical treatment. George Willison numbers the Algonquian among the Saints, and Judge John Davis, the fifth editor of *New-England's Memorial* 1826, writes: "Governor Bradford's pen was worthily employed in the tender notice taken of the death of this child of nature. With some aberrations, his conduct was generally irreproachable, and his useful services to the infant settlement entitle him to a grateful remembrance."[22]

The warrior-*pniese* was hardly a child, but the sentiment is appreciated. Tisquantum moved rather quickly from American history into American life and letters, and he still operates as the living, functioning American Indian Word. His *Yes, Ke-mo-sabe* supports our heroes, both real and literary, now just as it did in the past. Replicated by Crispus Attucks (Wampanoag) on Boston Common, echoed by Ira Hayes (Pima) at Iwo Jima, and translated by Charles Chibitty (Comanche) on Utah Beach, the American Indian Word stands ready. Tisquantum's fictional adumbrations range from Natty Bumppo to Tashtego to Huck Finn to Lew Wetzel. In a less glorious capacity, he annually reminds American schoolchildren of the American Indian contributions to the first Thanksgiving and to the development of the nation. The many other mirror reflections of the *pniese* underline the American Indian presence in our literature, our culture, our language, and our reality to the extent that Tisquantum's place in American letters is secure.

Something like a Janus figure, he appropriately came to Plymouth in the old New Year, March. That he arrived in corn planting season, taught the Plymoutheans to grow it, and died while trading for it connects Tisquantum to the Native sacramental and reaffirms his position as a creative force in European American letters. Emblematic of American literature before Contact, the agent of the Massasoit became European American literature after Contact. Tisquantum stands for American literature past and future, the old and the new.

It is also intriguing to see that Tisquantum's personal history is paradigmatic for the history of Bradford's original manuscript. Exactly like Tisquantum, the Bradford holograph was born in America. It was captured and taken to England by the British and finally returned to America, only to find its family dead and its village decimated. The phenomenon inherent in traditional American Indian oral narratives—in which signified and signifier meld—occurs in and with *Of Plimoth Plantation,* and this event has much prototypical significance for European American letters.

8 | THE INDEANS
DΘLƆ'C

DΘLƆ'C. As Bradford and Winslow, ⚭Ɉ ɈS⟊.Ɉ⚭Ɉ DƋ ΘhⱭG, journeyed through the strange New World, they felt compelled to mark their trails. To that end, the Principal Patriarch and his Deputy frequently kindled literary fires for memory, light, and safety. Their adroitly scattered writerly efforts served at least three purposes: they created historical records, encouragement for other colonists, and justification for their administrative actions. Happily for modern researchers casting about for Algonquian history, their fulgent fires, built with Indian timbers, survive as beacons drawing scholars through the interminable Puritan woodlands of sermons and meditations to the more intriguing shadows of Algonquian life and times. Bradford emerged from the forest as the tribe's official Fire Keeper, but his work was ably assisted by Winslow, who adroitly tossed on an occasional log. The records they left give off flickering images of Pilgrim musings and Algonquian movements.

Though not as prolix as Bradford, Winslow made his own inestimable contributions to Old Algonquia's written history. The embers from his fires often explode with fascinating vignettes of Algonquian men and women. He relished his encounters with American Natives, and his lively anecdotes of the indigenous people he met covered subjects ranging from Native foods to individual character traits and peculiarities. On his many travels outside the Colony, the Deputy Pilgrim recorded occurrences trivial, hostile, and poignant. One day en route to Sowams, Mourt meets people from Nemasket and detours to their village. "The inhabitants entertaining us with joy, in the best manner they could, giving us a kind of bread called by them *maizium*, and the spawn of shads, which they got in abundance, insomuch as they gave us spoons to eat them. With these they boiled musty acorns, but of the shads we ate heartily."

In return for the hospitality, the Plymoutheans graciously kill fourscore crows for the Nemaskets. The Nemaskets had been complaining about the birds but would not harm them because in their culture crows were "agent[s] of good and ill fortune, . . . marginal creatures[s] that [commute] between the world of the living and the world of the dead."[1] Having non-Indians do potentially hurtful tasks is an old Indian trick, one more common actually than burning forts. This incident illustrates the bicultural, adaptive interplay occurring at the time. Here the Europeans are trying to help the less fortunate, and the Indians are making good use of their new whipping boys.

Not all encounters were so mutually satisfying. In a famous exchange with Corbitant, Winslow asserts that the headman remarked that if Tisquantum "were dead, the English had lost their tongue." That declaration threw the Plymoutheans into a worried frenzy, but one snide comment maketh not a broil. Nothing happened as a result of that utterance, so in context or out, little can be gleaned from Corbitant's conceit except the observation that the remark was rather astute and the metaphor appropriate.

Corbitant, usually portrayed as an unfriendly type, was not always the unpleasant brute that Bradford and Winslow made him out to be. In *Good Newes from New England,* the Deputy Patriarch shows us Corbitant's gentler side. "That night, through the earnest request of Conbatant [Corbitant], who till now remained at Sawaams, . . . we lodged with him at Mattapuyst. By the way I had much conference with him, so likewise at his house, he being a notable politician, yet full of merry jests and squibs, and never better pleased than when the like are returned again upon him."

Winslow's recollection of this evening's conversation gives us one of the best portraits of Algonquians ever drawn in early American letters. Here we see an American Indian portrayed as a unique individual, not a generic savage or stoic mute. The selection also provides valuable insights into American Indian cultural practices. Kind-hearted teasing is a kind of metaphorical truth seeking and is an integral part of American Indian life.[2]

Winslow's passages sometimes demonstrate the fact that certain Algonquians could be intellectually perceptive and diplomatically astute. He writes that Corbitant asked why he, Hobomok, and their companion, John Hamden, a visiting "gentleman" from London, ventured so far from Plymouth alone. Were they not afraid? Winslow replies that "where was

true love, there was no fear; and [his] heart was so upright towards them
. . . [he] was fearless to come among them." Corbitant's response is thought
provoking:

> But, said he, if your love be such . . . how cometh it to pass, that when
> we come to Patuxet, you stand upon your guard, with the mouths of
> your pieces presented towards us? Whereupon I answered, it was the
> most honorable and respective entertainment we could give them; it
> being an order amongst us so to receive our best respected friends.
> . . . But shaking the head, he answered, that he liked not such saluta-
> tions. (325)

After a day of conversation, the evening meal was served, and Corbitant
asked Winslow to return thanks. The Deputy Patriarch obliged. When
the prayer was finished, Corbitant then asked Winslow why he prayed.
Winslow rattled off a hastily-put-together reply paraphrased haphazardly
from the 1563 *Heidelberg Catechism*. After listening to the homily politely,
the Algonquian replied that "they believed almost all the same things, and
that the same power that we called God, they called *Kiehtan*. Much profitable conference was occasioned hereby, which would be too tedious to
relate, yet was no less delightful to them, than comfortable to us."

Oh, Winslow. Ʂ ꝞꟆ? What would we not give to know what they
said. Not even the extradiegetic text can help us here. We know that early
American Indian thought was not informed by the *Heidelberg Catechism*
and the 1562 *Second Helvetic Confession*, two ecclesiastical instruments
encapsulating Reformed theology, but American Indians have from time
immemorial recognized a Prime Mover and have given thanks for beneficence. Winslow, who heard sufficient exposition to realize that the Algonquians were not godless savages, was apparently Renaissance man enough
to find the discourse "comforting," and not threatening.

Unfortunately, not all the dialogue between the Plymoutheans and the
First Families of Massachusetts was convivial. In a meeting with several
Massachuset warriors and Miles Standish, the General and Wituwamat
had one of their several verbal confrontations. Winslow describes the Algonquian sachem and the encounter this way:

> The chief of them [the Massachusets] was called Wituwamat, a no-
> table insulting villain, one who had formerly imbrued his hands in

the blood of English and French, and had oft boasted of his own valour, and derided their weakness, especially because, as he said, they died crying, making sour faces, more like children than men. This villain took a dagger from about his neck, which he had gotten of Master Weston's people, and presented it to the sachim [Canonicus]; and after made a long speech in an audacious manner, framing it in such sort, as the Captain, though he be the best linguist amongst us, could not gather anything from it. (310)

After hearing this exchange, which none of the English could understand, Winslow concludes that there was a conspiracy to destroy Weston's settlement and Plymouth. As a result, Standish is ordered to march on Wessagusset, and this ill-advised sortie ends in the previously mentioned deaths of Wituwamat, his brother, and six or seven other Massachusets.

The Plymoutheans' violent response to what was only an unintelligible conversation was irrational. At that particular instant, Wituwamat was merely expressing his views. Even though his opinions were extreme, it would have taken much deliberation to have incited an Indian attack because the involved parties would first have to reach a consensus agreeing to it. In reality, what is happening here is that Wituwamat was initiating what would become an ongoing intellectual debate about the immigration problem. The certainty that emerges from this incident is that Wituwamat's words and demeanor were powerful enough to provoke literary and military action. The warrior's narrative strategies grabbed hold of the European American imagination and held it fast for years. His oratorical stance frightened the Pilgrims witless and kept fort builders and the Seventh Calvary in business for centuries.

Wituwamat's political/literary proclivities, expressed later by leaders such as Dragging Canoe (Cherokee), Pushmataha (Choctaw), Tecumseh (Shawnee), Arpeika (Seminole), Black Hawk (Sauk), Crazy Horse (Lakota), Chitto Harjo (Mvskogee), Geronimo (Apache), and countless others, have had an enormous political impact on American Indian nations and their relations with the United States. With Wituwamat's convictions echoing in their minds, many American Indian Nations have attempted armed resistance to European expansion.

At issue with all these leaders and their respective tribes was their refusal to give up their land, the American Indian primal text. American land is the narrative that contains them and allows them to act. These Native chiefs/medicine men/poets would not sign treaties. To do so would vitiate their narrative integrity. By refusing to infuse English letters with their own power, symbolized by signing their names to documents written in English, an act which would transfer land or Native narrative sources to Europeans, they resisted the implementation of foreign letters in the New World. They sought to preserve Native epistemological and teleological sovereignty as manifested in the American Indian oral tradition. In other words, they balked at entering an alien, literate ontology.

Their verbal power, however, remains strong, and metaphorically these critic/warriors are with us still. Eternally recalcitrant, they ambush unsuspecting whites in Hollywood westerns; they stamp their names on our mightiest helicopters. They loom larger than life in our national parks, and their names literally lunge out of our mouths when we parachute from airplanes.[3] Their tribal appellations, like Omaha and Utah, mark our military's secret invasion sites. Wituwamat, together with his real and fictional adumbrations, has transcended Winslow's historical account by virtue of his intellectual strength and verbal courage. Even though he is largely ignored by scholars, he still exists in the American imagination, and, using names like Vine Deloria Jr. and Sherman Alexie, takes occasional potshots at American political leaders. He is certainly Winslow's most fiery spark.

While sitting near his own small fire during long Algonquian winters, Bradford, too, burns images into our minds as he paints unforgettable Indian stories on his buckskin canvas. His winter count, the second part of his history, is artistically decorated with myriad Algonquian signs and tracks. These imprints give the reader illuminating glimpses of Algonquian interactions with Plymoutheans. Some of the Principal Patriarch's remarks are simply observations-in-passing while others are thought-provoking assessments. For example, Bradford's readers learn that the "Tarentins" (probably the Micmacs) are the fiercest of the Algonquians, and the Massachusets are "much affraid" of them. In the trouble between Miantonomo and Uncas, we see that Bradford favors Uncas because the headman appears to be unequivocally loyal to the English.

The Bradford winter count also demonstrates that the Principal Patriarch is sensitive to Native predicaments and attentive to indigenous politics. He notes that Corbitant is "shie to come neare" Plymouth, and when the Mohawks behead the Pequot chief Sassacus, Bradford wonders whether the Mohawks did that deed "to satisfie ye English, or rather ye Narigansets, (who I have since heard, hired them to doe it,) or for their owne advantage."

Of Plimoth Plantation's second part is very different from the history's first section in tone and scope, a difference that will be discussed at some length in the following chapter. His 2. Booke is something like a winter count that artistically depicts Native history on large animal hides. Unlike the congenial Winslow, Bradford was not on intimate terms with Algonquians outside the Colony, but he was constantly alert to indigenous people as a reckoning force. Speculative wars with Indians and rumors of wars among Indians take up considerable space in his history. In Bradford's final chapters, the Pequots, the Narragansetts, and their military maneuvers emerge from the depths of the hypodiegetic narrative and move into the diegetic stratum of narrative. *Of Plimoth Plantation's* concluding portion gives voice to the penultimate agony of the Pequots at Mystic, the dismay and terror of the Narragansetts as they witness the massacre, and the Narragansett determination to remedy the deteriorating political situation after the First Puritan Conquest. Bradford's "Anno Dom: 1637" begins: "In ye fore parte of this year, the Pequents fell openly upon ye English at Conightecute, in ye lower parts of ye river, and slew sundry of them (as they were at work in ye feilds,) both men & women, to ye great terrour of ye rest; and wente away in great prid & triumph, with many high threats."

The Bradford history relates that the Narragansetts joined the English against the Pequots because they wanted revenge for former injuries even though they were cognizant of the fact that all Algonquian groups needed to unite against the settlers. Convinced by Winthrop to assist Massachusetts Bay in its machinations against the Pequots, the Narragansetts connected with European war parties from Connecticut and Boston and led the English soldiers to Mystic, an enclosed Pequot village housing women, children, and elders. The Pequot warriors were awaiting attack elsewhere. Bradford continues:

> They approached . . . [the fort] with great silence, and surrounded it both with English & Indeans, that they might not breake out; and so assualted them with great courage, shooting amongst them, and entered ye forte with all speed; and those y^t first entered found sharp resistance from the enimie, who both shott at & grapled with them;

others rane into their howses, & brought out fire, and sett them on fire, which soone tooke in their matts, &, standing close togeather, with yᵉ wind, all was quickly on a flame, and therby more were burnte to death then was otherwise slain; it burnte their bowstrings, and made them unservisable. Those yᵗ scaped yᵉ fire were slaine with yᵉ sword; some hewed to peeces, others rune throw with their rapiers, so as they were quickly dispatchte, and very few escaped. It was conceived they thus destroyed about 400. at this time. It was a fearfull sight to see them thus frying in yᵉ fyer, and yᵉ streams of blood quenching yᵉ same, and horrible was yᵉ stinck & sente ther of; but yᵉ victory seemed a sweete sacrifice, and they gave the prays therof to God. (425–26)

This passage makes contradictory impressions and raises questions. Astute enough to know that Winthrop's real motive for provoking the Pequots was real estate acquisition, not enemy threat, Bradford sent his terse regrets when Winthrop demanded that Plymouth join this expedition.[4] Even though Bradford gives a chilling account of the massacre, he did not witness the carnage. His moving recapitulation of the Pequot massacre is hearsay. Why does Bradford insert the passage into his text? Does he countenance the English actions?

Most of Bradford's Mystic interpolation is given over to the brutality inflicted upon the Pequots. The prose is graphic. The reader sees the blood. He hears the shrieks. He is perhaps moved to pity, and Bradford himself seems horror-stricken by his vivid retelling of the Pequots' final moments. As customary, he punctuates his account with a biblical allusion; this one, the "sweete sacrifice," is usually glossed as Leviticus 2:1–2, but the reference is modified. He does not say the sacrifice "is" sweet; instead he says it "seems" sweet. It is not like Bradford to equivocate. With the exception of "to be," he is not fond of copulative verbs, so this qualified allusion appears to be slightly at odds with the aims of Bradford's diegetic narrative, which ostensibly celebrates a victory over "so proud & insulting an enimie." Leviticus 2:1-2 reads:

And when any will offer a meate offring unto the Lord, his offering shall be of fine floure, and he shall powre oyle upon it, and put the incense theron. And shall bring it unto Aarons sonnes the Priests, and he shall take thence his handfull of the floure, and of the oyle with all the incense, and the Priest shall burne it for a memoriall upon the altar: for it is an offering made by fire for a sweete sauour unto the Lord. (Geneva Bible [1560])

Bradford, a meticulous Bible scholar, chooses sacred referents carefully. The Old Testament law from which this allusion is drawn pertains to the sanctioned way of making grain sacrifices, not flesh or burnt offerings, and is quite specific.[5] Since human sacrifice is neither required nor desired by the Hebrew God, one wonders if the disparity between the requirements of Old Testament law and the Pequot human offering is the point Bradford's hypodiegetic text is ironically making. Leviticus 2, with its explicit directions for including flour, oil, incense, and priestly office with the sacrifice, could suggest that Bradford did not condone this behavior. The Massachusetts Bay atrocity demanded a moral explanation especially since it reflected badly on the other colonists, and the Leviticus 2 "spin" may have been the best he could muster.

At the close of his Pequot relation, Bradford again picks up the thread of his Narragansett narrative as he conveys Narragansett reaction to the Pequot slaughter. As the attack rages, the "Narigansett Indeans, all this while, stood round aboute, but aloofe from all danger, and left ye whole execution to ye English, except it were ye stoping of any y^t broke away."

The Narragansetts have certainly not been innocent bystanders in this carnage. They have guided the expedition, taken part in the killing, and exulted at the deaths, but after the Mystic massacre they forsook the English both militarily and politically. The English were much too bloodthirsty for their tastes. Captain John Underhill, one of the English commanders at Mystic, later wrote that the Narragansetts explained their defection by saying that the British way of war was "too furious, and slaies too many men."[6]

As Bradford's chronicle, filled with administrative and financial minutiae, winds down, Algonquian affairs continue to dominate the diegetic narrative. The history recounts the Algonquian murders of John Oldham and John Stone, and the "strang and remarkable" deaths of nine hundred American Indians enclosed in a fort "up above in ye river of Conigtecut."[7] Bradford goes on to write that smallpox visits the Algonquians living near Plymouth's Windsor trading post and many Natives die. The Plymoutheans nurse those stricken and bury their dead.

In Bradford's winter count, Algonquian place names appear with increased frequency, empowering and recasting his text. The inclusion of so many Algonquian words, which are narratives in themselves, changes the history's language to the extent that it is no longer entirely English. It has become American, and the Algonquian power words function as agents of authority for the claims the text asserts.

For example, the 2. Booke acknowledges that Plymouth found herself in a boundary dispute with Massachusetts Bay and must rely on the Algonquian knowledge of rivers, streams, and the naming of same to substantiate her land base. Massachusetts Bay claims that from the "Charles-river, or any branch or parte therof, they [Massachusetts Bay] were to extend their limits, and 3. myles further to ye southward."

Bradford's reply to this extortionate demand is classic: "Now they y^t first named it have best reason to know it, and to explaine which it is."
Really! Oᴼ**V**.Ꙡ**G**.Ꙡ!

Plymouth asserts that the territory in question encompasses an area reachable only as far as the Charles can be navigated by boat. Massachusetts Bay, making a very interesting counter, claims all the land drained by the Charles or the land bordering "every runlett or small brooke, y^t should, farr within land, come into it, . . . and *were by ye natives called by other & differente names from it.*" When the matter is settled officially, Bradford uses Algonquian designations to make the boundaries legally binding. "Y^e marshes at *Conahasett* y^t lye of ye one side of ye river next to Hingam, shall belong to ye jurisdition of Massachusetts Plantation; and all ye marshes . . . next to *Sityate*, shall be long to ye jurisdiction of New-Plimoth." What is remarkable here is that both Plymouth and the Bay are basing their claims on Native proofs.

As Plymouth Colony dispersed over a larger area, new villages were established and William Bradford was asked to surrender some of his holdings to the fledgling towns. "The which he willingly did." Again, in issuing title, Bradford uses Native names to mark the lines "3. miles to ye eastward of *Naemschatet*. . . . to *Acoughcouss* . . . to the *Acushente* river . . . to *Nacata*." He reserves for the Indeans their "cheefe [place of] habitation" from the "*Sowansett* river to *Patucket* river, (with *Cawsumsett* neck, . . . extending into ye land 8. myles through ye whole breadth therof."

The final chapters of Bradford's second part take up some of Plymouth's more notable internal affairs, incidents that include the Thomas Granger scandal and the death of the elder, William Brewster. As Bradford concludes his lament for Brewster, he once again picks up the thread of his Narragansett narrative and describes in great detail the Articles of Confederation, which the United Colonies devise "by reason of ye plottings of the Narigansets."

As *Of Plimoth Plantation* draws to its end, Plymouthean and Algonquian lives merge. Plymouthean history, which first adumbrates Patuxetan, begins to presage future events for nearly all American Indian Nations. As time passes, Massachusetts Bay and the other colonies begin to outstrip Plymouth in size and prestige, and the later arrivals cut into nearly every economic pursuit the Plymoutheans had begun. Soon Plymouth has to work more diligently to keep her place in trade and commercial ventures. Since Plymouth never acquires a viable patent from the Crown, her bargaining power remains limited. Like the Algonquians, she finds herself shrinking in size and in fortunes. Too often she is obliged to negotiate with those whom she would prefer to ignore, particularly Massachusetts Bay. The Bay, Plymouth's traditional enemy, frequently bullies Plymouth and attempts to move her off her formerly claimed trading territories. To stave off these encroaching enemies, Bradford writes Winthrop that "you cast rather a partiall, if not a covetous eye, upon that wch is your neigbours." Winthrop, fallaciously and sanctimoniously, replies that the land in question is the "Lords wast." Bradford, taking straight aim, fires back, "If it was ye Lords wast, it was . . . [you] that found it so."

In "Anno Dom: 1644," the Plymouth church becomes seriously weakened by its members' leaving for other places "by reason of ye straightnes & barrennes" of Plymouth's environs. "Many meetings and much consultation was held hearaboute, and diverse were mens minds and opinions. Some were still for staying togeather in this place, ... Others were resolute upon removall." [8]

This passage reveals that Plymouth faced the difficult decision that nearly all American Indians were forced to consider after Contact. It is a sad fact that as American Indians became confined to small areas, and as their homelands were rendered barren and their food supplies depleted or cut off, their choices were the same as Plymouth's. They could stay and die, or leave and live. Leaving was actually a kind of death because removal from a Nation's traditional home meant a total severing from ceremonial grounds, the Nation's moral center. It meant leaving behind all the natural accoutrements of the traditional ritual world. The basic difference between the two groups is that the Plymoutheans could freely choose their new dwelling places, but most American Indians were militarily forced to unfamiliar locations far away from their homelands.[9]

Bradford's lament that Plymouth church's "anciente members [were] . . . worne away by death; and these of later time being like children translated into other families" describes not only the Plymoutheans, but also epitomizes the predicament of thousands of displaced American Indians who were forced to find homes with neighboring tribes hundreds of miles from the bones of their ancestors, their blood relations, their clan relatives, and their friends. The Pequots not killed or sold into slavery were coerced into blending with the Narragansetts, Mohegans, and Niantics. Other Algonquians later joined tribes to the north and west.[10]

Over the course of things, Plymouth, like so many American Indian villages throughout the nation, finally ceased to exist in its original form. Today modern Plymouth resembles an amusement park. Cold drinks and tee shirts are hawked beside the hallowed Rock. Nearby a rebuilt Plymouth, Plymouth Plantation, is a Massachusetts state tourist attraction much like Chaco Canyon or Aztec Ruins in New Mexico, where visitors are allowed to walk through former American Indian homes and see how the Ancient Ones lived. In Plymouth Plantation now sightseers stroll through the compound and watch Wampanoags hollow out canoes while pretend Pilgrims flake codfish.

Not only cultural decay, but repatriation of grave contents has become an issue for the ancient Pilgrims. Like many American Indian remains, Pilgrim bones have been washed into the sea or randomly scattered while Progress moved through the area. Burial grounds have been desecrated, and grave markers destroyed. For the most part, though, Pilgrim remains have escaped being placed in museums for public display or scientific experimentation.

Also like dispossessed American Indians, descendants of the original Plymoutheans are scattered, but they have managed, like their Indian colleagues, to preserve the record of their lineage by incomplete written records and their own oral tradition. Just as it is not uncommon today to meet a European American who claims descent from a Cherokee "princess," neither is it unusual to encounter a person who alleges succession from a *Mayflower* passenger. The *Mayflower* Society attempts to document Plymouthean lineage by issuing official bloodline lists that certify true *Mayflower* descent. Similarly, American Indian tribal registries and instruments like the Dawes Roll guarantee, quantify, and specify American Indian blood. Such agencies also issue certificates verifying same.[11]

The final pages of Bradford's text examine the internal problems of the Algonquians, while the interference of Massachusetts Bay in Algonquian affairs gets little attention. Uncas murders Miantonomo at Massachusetts Bay's request. He consolidates power and toadies to the English until 1675, when Metacomet declares war, a conflagration Bradford did not live to see. During the year 1644, the Narragansetts make several gestures that frighten the colonists. Concomitantly, internal strife between the various Algonquian tribes increases. In 1645, an agreement signed by Pessecous, Meekesano, Witowash, Aumsequen, Abdas, Pummash, and Cutchamakin, representatives of the major tribes, pledges to keep peace among the Narragansetts, Wampanoags, Niantics, Massachusets, Mohegans, Pawtuckets, and the English. As he records this agreement, Bradford spells his usual "Indean" *Endean,* and it is this document that brings his text to a close. In his manuscript, the Principal Patriarch laboriously replicates each Native signer's mark beside his name. For example, the name Witowash appears *Witowash his mark,* CCC. When this document, and the many, many others like it, was signed, American Indians physically, spiritually, metaphorically, and indelibly marked English letters.

These treaties, and the various land transactions also so marked, can be considered the official entry points of American Indian influence on American letters. The American Indian pictographic signatures bestowed authority and authenticity on English letters, words, acts, and narratives. After signing these agreements, European Americans became Algonquian land holders and holders of the American Indian literary tradition in trust.

Constance Rourke, in *The Roots of American Culture* (1942), finds the elaborate ceremonies surrounding treaty signings to be the originating point of American drama. She calls these events "interplay[s] of action" between American Indians and Europeans:

> These treaties were essentially plays-chronicle plays—recording what was said in the parleys, including bits of action, the exchanges of gifts, of wampum, the smoking of pipes, the many ceremonials with dances, cries and choral songs. Even the printed form of the treaties was dramatic: the participants were listed like a cast of characters, and precise notations were made as to ceremonial action. Symbolic phrases were used to seal promises, even to raise questions.[12]

Lisa Brooks (Abenaki), in *The Common Pot* (2008) asserts that, taken col-
lectively, the body of treaties made with American Indians constitutes a
genre that she calls "treaty literature."[13] *Bradford's Indian Book* agrees that
both Rourke and Brooks are correct in citing the importance of treaties to
American letters. The treaty literature represents a melding of European
letters with Native narrative sources, the land, and with Native authority,
the people who signed the documents with tribal symbols. Treaty literature is a hybrid genre. It is highly significant because it is the representation of a generative act, but it does not trigger the power that a medicine
text does. The American Indian poetics informing the medicine texts have
permeated American letters, and this transculturation was facilitated by
the human interplays, which were all-encompassing. They were physical,
intellectual, psychological, emotional, and theological, and they touched
every aspect of the American experience, including the writing.

It is American Indians who have given our national literature much of
its texture, its thematic directions, its imagery, its strength, and its amazing
vitality. There is an American Indian presence in European American literature that guides its thematic impulses and gives dignity to its measures.
The American Indian presence in our major works fills out our national
memory by recalling a past informed by Native people. American Indian
concepts broaden our thinking just as American Indian words extend and
enrich the English vocabulary. Identifying the obvious Indian markers in
American works is straightforward. Native characters, words, and themes
are not obscured, since they are often dressed in buckskin. It is the subtle
connections to the oral tradition—the Native poetics—that are elusive,
and it is those inscriptive markers that we must also consider and calibrate.

9 OF PLIMOTH PLANTATION AS MEDICINE TEXT

JA℘P

Of Plimoth Plantation is an artfully designed narrative construct divided into two parts that differ in form, length, style, and content. The first book, consisting of 104 pages, bears the title, *Of Plimoth Plantation,* and is divided into chapters designated "1. Chapter.," "2. Chap.," and the like. Bradford's book 1 displays characteristics of an American Indian creation account, a very common Native genre complete with legendary heroes and miraculous events described in ancient language. Written like a sacred text, the first section has a solemn tone. Its commentary contains many broad generalizations concerning information that in standard histories is usually much more specific, especially in terms of causation, names, dates, places, and officials. It has mythic overtones, scriptural referents, and elevated language. Illustrative of book 1's many lofty passages is the following selection, which is written in elegant prose and contains references to Deuteronomy 26:5–7, and to Psalms 107:1–5, 8:

> May not & ought not the children of these fathers rightly say: *Our faithers were Englishmen which came over this great ocean, and were ready to perish in this willdernes; but they cried unto ye Lord, and he heard their voyce, and looked on their adversitie, &c. Let them therfore praise ye Lord, because he is good, & his mercies endure for ever. Yea, let them which have been redeemed of ye Lord, shew how he hath delivered them from ye hand of ye oppressour. When they wandered in ye deserte willdernes out of ye way, and found no citie to dwell in, both hungrie, & thirstie, their sowle was overwhelmed in them. Let them confess before ye Lord his loving kindnes, and his wonderfull works before ye sons of men.* (96–97)

Prefatory to the first chapter of Bradford's creation account runs this caption and introduction:

Of Plimoth Plantation

> And first of yᵉ occasion and indusments ther unto; the which that
> I may truly unfould, I must begine at yᵉ very *roote & rise* of yᵉ same.
> The which I shall endevor to manefest in a plaine stile, with singuler
> regard unto yᵉ simple *trueth* in all things, at least as near as my slender
> judgmente can attaine the same. (3, emphasis mine)

Of Plimoth Plantation is introduced as a ceremony of truth and a construct
of balance. Bradford's equipoised plant metaphor, "roote and rise," or source
and development, refers to his examination of the factors contributing to
the Brownists' decision to migrate to the New World and their subsequent
history in that place. His introduction proposes to portray "occasion and
indusments," or cause and rationale, for the migration and the planting,
and in very general, and occasionally overreaching terms, book 1 does this.
Because Bradford promises to tell the truth, his narrative has to relate
the wicked events that transpired in the Colony as well as the good. This
promise is made good in The 2. Booke.

In its entirety then, *Of Plimoth Plantation* is a dichotomized account
designed to preserve both the history and the integrity of a political
creation by relating its engendering motions, its initial actions, and the
justifications for same. By setting down acts both virtuous and non-virtu-
ous, Bradford puts Plymouth's history and the actions of its citizens into
ethical balance. Unencumbered with postmodern sensibilities, Bradford
believes that truth can be uncovered, and he designs a metanarrative to
reveal it.

Like American Indian creation accounts, the first book of Bradford's
history is more mythic and epic than historical. The opening chapters
tell of struggles, travails, adventures, journeys, heroes, and monsters. The
old serpent, heathen Emperors, and Arians rage against the **DhBΘⱳ** of
God. Theological debates assume Homeric proportions, as do the griefs of
the persecuted. Inhabiting a world overcrowded and hostile, the Pilgrims
must, like the defeated Trojans, migrate to a new world. They send out
Robert Cushman and John Carver, designated in the text only as "messengers," to arrange the details of the move.

The first four chapters detailing the migration lack historical precision. Events taking place before and during the migration into the present world occur in "ignorante & superstitious times." In this section Bradford rarely mentions dates, times, specific events, and persons. John Wycliffe's work is referenced as "yᵉ first breaking out of yᵉ lighte of yᵉ gospell in our Honourable Nation of England," the Low Country destination of the exiles is a "desired Haven," and various Anglican rituals are alluded to as "popish trash." The Separatists' various adventures are described in solemn accents that reverberate with biblical overtones to the extent that Bradford's historical personages assume the characteristics of holy martyrs. "Yea, though they should loose their lives in this action, yet might they have comforte in the same, and their endeavors would be honourable" (35).

Most Americans instinctively understand that portions of Bradford's history are important American sacred and mythic traditions. They tend to tell their schoolchildren about Plymouth's corn-planting rituals and the first Thanksgiving primarily when the thunder and snakes are asleep. These autumnal oral narratives, often accompanied by singing, dancing, school pageants, parades, football games, worship services, and feasts, replicate the American Indian Corn Harvest festivals of an earlier era when clans gathered to celebrate the harvest and requicken life. Modern Americans frequently participate in exercises in charity during this period just as in the old days Algonquians collected corn tributes and distributed them to the needy as part of the harvest ritual. Not only children, but adults, too, are moved by Bradford's inspired account. Morison relates that the Honorable George F. Hoar, senator from Massachusetts, declared that "there was nothing like the Bradford History 'in human annals since the story of Bethlehem.'"[1]

Creation accounts often contain emergence myths. Generally speaking, there are two kinds of American Indian emergence stories. Natives, like the Cherokees, either come into the present world from an overcrowded sky vault above, or, like the Hopis, they work their way up to this world from lower regions in a long emergence process through succeeding worlds, each of which teaches lessons in living. In the former method, water animals dive into oceans or lakes, bring up earth, and prepare a new world that accommodates the overflow from the sky vault. **DꙄƖr** or **ᏝᏩhᏏ** does this for the Cherokees; **ᏦWᎽᏜᏆ** accomplishes it for the Wampanoags. People who come to the present world in this manner are called earthdivers.[2] The Pilgrims were not earthdivers. Neither were they emerging people or tunnelers. The Pilgrim Progenitors reached their new world by means of a Great Migration. They were carried across a vast expanse of water while cradled in the bosom of a giant May flower that deposited them on a magic rock.

The geographic location of one of these mythic events is preserved as a national memorial. Pieces of the sacred rock upon which the Pilgrims are said to have been deposited are protected by a monument. That rock, called Plymouth in remembrance of their place of departure, has its own narrative. It seems to be as mobile as the famous Shiprock that once flew Navajo warriors to safety in northwestern New Mexico. Plymouth Rock has been moved, defaced by sightseers, sold by the ounce, lifted into the air by a crane, and repositioned nearer the water than it was originally. Fragments of the holy stone have been carried away by tourists. At one time the rock was enshrined under a box of bones reported to be the remains of some Pilgrims. The boulder is now enclosed in a pit surrounded by an iron railing. As tourists view the rock, they cannot help noticing cigarette butts that have been tossed in from above lying near it. One can only suppose that certain passersby have made tobacco offerings to the venerable stone. It seems that European Americans have made the pit a memory hole like those of the Algonquians described by Edward Winslow in *Good Newes from New England*. Winslow's account further supports the Native principle that the earth is indeed a text as well as a generator of narrative:

> Instead of records and chronicles, they take this course. Where any remarkable act is done, in memory of it, either in the place, or by some pathway near adjoining, they make a round hole in the ground, about a foot deep, and as much over; which when others passing by behold, they inquire the cause and occasion of the same, which being once known, they are careful to acquaint all men, as occasion serveth, therewith; and lest such holes should be filled or grown up by any accident, as men pass by, they will oft renew the same; by which means many things of great antiquity are fresh in memory. So that as a man travelleth, if he can understand his guide, his journey will be the less tedious, by reason of the many historical discourses [which] will be related unto him. (367)

Creation accounts are central to a medicine text because they prescribe the normative, prelapsarian standard by which subsequent action in the text is evaluated. It is only after creation accounts are well established and a group of people has developed a sense of cohesiveness and identity that historians can begin recording the people's past. In some American Indian societies, these histories are called winter counts. Strictly speaking, winter counts are pictures painted on hides or birch bark and carefully preserved. Other histories were woven into wampum belts while others were committed to memory. Oral histories, either incorporated within medicine texts or existing extraneous to them, relate a group's past and are manifested in works as disparate as the visionary Pima bird songs, the fragmented Cherokee *E Lo Hi*, **R Ꮐ.Ꮍ**, and the Iroquois Rite of Condolence. These tribal histories, which I loosely designate here as winter counts whether they are painted or oral, were called winter counts because it was primarily during the winter that historians had time to write. Hunting and food-procuring chores were diminished. Winter was quiet time, a good time to sit inside the home, recall the year's events, and record the most outstanding.

When his creation account was finished, the Principal Patriarch began his winter count, or notation of important events chronicled annually. The second and longest portion of the history is simply entitled *The 2. Booke.* Its 429 pages are not divided into chapters but into sections entitled "Anno" with the date. For example, the first division of the second part is entitled "The remainder of Anº: 1620." The succeeding section is designated "Anno. 1621," and so it continues through "Anno Dom: 1646." The final entries have no narrative at all, but are simply entered as "Anno. 1647. And Anno 1648." In his 2. Booke, *Of Plimoth Plantation's* form and content noticeably alter. Book 2 notes "only the heads of principall things, and passages as they fell in order of time, and may seeme to be profitable to know, or to make use of."

Bradford commences his winter count with a transcript of the Mayflower Compact and the notation that the company "mette and consulted of lawes & orders" for their civil and military well-being. Much of his subsequent commentary delineates the many ways in which these laws were amended and/or broken as it depicts a Colony often driven more by necessity than by law. Bradford thus sets into motion a theme that will reverberate through American letters—especially sermons—for the next four hundred years, and that is the theme of declension or a falling away from a theoretical ideal.

Of Plimoth Plantation's second portion details minutiae; its tone is seldom elevated, but sometimes exasperated, weary, bewildered, and annoyed. It is a multifaceted and complex text. Its fundamental tension extends from the exacting demands of the Almighty and the Principal Patriarchs to the pathetic responses of most fallible man. The history fully delineates where and how mistakes were made in maintaining a covenanted undertaking. *Of Plimoth Plantation* is not the celebratory account of the founding of a new nation, but is rather a confession, a lament, an exegesis of an effort gone wrong, and a validation of human effort. It is an attempt to preserve the good names and righteous intentions of the Colony's leaders and their actions lest history find fault. It is an expression of nobility of spirit and a leader's personal grief intensified by the wearing away of Plymouth's church. It is a step toward healing a wounded spirit.

On one hermeneutic level, the winter count is a cautionary tale told to prevent other communions from forsaking the old ways. *Of Plimoth Plantation* is the history of a group whose professed intention in coming to the New World is to consolidate their faith by making and keeping converts, maintaining their children in that faith, and propagating their beliefs. In short, their purpose is preserving their medicine. "Lastly, . . . a great hope & inward zeall they had of laying some good foundation, . . . for ye propagating & advancing ye gospell of ye kingdom of Christ in those remote parts of ye world; yea, though they should be but even as stepping-stones unto others for ye performing of so great a work."

Of Plimoth Plantation's characters, ranging from King James I to the murderer John Billington, are myriad. Its story lines are complicated. *Of Plimoth Plantation* reveals evil and validates goodness. It details the sodomy of Thomas Granger, the adulteries of John Lyford, and the suspected fornications of Visitor Fells. The history bewails the accounting incompetence of Josiah Winslow, cites instances of the duplicity of Massachusetts Bay, and reveals the land-grabbing machinations of the Archbishop of Canterbury. Although wrongdoers take up a significant portion of Bradford's text, the history does not fail to remember virtuous people who performed noble acts for the settlement. Bradford is especially thankful to William Brewster and Miles Standish, who nurse the sick and bury the dead during the first epidemic that strikes the Colony:

> [They] spared no pains, night nor day, but with abundance of toyle and hazard of their owne health, fetched them woode, made them fires, drest them meat, made their beads, washed their lothsome cloaths, cloathed & uncloathed them; in a word, did all ye homly & necessarie offices for them wch dainty & quesie stomacks cannot

endure to hear named; and all this willingly & cherfully, without any grudging in yᵉ least, shewing herein their true love unto their freinds & bretheren. (111)

Not only is the winter count concerned with Plymouth's ecclesiastical and political accomplishments and shortcomings, but it is a personal reflection as well. The Governor's deontological relation creates historical balance as it advances him toward humiliation, the final stage in Calvinist preparation for spiritual repair, salvation.[3]

> I have been happy, in my first times, to see, and with much comforte to injoye, the blessed fruits of this sweete communion, but it is now a parte of my *miserie* in old age, to find and feele yᵉ *decay* and wante therof (in a great measure), and with greefe and sorrow of hart to lamente & bewaile yᵉ same. And for others *warning* and *admonnition*, and my owne *humiliation*, doe I hear note yᵉ same. (42, emphasis mine)

For its author, the work engenders humiliation, Bradford's requisite for spiritual healing. Simultaneously, it offers its readers a paradigm for avoiding problems endemic to new settlements. *Of Plimoth Plantation* is a medicine text with a twofold purpose. It is designed to put both Bradford and Plymouth in harmony with humanity and the universe.

The history has social, political, theological, psychological, and curative properties. As a medicine text, it is the record of an experimental New World antidote for the Roman Catholic "vile ceremoneys" and the Anglican "unproffitable cannons & decrees, which have since been as snares to many poore & peaceable souls" in England. Rich in biblical allusions and weighted with commentary on moral rectitude, the history has spiritual, cultural, political, and didactic functions. It asserts Eternal Providence and points the way to a Christian center. By recalling the ancient good, invoking the covenant, restating the aspirations, reviewing the contracts, and detailing lapses in integrity, a formula is implied, if not actually given, for returning to center or original purpose. *Of Plimoth Plantation* is a new ceremony. It is *Covenantway*.

American Indian sacred texts, concerned with physiological and emotional disease, assert medicine and open an avenue for healing and psychological insight. Designed to effect balance and harmony by putting

together the right combination of powerful words and sacred stories, medicine texts integrate the patient with the land, the heavens, and the culture.
They put him into balance with the power of the universe and leave him
either healed or spiritually comforted. Manitonquat points out that the
universe is a web of creation. Everything is related. Illness, both personal
and societal and physical or mental, is caused by being out of rhythm with
the universe.[4]

In *Beautyway: A Navajo Ceremonial* (1957), the anthropologist Leland
Wyman offers additional insights into the teleology underlying Navajo ceremonials, and these observations apply to the traditional beliefs of many
other American Natives as well. Wyman's remarks are a starting place for
understanding the metaphysics of many American Native societies:

> Briefly, the universe, viewed as an orderly system of interrelated ele-
> ments, is an all-inclusive unity. Hence it contains both good and evil
> and is therefore both benevolent and dangerous. Many things in the
> universe are inherently dangerous: certain animals, lightning, winds,
> the ghosts of the dead, the Holy People themselves. Improper con-
> tact with them may cause disease. Moreover, evil, disease, or other
> disaster may result from disturbance of the normal order, i.e., the
> harmony or balance between elements in the universe. . . . Evil may
> be dispelled, dangerous elements may be brought under control by
> means of knowledge and applications of orderly procedures, that is,
> by ritual.[5]

This passage should not be taken to mean that by ritual an individual
is given power over the universe. Manitonquat explains that the power
one seeks in a ritual is not power or domination over something. To get
power over something is a "contradiction to itself, since everything is part
of the whole." Rituals enable individuals to tap into the imaginative, creative power within themselves to effect a cure. "The only true power is that
which functions . . . in harmony with . . . Creation."[6]

It seems that Bradford's two books, considered in conjunction with the
history of Bradford's original manuscript—its posthumous emendations,
its travels and travails, together with its physical form—have become
Bradford's own personal medicine bundle, a collection of carefully chosen
articles which can protect the owner and help him work his will. In Bradford's bundle are the creation account, which is a repository of holy power

words, and the winter count, which contextualizes the words and situates them in space and time. Medicine bundles are a kind of sacred text and must be kept intact.

On the flyleaves in the front of Bradford's manuscript are words written in the Governor's hand from a language that he considers holy, Hebrew. There are also scriptures inscribed in Hebrew, Hebrew word lists, and verb conjugations. On one of the flyleaves is a note written by the Governor's great-grandson certifying authorship, transmission, and ownership of the manuscript. Pasted inside the front cover are verses eulogizing the Principal Patriarch's widow, Alice Carpenter Southworth. These lines were probably written by her nephew Nathaniel Morton, who inserted them years after her death. Scribbled on the cover of the manuscript is the signature of Mercy Bradford, the Governor's daughter.[7] Bradford's own words then are prefaced by holy words, authenticating words, and words recognizing women who somehow metaphorically emanated from his body—his rib, his loins. The work is certifiably his, but it has been modified to meet the requirements of a medicine text.

The manuscript that Bradford produced is a masculine text. It records primarily the acts of men, not women. *Of Plimoth Plantation* rarely mentions females, so its female narrative is muted. Mrs. Carver, Mrs. Lyford, Fell's maidservant, Hobomok's wife, and an old Pequot woman represent most of the women mentioned. That a female counternarrative in the form of his daughter's mark and a poem delineating the personal history and character traits of his second wife were added to the text without the author's knowledge or intention indicates that *Of Plimoth Plantation* is a powerful work, a medicine text. It righted itself in terms of gender balance. To be a truly balanced medicine narrative, one that conforms to the requirements of the sacred oral tradition, the work must have both feminine and masculine components, because a text without gender balance has neither efficacy nor potency. It is quite interesting, too, that according to Willison there were ten women among the Saints who arrived on the *Mayflower*. They were Mary Allerton, Dorothy Bradford, Mary Brewster, Catherine Carver, Desire Minter, Anne Tilley, Elizabeth Tilley, Susanna White, Elizabeth Winslow, and one whose name Bradford could not remember. She is Leyden Citizen's wife.[8] These women are Plymouth's clan mothers. That Bradford's creation account has ten chapters, perhaps in honor of the Principal Matriarchs, is appropriate. Passaconaway knew what he was doing even if Bradford did not.

When he died, Bradford left his text to his eldest son, William, who passed the manuscript to his son, and so on. That progression is acceptable, though not optimal, because a medicine bundle must remain private. Through excess lending over the years, the manuscript was, in the way of medicine, lost to the family because it had not been properly handled. Eventually it was housed in the Old South Meeting House's library in Boston, and from there made its way back to its point of narrative origin, England, after having been stolen and carried across the Atlantic. By the time it arrived in London, Bradford's medicine bundle had escaped fire at Increase Mather's, had survived both the Second Puritan Conquest and the American Revolution, and had likely been sold on the streets of London, until, presumably, a browsing ecclesiastic bought it and relocated it.

In England, the bundle underwent a one-hundred-year Anglican captivity and, in the Bishop of London's library where it was lodged, it successfully resisted cataloging. After being discovered Providentially by American historians, it was not, however, released. Instead, the manuscript was subjected to a forty-year period of negotiations between the United States and Great Britain. These high-level exchanges included the refusal of a dispensation by the Archbishop of Canterbury and a Royal Snub by the Squaw Sachem Victoria. After wandering in a bureaucratic wilderness for the requisite forty years, the bundle transformed itself into a ship's log in 1897 and, in that form, returned to the United States where it materialized again into a history book. For years the bundle suffered glass imprisonment in the State House in Boston where it could be viewed by visitors, but now it lies in a climate-controlled vault in an "undisclosed place," for reasons of security, but presumably within the State House.[9]

Medicine bundles are personal objects that should never be tampered with by others. When death approaches, a medicine person either buries his bundle in a secret place or passes it to a specially chosen and deserving recipient. Because it is so powerful, a medicine bundle tends to have a life of its own. Bradford's certainly does.

Bradford's bundle has been treated irresponsibly since his death. It should never have been lent to anyone outside the family. Like the medicine bundles of many American Indians, it is currently warehoused in a museum-like environment, a highly inappropriate place. ☽ If repatriation to Bradford's heirs proves impossible, this bundle should be wrapped in deer skins of an animal not killed with metal weapons, covered with woven Wampanoag mats, and buried somewhere in the environs of Old

Plymouth. Since that relocation is not likely to occur, the document should certainly be stored with more respect and dignity than it now receives. The bundle should be given a ceremony and allowed to rest in a place less hostile to its owner. ٥ Not even the most careless Americanist would venture to say that Bradford would want his sacred belongings reposing in the territory of Massachusetts Bay.

Early American writers like Bradford did as Passaconaway directed even though they understood neither the request nor the task. Assisted by Tisquantum, Hobomok, the land, and American Indian medicine, Plymouth's governor contrived an Indianized text that records English and Algonquian history while simultaneously replicating American Indian poetics and narrative strategies. In so doing, Bradford created the first American literary work. Of all the extant early American narratives, *Of Plimoth Plantation* gives us the clearest and most complete example of the Indianization of American letters. Through the centuries, many writers have subconsciously continued this process and created the American canon, but only Bradford did it quite so fully. He is America's Venerable Bede and, like the Bede, he originated in Northumbria. *The Ecclesiastical History of the English People* (731 AD) reveals Britain primeval and lays the groundwork for subsequent British histories, while *Of Plimoth Plantation* sets forth North America primordial and permanently fixes American Indian literary conventions in American literature.

The Indianization of Bradford's history is especially evident on *Of Plimoth Plantation*'s final page of official narrative. There is no obvious culmination or closing statement. The writing simply stops. By not bringing his history to a formal conclusion, but by leaving it open for additional Annos, Bradford devises a deliberate flaw or opening in his text. In American Indian artistic theory, the constructed flaw in a work of art is a spirit line that allows the artist's creative mind to walk away from his work with his soul intact and unencumbered. In other words, the artist is not caught in his own creative web. The spirit line also leaves the work itself open to change.[10] Since works with spirit lines are not tightly bound either to their authors or to their own forms, they can transform. *Of Plimoth Plantation*, therefore, is not an artifact confined to periodicity, but is an animate word flow that can breathe life into other works. Bradford's history, like American Indian art, does not accept the idea of closure.

٥ The People of the Eastern Light have surely prevailed. They began the process of re-forming American colonials, and they carefully molded their chosen scribe. Even in death, Bradford followed Algonquian ritual practices. It was a day in planting season when he knew, with certainty, he would return to earth. The Pilgrim *pniese*, slowly and painfully, banked his fires. His life's work was finished. He had governed the Colony and set American literature on its course. Too weak to write, he dictated a nuncupative will, or, in American Indian terms, he sang his death song. Having disposed of his property, he entrusted his medicine bundle to his nephew, bade his family farewell, and joined the spirits.

9 May Anno Dom: 1657

Ɔ

CHEROKEE GLOSSARY
ᏣᏩᏯ ᎠᎣᎠᏣ

Cherokee exhibits many variants that are often regional.

Ꭰ ᏓᏓᏓᏓ. Ꮈ ᏬᏟᏖᏙᏖ,ᎾᎯᎢᏫ!: Ah ha ha hah ha. That's all folks!

Ꭰ Ꮷ: And

ᎠᎾᏝᏬᏨ: Brothers

ᎠᎲ: -s. Designates plurality

ᎠᎲᎡ Ꮃ ᏫᎫ ᏫᏯ: Troublemakers

ᎠᎲᏣ Ꮞ or ᎠᎲᎠᏣ Ꮞ: Mvskogee Creeks

ᎠᎲᏣᏝᏬᎥᏫᏯ: Medicine people

ᎠᎲᏣᏩᏯ: Cherokees

ᎠᎲᎦᎥᏫ: Real People; Cherokees

ᎠᎲᎦᎥᏫ ᎠᎣᎬᎡᏖ ᎠᏨᏫᏣ: People of the Eastern Light

ᎠᏝᏨᎲᏛ: It is beginning.

ᎠᏝᎦᎠᏣ ᎣᏃᏈᎬ ᏫᏯ: Adultery narrative

ᎠᏣᎮ: Water bug

ᎠᏣᏩᏣ ᎾᎲᏫᏣ: Edward Winslow

ᎠᏰᎮ: Center

ᎠᎦᏝᏓᎦᏫᎡ: Thunder

Ꭱ Ꮃ Ꭺ: : Down

Ꭱ Ꮳ.Ꮽ: Earth

Ꭱ Ꮏ Ꭲ: Animals, undomesticated

Ꮼ Ꮴ.ᎯᏣ.Ꮽ: Really

ᏬᎧᎾᏣ: Rattlesnake

ᏕᎵᏊᎩ: Seven
ᏕᎵᏊᎩ ᏂᏚᎣᏚᏞᏓᏥᏎᎬ: Seven generations
ᏕᏦᎮᏫᏣᏍᎠᎢ: He habitually tricks.
ᏕᏛᏪᎫᎵ: Up
ᏕᏌᎭ: : Land
ᏕᏙᏃ or ᏕᏙ: Why

ᏍᎦᎠᎧᎢ: Truth

Ꭴ: Function word indicating importance
ᎤᏁᎦ: Word
ᎤᏃᎮᏢᏍᎩ: Narrative, story

ᎠᏫᎧ or ᎠᏪᎾ: Raven
ᎠᏫᎵ: Book
ᎠᏫᎵᎧᎧ or ᎠᏫᎵᎧᏍᏣᏞᎧ: Literature

ᎬᎾ: Turkey
ᎬᏓ or ᎬᎵ: Raccoon

ᏂᎬᎢ: All over

ᏁᏫᎭ: Spirit people

ᏫᏍᎣᎦᎤᎾᏪ: Passaconaway
ᏫᏣ ᏪᏣ ᎧᎧᎢ: Betty Booth Donohue

ᏎᏪᎩᏍᏓ or ᏎᏪᏫᏍᏕ: Muskrat
ᏎᎷ: Selu, the Cherokee Corn Mother

Ꭷ Ꮅ: Buzzard
ᏟᎦᏂᏞ: Water beetle

ᏨᏕᏕᎦᎾ: Automobile
ᏨᎤᏫᎢᏍᏨ: Word list
ᏨᎤᏁᎬᎢ: East
ᏨᎠᏫᎵ: Books
ᏨᎵ ᏫᎾ: Skunk bear, wolverine

ᏗᏂᏓᏅᏫᏍᎩ: Medicine men (variant)
ᏗᏓᏅᏫᏍᎩ: Medicine man
ᏗᏓᎴᏂᏍᎬ ᎤᏂᏃᎮᎸ: The beginning they told.

ᏙᏯ: Beaver

ᏣᎳᎩ: Cherokee

ᏥᎪᏯ: Bug, variant for water beetle
ᏥᏌ ᎦᎶᏁᏛ: Jesus Christ
ᏥᏍᏚ: Rabbit
ᏥᏯ: Otter

ᏧᎦᎾᏮᎢ or **ᎤᎦᎾᏭ**: South
ᏧᎳ or **ᏧᏟ**: Fox
ᏧᎾᎵᎢ: Friends
ᏧᏴᏢᎢ or **ᎤᏴᏢ**: North

ᏩᏙ: Thank you
ᏩᏯᏑ: Coyote

ᏫᎵ ᏬᏗ ᏗᎦᏐᎧᏍᏗ: William Bradford

ᏭᎦᎵᎬᎢ: West

ᏴᏩᏁᎬ: American
ᏴᏫ: Human

NOTES

Author's Note

In addition to the sources cited below, the following interviews and readings inform this study: personal interview with Cherokee linguist Harry Oosahwee (September 9, 2010); telephone interview with Professor Gerald Prince (November 21, 1997); personal interview with Croslyn Smith (August 12, 1997); poetry reading by Joy Harjo, Rogers State University, Tulsa, Oklahoma (March 22, 1998).

Preface

1. Samuel Eliot Morison, ed., introduction to *Of Plymouth Plantation*, vii–xliii.

2. In this volume I use the term *literature* as an expedient to refer to American Indian literary compositions that were transmitted verbally since terms like *orality* and *orature* do little to illuminate the issue under discussion. For a brief summation of this problem see William Bright. I use the word *writer* to refer to a Native author whether his work was written or not primarily for the same reasons of expediency. Granted, most ancient Native works were not written, but that notation should not obscure the fact that creative compositions existed and traces of them remain.

3. See Bob Blaisdell, George W. Cronyn, A. Grove Day, Karen Kilcup, Brian Swann, and Jack and Anna Gritts Kilpatrick for examples of these genres.

4. See James Axtell, Francis Jennings, and Susan Faludi for detailed analyses of Indianization.

5. George Willison, *Saints and Strangers*, 185.

6. Fannie Hardy Eckstorm, *Old John Neptune*, 101.

7. Neal Salisbury, "Squanto," 230.

8. Jessie Little Doe, telephone interview with the author, March 10, 2009.

9. Russell Thornton, *American Indian Holocaust and Survival*, 36, and Henry F. Dobyns, "Estimating Aboriginal American Population," 415.

10. John Winthrop, "Reasons for the Plantation in New England."

11. Gerald Prince, *Narratology*, 164.

12. Paul Chaat Smith, "Terrible Nearness of Distant Places," 382–83.

13. Paul Chaat Smith, "Terrible Nearness of Distant Places," 392.

14. See Ron Carpenter, "Pitfalls of Tribal Specificity," 209–16.

15. "Returning the Gift" was the title of a Native writers' conference held in Norman, Oklahoma, in July 1992. The title evokes the pan-tribal tradition of reciprocal giving. Since this conference, the phrase "returning the gift" has become common parlance in Native literary writings and often denotes a writer's desire to acknowledge writers who paved the way for others' success.

16. Daniel Heath Justice, *Our Fire Survives the Storm*.

17. Richard West, "The National Museum of the American Indian: Reflections on a Journey," keynote address at Purdue University, West Lafayette, Indiana, April 3, 2008.

18. Randolph Jacob, personal interview with the author, October 12, 1997. See also Donohue.

19. James Axtell, *Beyond 1492*, 10.

20. Michael J. Colacurcio, lecture, University of California Los Angeles, February 17, 1993.

Prelude

1. T. J. Garrett and Michael Garrett, *Medicine of the Cherokee*, 137.

Chapter 1. Land and Medicine

1. American Indian literature has its own theory, which is well defined in the sacred chants of the oral tradition and explicated in this volume. As many current American Indian literary critics realize, imposing a European theory on Native literature is, for the most part, unremunerative.

2. An anonymous Wampanoag woman of the Gay Head Agency, in a telephone interview with the author on January 6, 1997, verified that Wampanoags use juniper and cedar interchangeably for rituals or purification rites.

3. Historians think this body was that of a sailor who either jumped ship or was shipwrecked. It appears that he married an Algonquian woman and was buried with their child. The two may have succumbed to the pestilence that devastated the area. It is unlikely that a sailor would have taken an infant on a sea voyage as some scholars have theorized. If both inhabitants of the grave were Europeans, however, then Algonquians went to great pains to bury strangers.

4. William Simmons, *Cautantowwit's House*, 60.

5. Simmons, *Cautantowwit's House*, 60.

6. Simmons, *Cautantowwit's House*, 60.

7. Simmons, *Cautantowwit's House*, 57.

8. See Evan T. Pritchard's *No Word for Time* as well as Susan Scarberry-Garcia's *Landmarks of Healing* for explanations of informing essences.

9. William Wood, *New Englands Prospect*, 100–101.

10. Manitonquat, *Return to Creation*, iv.

11. There is a discrepancy in dates given by Mourt and Bradford for the expedition. Mourt gives the date of the expedition to rescue John as June 11. Alexander Young, editor of *Chronicles of the Pilgrim Fathers*, believes Bradford is correct.

12. See James Axtell's "White Indians of Colonial America" in *The European and the Indian* for additional information on Indian captives.

13. For more on the relation of metaphor to reality and language see Terence Hawkes' *Metaphor*.

14. For a discussion of wampum as literature and guaranty see this volume's chapter 4.

Chapter 2. The Earth as Narrative Source

1. Susan Scarberry-Garcia, *Landmarks of Healing*, 9.

2. Milton A. Travers, *Wampanoag Indian Federation*, 1957 ed., 161.

3. Travers, *Last of the Great Wampanoag Indian Sachems*, 89.

4. Charles G. Leland, *Algonquin Legends of New England*, 62.

5. Evan T. Pritchard, *No Word for Time*, 131.

6. Russell M. Peters, *Clambake*, 38.

7. Croslyn Smith, Keeper of the Redbird Grounds, personal interview with the author, February 14, 1997.

8. Each American Indian tribe has its own directional color scheme.

9. Michael Running Wolf, telephone interview with the author, September 17, 1997.

10. Betty Jacob, telephone interview with the author, October 2, 1997.

11. James W. Mavor and Byron E. Dix, *Manitou: The Sacred Landscape of New England's Native Civilization*, 132.

12. Mavor and Dix, *Manitou*, 126.

13. Mavor and Dix, *Manitou*, 304.

14. Joseph Nicolar, *Life and Traditions of the Red Man*, 134–38.

15. Michael Running Wolf, telephone interview, September 17, 1997.

16. Laurie Weinstein-Farson, *The Wampanoag*, 27–31.

17. Kathleen Bragdon, *Native People of Southern New England, 1500–1650*, 108.

18. The individual ownership of land was a foreign concept to American Indians.

19. James Axtell, ed., *Indian Peoples of Eastern America*, 22.

20. Elisha Potter, "Early History of the Narragansett," 178.

21. Myra Jehlen, "Literature of Colonization," in *Cambridge History of American Literature*, v. 1, 99.

22. Joseph Epes Brown, "Becoming Part of It," 13.

23. Travers, *Last of the Great Wampanoag Indian Sachems*, 89.

24. Mavor and Dix, *Manitou*, 129–30.

25. John Winthrop, "Reasons for the Plantation in New England."

26. Richard Slotkin, *Regeneration Through Violence*, 223.

Chapter 3. The Ritual Meeting of Two Cultures

1. John Humins, "Squanto and Massasoit," 56.

2. The claim that Tisquantum was the last of the Patuxets is not altogether true. A few members of his village, including at least one of his relatives, escaped the plague. The few survivors went to live with other bands and were absorbed by them. Tisquantum may have been the last unabsorbed Patuxet.

3. William Simmons, *Cautantowwit's House*, 53–59.

4. Thomas Morton, *New English Canaan*, 19.

5. Kathleen Bragdon, *Native People of Southern New England, 1500–1650*, 229.

6. Alvin G. Weeks, *Massasoit of the Wampanoags*, 108.

7. *Records of the Colony of New Plymouth* (Shurtleff and Pulsifer, eds.) indicates that the land was a gift in return for protection, but in the Pilgrims' view they "paid" for the land with three knives, a copper chain with a "jewel" in it, an earring, a pot of strong water, biscuits, and butter. Since many American Indians are lactose intolerant, the butter was somewhat problematic.

8. The number seven is considered a sacred number by many American Indian tribes because it represents the cardinal directions: north, south, east, west, up, down, and center. Seven has numerous other symbolic functions that vary tribally as well.

9. Evan T. Pritchard, *No Word for Time*, 137–38.

10. George Willison, *Saints and Strangers*, 182.

11. Bragdon, *Native People*, 140

12. Paula Gunn Allen, *Grandmothers of the Light*, xiv.

13. Benjamin Thatcher, *Indian Biography*, 140. Bragdon, along with other major historians, also agrees with Thatcher on this issue.

14. Willison, *Saints and Strangers*, 181–82.

15. For a discussion of similarities between Puritans and Indians, see Charles M. Segal and David C. Stineback, *Puritans, Indians, and Manifest Destiny*, and Ann Kibbey, *Interpretation of Material Shapes in Puritanism*.

16. Bragdon, *Native People*, 141–42.

17. For more information on Europeans who went Native see James Axtell, *European and the Indian*, 168–206.

18. In the inevitable course of things, many American Indians did become, and remain, thoroughly Europeanized and Christianized. Much tribal knowledge and many Native languages have been lost, but a remarkable amount remains. A significant number of American Indians still practice traditional lifestyles in a limited way and many Native languages are still spoken and are being taught and preserved. Indians change with the times, but they do not vanish.

19. Joseph Epes Brown, "Becoming Part of It," 11.

20. James W. Mavor and Byron E. Dix, *Manitou: The Sacred Landscape of New England's Native Civilization*, 60–62. Pritchard, in *No Word for Time* (65–105), further substantiates the claim that seventeenth-century Algonquians participated in vision quests.

21. Walter Ong, *Presence of the Word*, 12.

22. Michael Runyan, ed., *William Bradford*, 76.

23. Ong, *Presence of the Word*, 12–13.

24. N. Scott Momaday, "Native Voice," 7.

25. Margot Astrov, ed., *Winged Serpent*, 19–20.

26. Joseph Epes Brown, "Becoming Part of It," 13.

27. For more information on Bradford see Perry Westbrook's *William Bradford*.

28. Elaine Jahner, "Spiritual Landscape," 201.

29. Nicholas Black Elk, *Black Elk Speaks*, 16–36. There has been a long-standing debate concerning the authenticity of Black Elk's words and the reliability of Neihardt as recorder. Having collated *Black Elk Speaks* with *The Sixth Grandfather* by Raymond DeMallie, who edited the transcripts of Neihardt's notes, I have no reason to doubt Neihardt to any appreciable degree.

30. Black Elk, *Black Elk Speaks*, 210.

31. In "Beginning Cherokee," a lecture given at Northeastern State University, Tahlequah, Oklahoma, in October 1986, Martin Cochran, Cherokee linguist and scholar, reported that in the sacred stomp dance rituals of the Cherokees, the names of Abraham, Isaac, and Moses are used as they have been for centuries, even before Contact.

Chapter 4. Corn and Wampum

1. Joseph Nicolar, *Life and Traditions of the Red Man*, 134–38.

2. Grady N. Lowrey, *Journey to Sunrise*, 17–28.

3. Frank Waters, *Book of the Hopi*, xxi.

4. Forrest Carter is a highly controversial figure in American Indian literature. His work has been called into question by critics like Geary Hobson and it has

been more positively re-evaluated by David Treuer. My reason for citing *The Education of Little Tree* is that it contains the most pronounced corn narrative in any American work that my research has to date uncovered. For more on this debate see Geary Hobson's letter in the spring 1995 volume of *Wicazo Sa Review*, and David Treuer's *Native American Fiction*, 159–93.

5. Trudy Griffin-Pierce, *Earth Is My Mother, Sky Is My Father*, 190.

6. Griffin-Pierce, *Earth Is My Mother, Sky Is My Father*, 191.

7. E-mail message from Hanay Geiogamah, subject line: Paula Gunn Allen, from the American Indian Studies List Serve at University of California Los Angeles, May 30, 2008.

8. Nicolar, *Life and Traditions of the Red Man*, 134–38.

9. Jerry Martien, *Shell Game*, 22.

10. Frank Speck, *Functions of Wampum*, 22–32.

11. Speck, *Functions of Wampum*, 71.

12. Richard Slotkin, *Regeneration Through Violence*, 43.

13. Speck, *Functions of Wampum*, 8.

14. Speck, *Functions of Wampum*, 9.

15. Speck, "Eastern Algonkian Wabanaki Confederacy," 501, and *Functions of Wampum*, 6–7.

16. Martien, *Shell Game*, 10.

17. William Weeden, *Indian Money as a Factor*, 14.

18. Early European American documents note that several headmen wore large necklaces of wampum on regular occasions, but whether the wearing was for ornamentation, status designation, or for storage purposes is not clear. Various Massasoits, such as Metacomet, wore impressive amounts of wampum, and I believe that the large amount of wampum worn by Metacomet signified his office of wampum keeper, not his chief status. Tribal chiefs were literary men as well as leaders. Metacomet, besides being a leader, was also a Wampanoag historian.

19. For detailed accounts of this war, see Francis Jennings, *Invasion of America*, and Eric B. Schultz and Michael J. Tougias, *King Philip's War*.

20. Herbert H. Rowen, ed., *Low Countries*, 70–74. An examination of the Articles of Utrecht 1579 indicates that there are significant differences between the Utrecht Articles and the Articles of the United Colonies. In the Utrecht document, meeting times and places are not spelled out, a uniform system of taxation to pay for common defense is established, potential enemies are not named, the number of commissioners is not established, and a third party for deciding disagreements is chosen. The Articles of the United Colonies admits that the alliance is established to combat American Natives, provides for a sliding scale of taxation, establishes a fixed number of commissioners, and determines that a majority vote will decide differences. The Colonial Articles also sets up meeting times and places, which the Utrecht document does not.

21. Since wampum is a written confirmation of an exchange, it is probable that the wampum was not "paid" because Miantonimo had not been released. Again, from an Algonquian point of view there had been nothing to confirm.

22. See Jennings, *Invasion*, Martien, *Shell Game*, and Weeden, *Indian Money*, for approximations of the monetary worth of the wampum tributes.

23. Schultz and Tougias, *King Philip's War*, 139–41.

Chapter 5. Animals and Tricksters

1. Charles G. Leland, *Algonquin Legends of New England*, 31.

2. Manitonquat, *Children of the Morning Light*, 20.

3. Leland, *Algonquin Legends*, 79.

4. Leland, *Algonquin Legends*, 32–36.

5. Leland, *Algonquin Legends*, 186–88.

6. Vernida Casuse (Navajo), personal interview with the author, October 16, 2007. Despite the many literary dimensions ascribed to them by critics like Gerald Vizenor (Chippewa), trickster tales are primarily children's stories even though, like Aesop's Fables or Grimm's Fairy Tales, they evidence adult appeal.

7. Alan R. Velie, ed. *American Indian Literature*, 55.

8. "Gluskabi/Gluskap Stories and Other Wabanaki Legends," http:/www.native-languages.org/Wabanaki-legends.htm.

9. The Joel Chandler Harris Uncle Remus stories bear a striking resemblance to Cherokee trickster tales featuring Rabbit. Some scholars believe African Americans heard the Cherokee stories and blended them with African folktales and Uncle Remus resulted. The important thing here is that Rabbit is a trickster for many Eastern tribes.

10. "Merchant Adventurers," http://www.mayflowerhistory.com/Genealogy/merchantadventurers.php.

11. George Willison, *Saints and Strangers*, 236.

12. "U.S. Presidents with *Mayflower* Lineages," http://reocities.com/hawaii1620/prez.html.

Chapter 6. The Native Hagiography

1. Many Americans have heard "Indian stories" or frontier-day tales that have been passed from generation to generation within families. These stories support the theory that a European oral tradition concerning American Indians in early America did come about.

2. That most of the American Indians represented in European American fiction are in some way or other stereotypical is a problem that many present-day Native people deplore. My aim in this book, however, is simply to call attention to

the types, not to critique them. It is with their presence, not their various ramifications, that this work is concerned.

3. Joseph Epes Brown, "Becoming Part of It," 11.

4. Joseph Epes Brown, "Becoming Part of It," 11.

5. Valarie Livingston (Navajo), personal interview with the author, January 3, 2006.

6. Margot Astrov, ed. *Winged Serpent*, 19.

7. Randolph Jacob, untitled sermon delivered at the Coal Creek Cumberland Presbyterian Church in Atoka, Oklahoma, February 23, 1991.

8. See Francis Jennings, *Invasion of America*, Howard S. Russell, *Indian New England before the Mayflower*, and Robert M. Utley and Wilcomb E. Washburn, *Indian Wars*, for additional information on Native warfare.

9. Samuel Eliot Morison, ed., introduction to *Of Plymouth Plantation*, xxvii–xxx.

10. *Mourt's Relation*, 73.

11. I am indebted to Ramona Peters (Wampanoag) for this observation. Peters, a present-day Wampanoag tribal leader, is the daughter of a medicine man.

12. Some present-day historians discount the Weymouth account assuming that the source of this information, Ferdinando Gorges, was mistaken. Other historians, such as Alexander Young, accept Gorges' relation.

13. Kathleen Bragdon, *Native People of Southern New England, 1500–1650*, 23.

14. William Simmons, *Cautantowwit's House*, 51.

15. Bragdon, *Native People*, 189–90.

16. Sydney V. James, ed. *Three Visitors to Early Plymouth*, 29.

17. James, ed. *Three Visitors*, 29.

18. Ramona Peters, telephone interview with the author, November 19, 1997. Peters reports that the Wampanoags are matrilineal, were matrilineal at Contact, and have always been involved in tribal government. Such information refutes earlier scholarship that either denies Algonquian feminine power, marginalizes it, or problematizes it. Peters' information is bolstered by the feminine authority illustrated in Hobomok's wife's narrative.

19. See Berard Haile, *Women Versus Men*.

20. To infer from this statement that metaphysical and actual Native life was/is clear-cut in terms of gender balance would be erroneous. Not all Native spirits or humans are definitively male or female. There are Native hermaphroditic spirits and Native homosexual persons, and it is probably safe to conclude that these types are considered to be anomalies. As a general rule, anomalies in Native life hold a special, respected status that is positioned outside the bifurcated complements. Anomalies are the exclamation points on the page. Because anomalies are valued in Native life, it is not unusual to find that they inspire many American

Indian names, such as Dreadfulwater, Sitting Bull, Black Elk, or Drywater. Usually water tastes good, not dreadful. Rarely do bulls sit, elk are brown, and water is wet.

Chapter 7. Tisquantum

1. In *Good Newes from New England*, Winslow writes a passage almost identical to Bradford's. For a recent interpretation of this passage see Cristobal Silva, *Miraculous Plagues*.

2. Neal Salisbury, "Squanto," 243.

3. James Phinney Baxter, *Sir Ferdinado Gorges and His Province of Main*, 105.

4. Although modern historians occasionally ascribe attributes of ventriloquism to many remarks made by American Natives and recorded by non-Indians, this one should be taken at face value. It is doubtful that Bradford would prevaricate. Bradford displays personal integrity, and his history's stated goal is to "manifest . . . yᵉ simple trueth in all things."

5. I am indebted to Paula Gunn Allen for this observation.

6. Several historians, including Francis Jennings, believe that "kingship" among the Algonquians was hereditary. If there was not a direct line of descent from father to son, then members of the same family ruled. In that case, Tisquantum could not have been brokering power, since he apparently did not descend from a ruling dynasty.

7. Frank Shuffelton, "Indian Devils and Pilgrim Fathers," 114–15.

8. Some recent historians now believe that the bundle of arrows wrapped in a rattlesnake skin was an invitation to trade or to establish a formal friendship. See Karen Ordahl Kupperman, *Indians and English*, and Paul Robinson, "Lost Opportunities," for additional insights.

9. Charles G. Leland, *Algonquin Legends of New England*, 261.

10. Leland, *Algonquin Legends of New England*, 111.

11. James W. Mavor and Byron E. Dix, *Manitou*, 149–50.

12. Many American Indian tribal names translate
"real people." For instance, the Cherokees' name for themselves is Aniyvwiya, which means the real people. The Navajos are Dine, the people.

13. Mavor and Dix, *Manitou: The Sacred Landscape of New England's Native Civilization*, 322. Also, William Hubbard in *A Narrative of the Indian Wars of New England* (1815) relates that the Algonquians held a "great dance (which solemnities are the times they make use of to tell their stories, and convey the knowledge of some past and most memorable things to posterity)" and that invitations to this feast are issued by sagamores or sachems (58).

14. Sydney V. James, ed., *Three Visitors to Early Plymouth*, 12.

15. Milton A. Travers, *Wampanoag Indian Federation*, rev. ed., 40.

16. Travers, *Wampanoag Indian Federation*, rev. ed., 40–45.

17. Mavor and Dix, *Manitou*, 322–23.

18. Travers, *Wampanoag Indian Federation*, rev. ed., 45–46.

19. Daniel K. Richter, *Ordeal of the Longhouse*, 32–33.

20. John Humins, "Squanto and Massasoit," 67.

21. Jennings, *Invasion of America*, 147–48.

22. Nathaniel Morton, *New-Englands Memoriall*, 86.

Chapter 8. The Indeans

1. William Simmons, *Cautantowwit's House*, 61–62.

2. Teasing and joking are essential elements of Native life. American Indians often use teasing to teach their children to sharpen their wits, to mature, and to analyze other speakers' motivations. Teasing helps a child become adept at using and detecting metaphors. Teasing is also a psychological tool for determining another's character. How much can a person take? Is the person short-fused? Is the person intelligent enough to determine one's real intentions? Basically, teaching a child to tease and to understand teasing is to give him societal skills. Not only is joking instructive, but it also relieves boredom in the primordial time before bingo halls and casinos.

3. When American parachute jumpers leap from planes, why do they shout "Geronimo," not a European American military giant's name? Why not Washington, Lee, Grant, Sherman, Patton, MacArthur, Eisenhower, Doolittle, or the like? I contend that they shout "Geronimo" because they instinctively realize that the Apache nomen is a power word that potentially can help them. They know this without being told. They can sense the potency because the word *is* powerful, just like Geronimo himself.

4. The diegetic text reveals that Bradford did not assist the Bay in the Pequot massacre because he was angry with Winthrop for not siding with Plymouth in an altercation between Plymouth and de Aulnay at Penobscot Trading Post. Following the Girling affair, the Bay actually assisted the French in trying to ruin Plymouth's venture. Without doubt this incident and the attendant insults were paramount in Bradford's decision not to take part in the attack; however, human beings are complex and their actions are often influenced by more than one consideration. That Bradford despised Winthrop is the primary reason he stayed home, but I really feel that another factor also important in his decision is that he did not approve of unprovoked killing and would not disappoint Robinson again.

5. The word *meate* Bradford read in Leviticus 2:1–2 is translated from the rather nonspecific Hebrew *mazown*, meaning food, meat, or victual. Like the Geneva

Bible, the King James Version also translates the word *meat*. More modern translations, however, write *grain* or *cereal* for *mazown*, and that rendering makes much more sense given the context. Whatever the translation variances may be, however, Bradford would have read *meate*, but the footnotes in the Geneva spell out the fact that *meate* means grain and the gist of the argument holds. Sacrifices must be properly done, and in this case would have involved flour, incense, and a priest.

6. John Underhill, *Newes from America*, 42–43.

7. Bradford writes that three or four Dutchmen spent the winter with this stricken group and it is probable they exposed the Indians to the disease. The same Dutch made their way to Windsor, and Bradford goes on to say that the Indians near Windsor came down with smallpox soon after, so it is likely that it was smallpox contracted from the Dutch that killed the nine hundred. Only one hundred of this group lived.

8. Bradford's recollection here is eerily duplicated word for word in the script played out in the Cherokee Nation by the Ridge and Ross factions years later—whether to sign the 1835 Treaty of New Echota and move to Oklahoma Territory or to remain in Georgia, Tennessee, and North Carolina and suffer indeterminate losses. Ridge advocated leaving while there was something to save, and he did, but Ross was of another mind. He stayed and waged a court battle, but was ultimately forced to walk to Oklahoma on The-Trail-Where-They-Cried.

9. The Five Tribes from the southeastern part of the United States were forcibly and illegally removed to Oklahoma by Andrew Jackson in defiance of the Supreme Court's decision to the contrary. Called the Trail of Tears, this forced removal claimed the lives of more than twenty-five thousand Choctaws, Chickasaws, Creeks, Cherokees, and Seminoles. The effects of it are still felt.

10. Removal affected nearly all tribes. The splintering and scattering of Natives is astounding. There are now Paiutes in hiding on the Navajo reservation midway up Navajo Mountain. They pass for Navajos, but speak both their own language and Navajo. Many tribes were moved into Oklahoma. The Yuchis (Euchees) are living with the Creeks in northeastern Oklahoma, but they do not like to be considered Creeks. They are working toward government recognition. The same can be said for many tribes. There are presently thirty-eight recognized tribes living in Oklahoma and twenty-seven unrecognized.

11. Blood quantum is usually designated on a white card issued by the Bureau of Indian Affairs while tribal affiliation is designated on a card of another color. Recognized Indians carry both. I suppose only the American Kennel Club engages in more meticulous record keeping.

12. Constance Rourke, *Roots of American Culture*, 61–62.

13. Lisa Brooks, *Common Pot*, 229.

Chapter 9. *Of Plimoth Plantation* as Medicine Text

1. Samuel Eliot Morison, ed., introduction to *Of Plymouth Plantation*, xxxviii.

2. Earthdivers is a term used descriptively by Andrew Wiget, "Oral Literature of the Southwest," and metaphorically by Gerald Vizenor, *Earthdivers*.

3. John Calvin, *Institutes of the Christian Religion*, i, 232.

4. Manitonquat, *Return to Creation*, 16.

5. Leland Wyman, ed. *Beautyway*, 6.

6. Manitonquat, *Return to Creation*, 80–81.

7. For the description of the manuscript I am indebted to Morison's edition of *Of Plymouth Plantation* (1952) and to Charles Deane's introduction to the 1856 edition.

8. George Willison, *Saints and Strangers*, 437–40.

9. Lacy Crews-Stoneburner (preservation librarian, State Library of Massachusetts), telephone interview with the author, March 18, 2010.

10. For more information on spirit lines see Noel Bennett, *The Weaver's Pathway*.

BIBLIOGRAPHY

Adams, Charles Francis. *Three Episodes of Massachusetts History.* 2 vols. Boston: Houghton Mifflin, 1892.

Adams, James Truslow. *The Founding of New England.* Boston: Little, Brown, 1921.

Addison, Albert Christopher. *The Romantic Story of the Mayflower Pilgrims and Its Place in the life of To-day.* Boston: L. C. Page, 1911.

Adolf, Leonard A. "Squanto's Role in Pilgrim Diplomacy." *Ethnohistory* 11 (1964): 247-61.

Alexie, Sherman. *The Toughest Indian in the World.* New York: Grove Press, 2000.

Allen, Paula Gunn. *Grandmothers of the Light: A Medicine Woman's Sourcebook.* Boston: Beacon, 1991.

———. *The Sacred Hoop: Recovering the Feminine in American Indian Traditions.* Boston: Beacon, 1986.

———. *The Woman Who Owned the Shadows.* San Francisco: Spinsters/Aunt Lute, 1983.

———, ed. *Studies in American Indian Literature: Critical Essays and Course Designs.* New York: Modern Language Association of America, 1983.

Andrews, Charles M., ed. *Narratives of the Insurrections, 1675-1690.* New York: Barnes and Noble, 1943.

Angoff, Charles. *A Literary History of the American People.* 2 vols. New York: Alfred Knopf, 1931.

Astrov, Margot, ed. *The Winged Serpent: American Indian Prose and Poetry.* Boston: Beacon, 1946.

Austen, Jane. *Pride and Prejudice.* London: T. Egerton, 1813.

Austin, Mary. *The American Rhythm: Studies and Reexpressions of Amerindian Songs.* New York: Harcourt, 1923. New York: Cooper Square, 1970.

———. *Earth Horizon: Autobiography.* New York: Literary Guild, 1932.

Axelrod, Alan. *Chronicle of the Indian Wars: From Colonial Times to Wounded Knee.* New York: Prentice Hall, 1993.

Axtell, James. *After Columbus: Essays in the Ethnohistory of Colonial North America.* New York: Oxford University Press, 1988.

———. *Beyond 1492: Encounters in Colonial North America.* New York: Oxford University Press, 1992.

———. *The European and the Indian: Essays in the Ethnohistory of Colonial North America.* New York: Oxford University Press, 1981.

———, ed. *The Indian Peoples of Eastern America: A Documentary History of the Sexes.* New York: Oxford University Press, 1981.

Bahr, Donald, Lloyd Paul, and Vincent Joseph. *Ants and Orioles: Showing the Art of Pima Poetry.* Salt Lake City: University of Utah Press, 1997.

Bailey, Alfred G. *The Conflict of European and Eastern Algonkian Cultures, 1504-1700: A Study in Canadian Civilization.* Toronto: University of Toronto Press, 1969.

Baker, Virginia. "Glimpses of Ancient Sowams." *Rhode Island Historical Society.* Vol. 2. Providence: Standard Printing, 1894.

Banks, Charles E. "Thomas Morton of Merrymount." *Proceedings of the Massachusetts Historical Society* 58 (December 1924): 157-93.

Barlow, Joel. *The Columbiad: A Poem.* 2 vols. Philadelphia: C. and A. Conrad, 1809.

Barsh, Russell Lawrence, and James Youngblood Henderson. *The Road: Indian Tribes and Political Liberty.* Berkeley: University of California Press, 1980.

Barthes, Roland. *S/Z.* Translated by Richard Miller. Paris: Editions du Seuil, 1970. New York: Hill and Wang, 1974.

Barton, Thomas. *Unanimity and Public Spirit: A Sermon Preached . . . soon after General Braddock's Defeat.* Philadelphia: B. Franklin and D. Hall, 1755.

Basso, Keith H. *Portraits of the "The Whiteman": Linguistic Play and Cultural Symbols among the Western Apache.* New York: Cambridge University Press, 1979.

Baxter, James Phinney, A.M. *Sir Ferdinando Gorges and His Province of Maine: Including The Brief Relation, the Brief Narration, His Defence, The Charter Granted to Him, His Will, and His Letters.* 3 vols. Boston: Prince Society, 1890.

Beck, Peggy, Anna Lee Walters, and Nia Francisco. *The Sacred: Ways of Knowledge, Sources of Life.* Tsaile, Arizona: Navajo Community College, 1992.

Bede, Saint (the Venerable Bede). *The Ecclesiastical History of the English People.* Translated and edited by A. M. Sellar. Mineola, New York: Dover, 2011.

Bennett, Noel. *The Weaver's Pathway: A Clarification of the "Spirit Trail" in Navajo Weaving.* Flagstaff, Arizona: Northland Press, 1974.

Bercovitch, Sacvan. *The Puritan Origins of the American Self.* New Haven: Yale University Press, 1975.

Bercovitch, Sacvan, and Cyrus R. K. Patell, eds. *The Cambridge History of American Literature.* Vol. 1, *1590-1820.* New York: Cambridge University Press, 1994.

Berkhoffer, Robert F., Jr. *The White Man's Indian: Images of the American Indian from Columbus to the Present.* New York: Vintage, 1978.

Beverley, Robert. *The History and Present State of Virginia in Four Parts.* London: Parker, 1705. Chapel Hill: University of North Carolina Press, 1947.

Black Elk, Nicholas. *Black Elk Speaks: Being the life Story of a Holy Man of the Oglala Sioux as Told Through John G. Neihardt.* New York: W. Morrow, 1932.

Blaisdell, Bob, ed. *Great Speeches by Native Americans.* Mineola, New York: Dover, 2000.

Boas, Franz. *Race, Language, and Culture.* New York: Macmillan, 1940.

Bohannan, Paul, and Fred Plog, eds. *Beyond the Frontier: Social Process and Cultural Change.* New York: Natural History Press, 1967.

Boorstin, Daniel. *The Americans: The Colonial Experience.* New York: Vintage Books, 1958.

———. *The Americans: The National Experience.* New York: Random House, 1965.

Bowden, Henry W., and James P. Ronda, eds. *John Eliot's Indian Dialogues: A Study in Cultural Interaction.* Westport, Connecticut: Greenwood Press, 1980.

Bradford, William. *Bradford's History "Of Plimoth Plantation" from the Original Manuscript.* Boston: Wright and Potter, 1901.

———. *History of Plymouth Plantation.* Boston: Little, Brown, 1856.

———. *Of Plymouth Plantation, 1620-1647.* New York: Modern Library, 1981.

———. *Of Plymouth Plantation 1620-1647.* Edited by Samuel Eliot Morison. New York: Knopf, 1952. New York: Knopf, 1994.

———. *William Bradford: The Collected Verse.* Edited by Michael G. Runyan. St. Paul, Minnesota: John Colet Press, 1974.

Bragdon, Kathleen J. *Native People of Southern New England, 1500-1650.* Norman: University of Oklahoma Press, 1996.

Brant, Beth, ed. *A Gathering of Spirit: A Collection by North American Indian Women.* Ithaca, New York: Firebrand, 1984.

Bright, William. *American Indian Linguistics and Literature.* New York: Mouton, 1984.

Brill de Ramirez, Susan Berry. *Contemporary American Indian Literature and the Oral Tradition.* Tucson: University of Arizona Press, 1999.

Brooks, Lisa. *The Common Pot: The Recovery of Native Space in the Northeast.* Minneapolis: University of Minnesota Press, 2008.

Brooks, Van Wyck. *America's Coming-of-Age.* New York: Octagon, 1975.

Brotherston, Gordon. *Image of the New World: The American Continent Portrayed in Native Texts.* London: Thames and Hudson, 1979.

Brown, Charles Brockden. *Edgar Huntly: or Memoirs of a Sleep Walker.* Port Washington, New York: Kennikat Press, 1799.

Brown, Joseph Epes. "Becoming Part of It." In *I Become Part of It: Sacred Dimensions in Native American Life,* edited by D. M. Dooling and Paul Jordan-Smith, 9-20. San Francisco: HarperSanFrancisco, 1989.

————. *The Spiritual Legacy of the American Indian*. New York: Crossroad, 1982.

Bruchac, Joseph, ed. *Returning the Gift: Poetry and Prose from the First North American Native Writers' Festival*. Tucson: University of Arizona Press, 1994.

Butterworth, Hezekiah. *The Wampum Belt or "The Fairest Page of History": A Tale of William Penn's Treaty with the Indians*. New York: Appleton: 1897.

Cadena, Marisol de la, and Orin Starn, eds. *Indigenous Experience Today*. New York: Berg, 2007.

Calef, Robert. *More Wonders of the Invisible World*. London: Hillar and Collyer, 1700.

Calloway, Colin G., ed. *Dawnland Encounters: Indians and Europeans in Northern New England*. Hanover, New Hampshire: University Press of New England, 1991.

————. *The Western Abenakis of Vermont, 1600-1800*. Norman: University of Oklahoma Press, 1990.

Calvin, John. *Institutes of the Christian Religion*. Geneva: Robert Estienne, 1559. Grand Rapids, Michigan: Eerdman's Publishing, 1983.

Carpenter, Ron. "Pitfalls of Tribal Specificity." *Studies in American Indian Literatures* 19.4 (2007): 209-16.

Carroll, Peter N. *Puritanism and the Wilderness: The Intellectual Significance of the New England Frontier, 1692-1700*. New York: Columbia University Press, 1969.

Carter, Forrest. *The Education of Little Tree*. Albuquerque: University of New Mexico Press, 1976.

Castro, Michael. *Interpreting the Indian: Twentieth-Century Poets and the Native American*. Norman: University of Oklahoma Press, 1991.

Catlin, George. *Letters and Notes on the Manners, Customs, and Conditions of the North American Indians*. 2 vols. New York: Dover, 1973.

Champagne, Duane, ed. *The Native North American Almanac: A Reference Work on Native North Americans in the United States and Canada*. Detroit: Gale Research, 1994.

Chapin, Howard M. *Sachems of the Narragansetts*. Providence: Rhode Island Historical Society, 1931.

Chase, Henry E. "Notes on the Wampanoag Indians." *38th Annual Report of the Board of Regents of the Smithsonian Institution Showing the Operations, Expenditures, and Condition of the Institution for the Year 1883*. Washington, D.C.: Government Printing Office, 1885.

Child, Lydia Maria. *Hobomok and Other Writing on Indians*. Edited by Carolyn Karcher. New Brunswick, New Jersey: Rutgers University Press, 1986.

Christie, Agatha. *And Then There Were None*. New York: Dodd, Mead, 1940.

————. *The Secret of Chimneys*. New York: Dodd, Mead, 1925.

Clifton, James A., ed. *The Invented Indian: Cultural Fictions and Government Policies*. New Brunswick, New Jersey: Transaction, 1990.

Cohen, Felix S. "Americanizing the White Man." *American Scholar* 21 (Spring 1952): 171-93.

Cohen, Hennig, ed. *The American Experience: Approaches to the Study of the United States*. Boston: Houghton Mifflin, 1868.

Colden, Cadwaller. *History of the Five Nations Depending on the Province of New-York in America*. Ithaca, New York: Cornell University Press, 1958.

Coleman, Emma, ed. *New England Captives Carried to Canada between 1677-1760 during the French and Indian Wars*. 2 vols. Portland, Maine: Southworth Press, 1925.

Cooper, James Fenimore. *The Last of the Mohicans: A Narrative of 1757*. Philadelphia: H. C. Cary and I. Lea-Chestnut-Street, 1826.

Cooper, John M. "Land Tenure among the Indians of Eastern and Northern North America." *Pennsylvania Archaeologist* 8 (1938): 55-59.

Cox, James. H. *Muting White Noise: Native American and European Novel Traditions*. Norman: University of Oklahoma Press, 2006.

Crevecoeur, Michael Guillaume St. Jean de. *Letters from an American Farmer*. Edited by Warren Barton Blake. New York: Dutton, 1957.

Cronyn, George W. *American Indian Poetry: An Anthology of Songs and Chants*. New York: Fawcett Columbine, 1991.

Culler, Jonathan. *Structuralist Poetics: Structuralism, Linguistics and the Study of Literature*. Ithaca, New York: Cornell University Press, 1975.

Cutler, Charles L. *O Brave New Words!: Native American Words in Current English*. Norman: University of Oklahoma, 1944.

Day, A. Grove. *The Sky Clears: Poetry of the American Indians*. Lincoln: University of Nebraska Press, 1951.

Deloria, Vine, Jr. *Custer Died for Your Sins: An Indian Manifesto*. New York: Macmillan, 1969. Norman: University of Oklahoma Press, 1988.

———. *The World We Used to Live In: Remembering the Powers Of the Medicine Men*. Golden, Colorado: Fulcrum, 2006.

Demos, John. *The Unredeemed Captive: A Family Story from Early America*. New York: Alfred Knopf, 1944.

Dobyns, Henry F. "Estimating Aboriginal American Population: An Appraisal of Techniques with a New Hemisphere Estimate." *Current Anthropology* 7 (1966): 395-416.

Donohue, Betty Booth. "Observations of Another Trotline Runner: A Critical Discussion of D. L. Birchfield's *Oklahoma Basic Intelligence Test*." *Studies in American Indian Literature* 11 (Fall 1999): 66-78.

Dooling, D. M., and Paul Jordan-Smith, eds. *I Become Part of It: Sacred Dimensions in Native American Life*. San Francisco: HarperSanFrancisco, 1989.

Drake, Samuel. *The Book of the Indians; or, Biography and History of the Indians of North America*. 8th ed. New York: AMS Press, 1976.

Drimmer, Frederick, ed. *Captured by the Indians: 15 Firsthand Accounts, 1750-1870.* New York: Dover, 1986.

Drinnon, Richard. *Facing West: The Metaphysics of Indian-Hating and Empire-Building.* Norman: University of Oklahoma Press, 1980.

Dundes, Alan, ed. *Sacred Narrative: Readings in the Theory of Myth.* Berkeley: University of California Press, 1984.

Eames, Wilberforce, ed. *John Eliot and the Indians, 1652-1657: Being Letters Addressed to Rev. Jonathan Hanner of Barnstaple, England.* New York: Adams and Grace Press, 1915.

Eastman, Charles A. *The Soul of the Indian: An Interpretation.* Boston: Houghton Mifflin, 1911. Lincoln: University of Nebraska Press, 1980.

Ebersole, Gary. *Captured by Texts: Puritan to Postmodern Images of Indian Captivity.* Charlottesville: University Press of Virginia, 1995.

Eckstorm, Fannie Hardy. *Old John Neptune and Other Maine Indian Shamans.* Portland, Maine: Southworth-Anthoensen Press, 1945.

Eidson, Tom. *The Last Ride.* New York: Putnam's, 1995.

Eliot, John. "A Late and Further Manifestation of the Progress of the Gospel amongst the Indians in New England. Declaring Their Constant Love and Zeal to the Truth: With a Readiness to Give Account of their Faith and Hope; as of Their Desires in Church to be Partakers of the Ordinances of Christ. Being a Narrative of the Examinations of the Indians, About Their Knowledge in Religion by the Elders of the Churches." Reprinted from the London 1655 edition. *Collections of the Massachusetts Historical Society,* 3rd series, vol. 4, 261-87. Boston: 1834.

———. "Tears of Repentance: Or, A Further Narrative of the Progress of the Gospel amongst the Indians in New-England: Setting Forth not Only Their Present State and Condition, but Sundry Confessions of Sin by Diverse of the Said Indians, Wrought Upon by the Saving Power of the Gospel; Together with the Manifestation of Their Hearts." Reprinted from the London 1653 edition. *Collections of the Massachusetts Historical Society,* 3rd series, vol. 4, 197-260. Boston: 1834.

Elliott, Emory, ed. *Columbia Literary History of the United States.* New York: Columbia University Press, 1988.

R G Ꝺ. *A Cherokee Vision of Eloh.'* Edited by Howard Meredith and Virginia Milan. Translated by Wesley Proctor. Muskogee, Oklahoma: Indian University Press, 1981.

Faludi, Susan. *The Terror Dream: Fear and Fantasy in Post-9/11 America.* New York: Metropolitan Books, 2007.

Farella, John. *The Main Stalk: A Synthesis of Navajo Philosophy.* Tucson: University of Arizona Press, 1984.

Faulkner, William. *Go Down, Moses*. New York: Modern Library, 1955.

———. *The Town: A Novel of the Snopes Family*. New York: Random House, 1957.

Fay, George E., ed. *Treaties between the Tribes of the Great Plains and the United States of America: Comanche and Kiowa; Arikara, Gros Ventre and Mandan; 1835-1991*. Greeley, Colorado: Museum of Anthropology, University of Northern Colorado, 1982.

Fiedler, Leslie. *The Return of the Vanishing American*. New York: Stein and Day, 1968.

Fish, Stanley. *Is There a Text in This Class? The Authority of Interpretative Communities*. Cambridge, Massachusetts: Harvard University Press, 1980.

Flannery, Regina. *An Analysis of Coastal Algonquian Culture*. Catholic University of America, Anthropological Series 7. Washington, D.C.: Catholic University of America Press, 1939.

Forbes, Jack. *The Indian in America's Past*. Englewood Cliffs, New Jersey: Prentice-Hall, 1964.

Ford, Worthington, ed. *History of Plymouth Plantation, 1620-1647*. Boston: Massachusetts Historical Society, 1912.

Foreman, Carolyn. *Indians Abroad: 1493-1938*. Norman: University of Oklahoma Press, 1943.

Gardiner, Lion. "Gardiner's Pequot Warres." *Collections of the Massachusetts Historical Society*, 3rd series, vol. 3. Boston, 1833.

Garrett, T. J., and Michael Garrett. *Medicine of the Cherokee: The Way of Right Relationship*. Santa Fe: Bear, 1996.

Genette, Gerard. *Narrative Discourse: An Essay in Method*. Translated by Jane E. Lewin. Ithaca, New York: Cornell University Press, 1980.

———. *Paratexts: Thresholds of Interpretation*. Translated by Jane Lewin. New York: Cambridge University Press, 1997.

Gibson, Susan, ed. *Burr's Hill: A 17th Century Wampanoag Burial Ground in Warren, Rhode Island*. Providence: Haffenreffer Museum, Brown University, 1980.

Gilkey, Langdon. *Nature, Reality, and the Sacred: The Nexus of Science and Religion*. Minneapolis: Fortress Press, 1993.

———. *Renaming the Whirlwind: The Renewal of God-Language*. Indianapolis: Bobbs-Merrill, 1969.

Gill, Sam. "The Trees Stood Deep Rooted." In *I Become Part of It*, edited by D. M. Dooling and Paul Jordan-Smith, 21-31. New York: HarperSanFrancisco, 1989.

Gill, Sam D., and Irene Sullivan. *A Dictionary of Native American Mythology*. New York: Oxford University Press, 1992.

"Gluskabi/Gluskap Stories and Other Wabanaki Legends." *Native Languages of the Americas*. Web site. http:/www.native-languages.org/Wabanaki-legends.htm.

Gookin, Daniel. *An Historical Account of the Doings and Sufferings of the Christian Indians in New England in the Years 1675, 1676, 1677.* Reprint, New York: Arno Press, 1972.

Grabo, Norman. "William Bradford: *Of Plymouth Plantation.*" *Landmarks of American Writing.* Edited by Hennig Cohen. New York: Basic Books, 1969.

Green, Rayna. *Women in American Indian Society.* New York: Chelsea House, 1992.

Greenblatt, Stephen J. *Learning to Curse: Essays in Early Modern Culture.* New York: Routledge, 1990.

Greenblatt, Stephen, and Giles Gunn, eds. *Redrawing the Boundaries: The Transformation of English and American Literary Studies.* New York: Modern Language Association of America, 1992.

Grey, Zane. *Riders of the Purple Sage: A Novel.* New York: Grosset and Dunlap, 1912.

———. *The Spirit of the Border: A Romance of the Early Settlers in the Ohio Valley.* New York: A. L. Burt, 1906.

Griffin-Pierce, Trudy. *Earth Is My Mother, Sky Is My Father: Space, Time, and Astronomy in Navajo Sandpainting.* Albuquerque: University of New Mexico Press, 1992.

Grinde, Donald A., Jr., and Bruce E. Johansen. *Exemplar of Liberty: Native American and the Evolution of Democracy.* Los Angeles: American Indian Studies Center, 1991.

Haile, Berard. *An Ethnologic Dictionary of the Navajo Language.* St. Michaels, Arizona: Franciscan Fathers, 1910.

———. *Legend of the Ghostway Ritual in the Male Branch of Shootingway Part One* [and] *Suckingway: Its Legend and Practice Part Two.* St. Michaels, Arizona: St. Michael's Press, 1950.

———. *Women Versus Men: A Conflict of Navajo Emergence, The Curly Tó Aheedlíinii Version.* Lincoln: University of Nebraska Press, 1981.

———, comp. and trans. *Beautyway: A Navajo Ceremonial.* Edited by Leland Wyman. New York: Bollingen Foundation, 1957.

Hale, Horatio, ed. *The Iroquois Book of Rites.* New York: AMS Press, 1883.

Hallowell, A. Irving. *Contributions to Anthropology: Selected Papers of A. Irving Hallowell.* Chicago: University of Chicago Press, 1976.

———. *Culture and Experience.* Philadelphia: University of Pennsylvania Press, 1955.

Handlin, Oscar. *Race and Nationality in American Life.* Garden City, New York: Doubleday, 1957.

Hanson, Elizabeth. *Thoreau's Indian of the Mind.* Lewiston, New York: Mellen, 1991.

Harris, Joel Chandler. *Uncle Remus, His Songs and His Sayings*. New York: Grosset and Dunlap, 1921.

Harrison, Jim. *Legends of the Fall*. New York: Dell, 1978.

Harrod, Howard. *Renewing the World: Plains Indian Religion and Morality*. Tucson: University of Arizona Press, 1987.

Hauptman, Laurence M., and James D. Wherry, eds. *The Pequots in Southern New England: The Fall and Rise of an American Indian Nation*. Norman: University of Oklahoma Press, 1990.

Hawkes, Terence. *Metaphor*. London: Methuen, 1972.

Hawthorne, Nathaniel. *The House of the Seven Gables*. Boston: Ticknor, Reed, and Fields, 1851.

———. "Young Goodman Brown." *Mosses from an Old Manse . . . in Two Parts*. London: Wiley and Putnam, 1846.

Heckewelder, John. *History, Manners, and Customs of the Indian Nations Who Once Inhabited Pennsylvania and the Neighbouring States*. Philadelphia: Historical Society of Pennsylvania, 1876.

"Heidelberg Catechism." *The Book of Confessions*. New York: Office of the General Assembly of the Presbyterian Church, 1983.

Hobson, Geary. Letter. *Wicazo Sa Review* (Spring 1995): 68-70.

Hoffer, Peter. *Indians and Europeans: Selected Articles on Indian-White Relations in Colonial North America*. New York: Garland, 1988.

Hogan, Linda. *Mean Spirit*. New York: Ballantine, 1990.

Hubbard, William. *A General History of New England, From the Discovery to MDCLXXX*. Cambridge, Massachusetts: Hilliard and Metcalf, 1815. Boston: C. C. Little and J. Brown, 1848.

———. *The History of the Indian Wars in New England from the First Settlement to the Termination of the War with King Philip in 1677*. Edited by Samuel Drake. 2 vols. Roxbury, Massachusetts: Woodward, 1865.

Hulme, Peter. *Colonial Encounters: Europe and the Native Caribbean, 1492-1797*. New York: Routledge, 1992.

Humins, John. "Squanto and Massasoit: A Struggle for Power." *The New England Quarterly* 60 (1987): 54-70.

Hurtado, Albert L., and Peter Iverson, eds. *Major Problems in American Indian History: Documents and Essays*. Lexington, Massachusetts: D. C. Heath, 1994.

Hutchinson, Thomas. *The History of the Colony and Province of Massachusetts Bay. From the First Settlement Therof in 1628 until its Incorporation with the Colony of Plimouth, Province of Main, etc. by the Charter of King William and Queen Mary, in 1691*. 2 vols. Boston: Thomas and John Fleet, 1764.

Hymes, Dell. *"In vain I tried to tell you": Essays in Native American Ethnopoetics*. Philadelphia: University of Pennsylvania Press, 1981.

Indian Treaties Printed by Benjamin Franklin, 1736-1762. Philadelphia: Historical Society of Pennsylvania, 1938.

Jackson, Helen Hunt. *A Century of Dishonor: A Sketch of the United States Government's Dealing with Some of the Indian Tribes.* New York: Indian Head Books, 1881.

———. *Ramona.* New York: Scholastic Book Services, 1973.

Jacobs, Wilbur R. *Dispossessing the American Indian: Indians and Whites on the Colonial Frontier.* New York: Scribner, 1972.

Jahner, Elaine. "The Spiritual Landscape." In *I Become Part of It: Sacred Dimensions in Native American Life,* edited by D. M. Dooling and Paul Jordan-Smith, 193-203 San Francisco: HarperSanFrancisco, 1989.

James, Sydney V., ed. *Three Visitors to Early Plymouth.* Plymouth: Plimoth Plantation, 1963.

Jameson, J. Franklin, ed. *Johnson's Wonder-Working Providence, 1628-1651.* New York: Scribner's, 1910.

———, ed. *Narratives of New Netherland, 1609-1664.* New York: Scribner, 1909. Barnes and Noble, 1937.

Jehlen, Myra. "The Literature of Colonization." *The Cambridge History of American Literature.* Edited by Sacvan Bercovitch and and Cyrus R. K. Patell. Vol. 1, *1590-1820.* New York: Cambridge University Press, 1994.

Jehlen, Myra, and Michael Warner, eds. *The English Literatures of America: 1500-1800.* New York: Routledge, 1996.

Jennings, Francis. *The Ambiguous Iroquois Empire: The Covenant Chain Confederation of Indian Tribes with English Colonies from Its Beginnings to the Lancaster Treaty of 1744.* New York: Norton, 1984.

———. *The Invasion of America: Indians, Colonialism, and the Cant of Conquest.* New York: Norton, 1976.

Johnson, Pauline E. *The Moccasin Maker.* Edited by A. LaVonne Brown Ruoff. Tucson: University of Arizona Press, 1987.

Jones, Howard Mumford. *O Strange New World: American Culture, the Formative Years.* New York: Viking, 1965.

Josephy, Alvin M., Jr. *The Indian Heritage of America.* New York: Knopf, 1968.

Journall of the English Plantation at Plimoth. London: John Bellamie, 1622.

Justice, Daniel Heath. *Our Fire Survives the Storm: A Cherokee Literary History.* Minneapolis: University of Minnesota Press, 2006.

Kappler, Charles J. *Indian Treaties: 1778-1883.* New York: Interland, 1972.

Kawashima, Yasuhide. *Puritan Justice and the Indian: White Man's Law in Massachusetts, 1630-1763.* Middletown, Connecticut: Wesleyan University Press, 1986.

Kelsey, Penelope Myrtle. *Tribal Theory in Native American Literature: Dakota and Haudenosaunee Writing and Indigenous World Views.* Lincoln: University of Nebraska Press, 2008.

Kesey, Ken. *One Flew Over the Cuckoo's Nest*. New York: Penguin, 1962.

Keyser, Charles S. *Penn's Treaty with the Indians*. Philadelphia: McKay, 1882.

Kibbey, Ann. *The Interpretation of Material Shapes in Puritanism: A Study of Rhetoric, Prejudice, and Violence*. New York: Cambridge University Press, 1986.

Kidwell, Clara Sue, Homer Noley, and George E. Tinker. *A Native American Theology*. Maryknoll, New York: Orbis Books, 2001.

Kilcup, Karen, ed. *Native American Women's Writings 1800-1924*. Oxford: Blackwell Publishers, 2000.

Kilpatrick, Jack, and Anna Gritts Kilpatrick, eds. *Run Toward the Night Land: Magic of the Oklahoma Cherokees*. Dallas: Southern Methodist University Press, 1967.

King, Thomas. *The Truth about Stories: A Native Narrative*. Minneapolis: University of Minnesota Press, 2003.

Kittredge, George. L. "Cotton Mather's Election into the Royal Society." *Publications of the Colonial Society of Massachusetts*. Vol. 14. Boston: Colonial Society of Massachusetts, 1913.

Klein, Laura, and Lillian Ackerman, eds. *Women and Power in Native North America*. Norman: University of Oklahoma Press, 1995.

Krupat, Arnold. *Ethnocriticism: Ethnography, History, Literature*. Berkeley: University of California Press, 1992.

Kupperman, Karen Ordahl. *Indians and English: Facing off in Early America*. Ithaca, New York: Cornell Press, 2000.

Larson, Charles R. *American Indian Fiction*. Albuquerque: University of New Mexico Press, 1978.

Leacock, Eleanor. "Women's Status in Egalitarian Society: Implications for Social Evolution." *Current Anthropology* 19 (1978): 247-55.

Leavitt, Robert M., and David A. Francis, eds. *Wapapi Akonutomakonol. The Wampum Records: Wabanaki Traditional Laws*. Fredericton, New Brunswick: Micmac-Maliseet Institute, University of New Brunswick, 1990.

Leland, Charles G. *The Algonquin Legends of New England; or, Myths and Folk Lore of the Micmac, Passamaquoddy, Penobscot Tribes*. Boston: Houghton-Mifflin, 1884. New York: Dover, 1992.

Lemay, J. A. Leo. *The Frontiersman from Lout to Hero: Notes on the Significance of the Comparative Method and the Stage Theory in Early American Literature and Culture*. Worcester, Massachusetts: American Antiquarian Society, 1979.

Lenz, Gunter, Hartmut Keil, and Sabine Brock-Sallah, eds. *Reconstructing American Literary and Historical Studies*. New York: St. Martin's, 1990.

"Letters of William Bradford." *Collections of the Massachusetts Historical Society*, 4th series, vol. 6, 156-61. Boston, 1863.

Levi-Strauss, Claude. *The Savage Mind*. Chicago: University of Chicago Press. 1966.

————. *Structural Anthropology*. Translated by Claire Jacobson and Brooke Grundfest Schoepf. New York: Basic Books, 1963.

Lincoln, Charles Henry, ed. *Narratives of the Indian Wars: 1675-1699*. New York: Barnes and Noble, 1966.

Lincoln, Kenneth. *Native American Renaissance*. Berkeley: University of California Press, 1983.

Lindman, Janet Moore, and Michele Lise Tarter, eds. *A Center of Wonders: The Body in Early America*. Ithaca: Cornell University Press, 2001.

Link, Margaret Schevill, comp. *The Pollen Path: A Collection of Navajo Myths Retold by Margaret Schevill Link*. Stanford: Stanford University Press, 1956.

Linton, Ralph, ed. *Acculturation in Seven American Indian Tribes*. New York: Appleton-Century, n.d.

Littlefield, Daniel F., and James W. Parins. *A Bibliography of Native American Writers, 1772-1924*. Metuchen, New Jersey: Scarecrow Press, 1981.

————. *A Bibliography of Native American Writers, 1772-1924: A Supplement*. Metuchen, New Jersey: Scarecrow Press, 1985.

Longfellow, Henry Wadsworth. "The Courtship of Miles Standish: And Other Poems." Boston: Ticknor and Fields, 1859.

————. *The Song of Hiawatha*. Boston: Ticknor and Fields, 1855.

Lowrey, Grady N. *Journey to Sunrise: Myths and Legends of the Cherokee*. Claremore, Oklahoma: Egi Press, 1977.

Manitonquat. *The Children of the Morning Light: Wampanoag Tales*. New York: Macmillan, 1994.

————. *Return to Creation: A Survival Manual for Native and Natural People*. Spokane: Bear Tribe Publishing, 1991.

Martien, Jerry. *Shell Game: A True Account of Beads and Money in North America*. San Francisco: Mercury House, 1996.

Martin, Wallace. *Recent Theories of Narrative*. Ithaca, New York: Cornell University Press, 1986.

Mason, John. "The History of the Pequot War." Boston: *Collections of the Massachusetts Historical Society*, 2nd series, vol. 8. Boston, 1819.

Mather, Cotton. *Magnalia Christi Americana*. 3rd edition. 2 vols. Hartford: Silas Andrus, 1853. Edinburgh: Banner of Truth Trust, 1979.

Mather, Increase. *Remarkable Providences Illustrative of the Earlier Days of American Colonisation*. London: Reeves and Turner, 1890.

Mavor, James W., and Byron E. Dix. *Manitou: The Sacred Landscape of New England's Native Civilization*. Rochester, Vermont: Inner Traditions International, 1989.

McMurtry, Larry. *Lonesome Dove*. New York: Simon and Schuster, 1985.

Melville, Herman. *Moby-Dick, or the White Whale*. New York: Harper and Brothers, 1851.

———. *Pierre: Or the Ambiguities.* London: S. Low, Son, and Company, 1852.

"Merchant Adventurers." *MayflowerHistory.com.* http://www.mayflowerhistory. com/Genealogy/merchantadventurers.php.

Meredith, Howard L., and Virginia E. Milan, eds. *A Cherokee Vision of Eloh.'* Translated by Wesley Proctor. Muskogee, Oklahoma: Indian University Press, 1981.

Meyer, Isidore S. *The Hebrew Exercises of Governor William Bradford.* Plymouth, Massachusetts: Pilgrim Society, 1973.

Mignolo, Walter D. *The Darker Side of the Renaissance: Literacy, Territoriality, and Colonization.* Ann Arbor: University of Michigan Press, 1995.

Miller, Perry. *Errand into the Wilderness.* New York: Harper and Row, 1964.

———. *The New England Mind: The Seventeenth Century.* Cambridge, Massachusetts: Harvard University Press, 1954.

Mitchell, Lewis, recounter. *Wapapi Akonutomakonol: The Wampum Records, Wabanaki Traditional Laws.* Edited by Robert M. Leavitt and David A. Francis. Fredericton, Canada: University of New Brunswick, 1990.

Molloy, Anne. *Wampum.* New York: Hastings House, 1977.

Momaday, N. Scott. *House Made of Dawn.* New York: New American Library, 1966.

———. "The Native Voice." *Columbia Literary History of the United States.* Edited by Emory Elliott. New York: Columbia University Press, 1988.

Morgan, Edmund. *The Puritan Dilemma: The Story of John Winthrop.* Boston: Little, Brown, 1958.

Morison, Samuel Eliot. *The Puritan Pronaos: Studies in the Intellectual Life of New England in the Seventeenth Century.* New York: New York University Press, 1936.

Morison, Samuel Eliot, ed. *Of Plymouth Plantation, 1620-1647.* New York: Knopf, 1952.

Morrison, Kenneth. "Towards a History of Intimate Encounters: Algonkian Folklore, Jesuit Missionaries, and Kiwake, the Cannibal Giant." *American Indian History: A Reader in Early Cultural Contact, 1492-1760.* Los Angeles: American Indian Studies Center, University of California Los Angeles, 1981.

Morton, George, ed. *A Relation or Iournall of the Beginning and Proceedings of the English Plantation Setled at Plimoth in New England, etc.* London: Iohn Bellamie, 1622.

Morton, Nathaniel. *New-England's Memorial.* Edited by John Davis. Boston: Croker and Brewster, 1826.

Morton, Nathaniel. *New-Englands Memoriall: Or a Brief Relation of the Most Remarkable. . . .* Cambridge, Massachusetts: John Usher, 1669.

Morton, Thomas. *The New English Canaan: Or New Canaan, Containing an Abstract of New England. . . .* Amsterdam: Jacob Frederick Stam, 1637.

Mourt's Relation: A Journal of the Pilgrims at Plymouth. Edited by Dwight B. Heath. Bedford, Massachusetts: Applewood Books, 1963.

Mwalim. *A Mixed Bag: Original Black Wampanoag Folklore.* Boston: Talking Drum Press, 1995.

Nabokov, Peter, ed. *Native American Testimony: A Chronicle of Indian-White Relations from Prophecy to the Present, 1492-1992.* New York: Viking, 1978.

Nash, Gary. *Red, Black, and White: The Peoples of Early North America.* Englewood Cliffs, New Jersey: Prentice Hall, 1992.

Neilson, Francis. *Manabozo: An Opera in Three Acts.* London: Chester, n.d.

Nelson, Robert M. *Place and Vision: The Function of Landscape in Native American Fiction.* New York: Peter Lang, 1993.

Nicolar, Joseph. *The Life and Traditions of the Red Man.* Edited by Annette Kolodny. Durham, North Carolina: Duke University Press, 2007.

Nobel, William C. "'Vision Pits,' Cairns, and Petroglyphs at Rock Lake, Algonquin Provincial Part, Ontario." *Ontario Archaeology* 11 (1968): 47-64.

Nolan, James. *Poet-Chief: The Native American Poetics of Walt Whitman and Pablo Neruda.* Albuquerque: University of New Mexico Press, 1994.

Nowell, Samuel. *Abraham in Arms: Or, The First Religious General with His Army Engaging in a War for which He Had Wisely Prepared, and by which, Not Only an Eminent Victory was Obtained, . . . 1678.* Boston: John Fosterm, 1678.

O'Brien, Sharon. *American Indian Tribal Governments.* Norman: University of Oklahoma Press, 1989.

O'Connell, Barry, ed. *On Our Own Ground: The Complete Writings of William Apess, a Pequot.* Amherst: University of Massachusetts Press, 1992.

Ong, Walter, S.J. *The Presence of the Word: Some Prolegomena for Cultural and Religious History.* New Haven: Yale University Press, 1967.

Owens, Louis. *Other Destinies: Understanding the American Indian Novel.* Norman: University of Oklahoma Press, 1992.

Parrington, Vernon Louis. *Main Currents in American Thought.* 3 vols. New York: Harcourt, Brace, 1926.

Pearce, Roy Harvey. *The Savages of America: A Study of the Indian and the Idea of Civilization.* Baltimore: Johns Hopkins Press, 1953.

———. *Savagism and Civilization: A Study of the Indian and the American Mind.* Berkeley: University of California Press, 1988.

Peters, Russell M. *Clambake.* Minneapolis, Minnesota: Lerner Publications, 1992.

———. *The Wampanoags of Mashpee: An Indian Perspective on American History.* Boston: Nimrod Press, n.d.

Plymouth Church Records, 1620-1859. Baltimore: Genealogical Publishing Company, 1975.

Posey, Alexander. *The Fus Fixico Letters.* Edited by Daniel Littlefield and Carol Hunter. Lincoln: University of Nebraska Press, 1993.

Potter, Elisha. "The Early History of the Narragansett." *Collections of the Rhode-Island Historical Society*, vol. 3. Providence, Rhode Island: Marshall, Brown, 1835.

Potter, Stephen. *Commoners, Tribute, and Chiefs: The Development of Algonquian Culture in the Potomac Valley.* Charlottesville: University Press of Virginia, 1993.

Prince, Gerald. *Dictionary of Narratology.* Lincoln: University of Nebraska Press, 1987.

———. *A Grammar of Stories: An Introduction.* The Hague: Mouton, 1973.

———. *Narratology: The Form and Functioning of Narrative.* Berlin: Mouton, 1982.

Prince, Thomas. *A Chronological History of New-England, in the Form of Annals, Being a Summary and Exact Account of the most Material Transactions and Occurrences Relating to this Country. . . .* Printed privately in installments. Boston: Kneeland and Green, 1826.

Pritchard, Evan. T. *Native New Yorkers: The Legacy of the Algonquin People of New York.* Tulsa, Oklahoma: Council Oak Books, 2002.

———. *No Word for Time: The Way of the Algonquin People.* Tulsa, Oklahoma: Council Oak Books, 1997.

Propp, Vladimir. *Morphology of the Folktale.* Translated by Laurence Scott. Austin: University of Texas Press, 1968.

Purchas, Francis Paul. *American Indian Policy in the Formative Years: The Indian Trade and Intercourse Acts 1790-1834.* Cambridge, Massachusetts: Harvard University Press, 1962.

———. *The Indians of American Society: From the Revolutionary War to the Present.* Berkeley: University of California Press 1985.

Radin, Paul. *The Trickster: A Study in American Indian Mythology.* New York: Schoken Books, 1972.

Reichard, Gladys A. *Navajo Religion: A Study of Symbolism.* New York: Bollingen Foundation, 1950.

Richter, Daniel K. *The Ordeal of the Longhouse: The Peoples of the Iroquois League in the Era of European Colonization.* Chapel Hill: University of North Carolina Press, 1992.

Roach, Joseph. *Cities of the Dead: Circum Atlantic Performance.* New York: Columbia University Press, 1996.

Robinson, Paul. "Lost Opportunities: Miantonomi and the English in Seventeenth-Century Narragansett Country." In *Northeastern Indian Lives,* edited by Robert S. Grumet, 13-28. Amherst: University of Massachusetts Press, 1996.

Rogers, Will. *The Cowboy Philosopher on the Peace Conference.* Stillwater, Oklahoma: Oklahoma State University Press, 1975.

Rogin, Michael Paul. "Liberal Society and the Indian Question." *Politics and Society* 3 (May 1971): 269-312.

Ronda, James P. "'We Are Well as We Are' An Indian Critique of Seventeenth

Century Christian Missions." *William and Mary Quarterly* 3rd series, vol. 34, no. 1 (January 1977): 66-82.

Rosenmeier, Jesper. "'With My Owne Eyes': William Bradford's *Of Plymouth Plantation*." *Typology and Early American Literature*. Edited by Sacvan Bercovitch. Amherst: University of Massachusetts Press, 1972.

Rourke, Constance. *American Humor: A Study of the National Character*. New York: Harcourt Brace, 1931. Doubleday, 1953.

———. *The Roots of American Culture and Other Essays*. New York: Harcourt, Brace, 1942.

Rowen, Herbert H., ed. *The Low Countries in Early Modern Times*. New York: Walker, 1972.

Rowlandson, Mary. *The Sovereignty and Goodness of God: A True History of the Captivity & Restoration of Mrs. Mary Rowlandson, a Minister's Wife.* . . . London: Joseph Poole, 1682.

Ruland, Richard, and Malcolm Bradbury. *From Puritanism to Postmodernism: A History of American Literature*. New York: Penguin, 1991.

Runyan, Michael, ed. *William Bradford: The Collected Verse*. St. Paul, Minnesota: John Colet Press, 1974.

Ruoff, A. LaVonne Brown, and Jerry W. Ward Jr., eds. *Redefining American Literary History*. New York: Modern Language Association of America, 1990.

Russell, Howard S. *Indian New England before the Mayflower*. Hanover, New Hampshire: University Press of New England, 1980.

Salisbury, Neal. *Manitou and Providence: Indians, Europeans, and the Making of New England, 1500-1643*. New York: Oxford University Press, 1982.

———. "Red Puritans: The 'Praying Indians' of Massachusetts Bay and John Eliot." *William and Mary Quarterly* 3rd series, vol. 31, no. 1 (January 1974): 27-54.

———. "Squanto: Last of the Patuxets." *Struggle & Survival in Colonial America*. Edited by David G. Sweet and Gary Nash. Berkeley: University of California Press, 1981.

Savage, William W., ed. *Indian Life: Transforming an American Myth*. Norman: University of Oklahoma Press, 1977.

Scarberry-Garcia, Susan. *Landmarks of Healing: A Study of House Made of Dawn*. Albuquerque: University of New Mexico Press, 1990.

Schaaf, Gregory. *Wampum Belts and Peace Trees: George Morgan, Native Americans, and Revolutionary Diplomacy*. Golden, Colorado: Fulcrum, 1990.

Schultz, Eric B., and Michael J. Tougias. *King Philip's War: The History and Legacy of America's Forgotten Conflict*. Woodstock, Vermont: Countryman Press, 1999.

Seals, David. *The Powwow Highway*. New York: Penguin, 1979.

Seaver, James. *A Narrative of the Life of Mrs. Mary Jemison: Who Was Taken by the Indians, in the Year 1755.* . . . New York: Citation, 1961.

"Second Helvetic Confession." *The Book of Confessions*. New York: Office of the General Assembly of the Presbyterian Church, 1983.

Segal, Charles M., and David C. Stineback. *Puritans, Indians, and Manifest Destiny*. New York: Putnam, 1977.

Sewell, Samuel. *The Diary of Samuel Sewall, 1674-1729*. 2 vols. New York: Farrar, Straus, and Giroux, 1973.

Shanley, Kathryn W., ed. *Native American Literature: Boundaries & Sovereignties*. Special edition of *Para.Doxa: Studies in World Literary Genres* 15 (2001).

Shepard, Thomas. "The Day-Breaking, If Not the Sun-Rising of the Gospell with the Indians in New-England." *Collections of the Massachusetts Historical Society*. 3rd series, vol. 4, 1-23. Boston, 1834.

———. "A Letter from the Rev. Mr. Thomas Shepard to His Son At His Admission into the College." *Publications of The Colonial Society of Massachusetts, 1911-1913*. Vol. 15. Boston: The Society, 1913.

Shuffelton, Frank. "Indian Devils and Pilgrim Fathers: Squanto, Hobomok, and the English Conception of Indian Religion." *The New England Quarterly* 44 (March 1976): 108-16.

———. *A Mixed Race: Ethnicity in Early America*. New York: Oxford University Press, 1993.

Shurtleff, Nathaniel B., and David Pulsifer, eds. *Records of the Colony of New Plymouth in New England*: Printed by Order of the Legislature of the Commonwealth of Massachusetts. 12 vols. in 6. Boston: William White, 1855-61. Reprint, New York: AMS, 1968.

Silva, Cristobal. *Miraculous Plagues: An Epidemiology of New England Narrative, 1616-1721*. New York: Oxford University Press, 2011.

Simmons, William. *Cautantowwit's House: An Indian Burial Ground on the Island of Conanicut in Narragansett Bay*. Providence, Rhode Island: Brown University Press, 1970.

———. "Conversion from Indian to Puritan." *New England Quarterly* 52 (June 1979): 197-218.

———. "Southern New England Shamanism: An Ethnographic Reconstruction." *Papers of the Seventh Algonkian Conference*. Edited by William Cowan. Ottawa, 1975: 217-57.

———. *Spirit of the New England Tribes: Indian History and Folklore, 1620-1984*. Hanover, New Hampshire: University Press of New England, 1986.

Simonds, Philip B. "Intercourse and Non-Intercourse with the Narragansett Indians." Providence, Rhode Island: Rhode Island Historical Society, 1979.

Slotkin, Richard. *Regeneration Through Violence: The Mythology of the American Frontier, 1600-1860*. Hanover, New Hampshire: University Press of New England, 1973.

Smith, Henry Nash. *Virgin Land: The American West as Symbol and Myth*. New York: Vintage, 1950.

Smith, Paul Chaat. *Everything You Know About Indians Is Wrong*. Minneapolis: University of Minnesota Press, 2009.

———. "The Terrible Nearness of Distant Places: Making History at the National Museum of the American Indian." *Indigenous Experience Today*. Edited by Marisol de la Cadena and Orin Starn. New York: Berg, 2007.

Snow, Edward Rowe. *Legends of the New England Coast*. New York: Dodd, Mead, 1957.

Sollors, Werner. *Beyond Ethnicity: Consent and Descent in American Culture*. New York: Oxford University Press, 1986.

Speck, Frank. "The Eastern Algonkian Wabanaki Confederacy." *American Anthropologist* 17 (July-September 1915): 492-508.

———. *The Functions of Wampum among the Eastern Algonkian*. Lancaster, Pennsylvania: American Anthropological Association, 1919.

———. *Midwinter Rites of the Cayuga Long House*. Philadelphia: University of Pennsylvania Press, 1949. Lincoln: University of Nebraska Press, 1995.

Speier, Hans. *The Truth in Hell and Other Essays on Politics and Culture, 1935-1987*. New York: Oxford University Press, 1989.

Spencer, Benjamin. *The Quest for Nationality: An America Literary Campaign*. Syracuse, New York: Syracuse University Press, 1957.

Spiller, Robert E., Willard Thorp, Thomas H. Johnson, and Henry Seidel Canby, eds. *Literary History of the United States: History*. London: Macmillan, 1946.

Stannard, David E. *American Holocaust: The Conquest of the New World*. New York: Oxford University Press, 1992.

Stiles, Henry R. *The History of Ancient Wethersfield, Connecticut Comprising the Present Towns of Wethersfield, Rocky Hill, and Newington; and of Glastonbury Prior to Its Incorporation in 1693 from Date of Earliest Settlement Until the Present Time*. 2 vols. New York: Grafton, 1904.

Strong, James, S.T.D., L.L.D. *The Exhaustive Concordance of The Bible: Showing Every Word of the Text of the Common English Version of the Canonical Books, and Every Occurrence of Each Word in Regular Order; Together with a Comparative Concordance of the Authorized and Revised Versions, Including the American Variations; Also Brief Dictionaries of the Hebrew and Greek Words of the Original, With References to the English Words*. New York: Abingdon-Cokesbury Press, 1890.

Sugden, John. *Tecumseh: A Life*. New York: John Macrae/Owl Book, 1997.

Sullivan, Lawrence E., ed. *Native American Religions: North America*. New York: Macmillan, 1987.

Swann, Brian, ed. *Coming to Light: Contemporary Translations of the Native Literature of North America*. New York: Vintage Press, 1994.

Sweet, David G., and Gary B. Nash. *Struggle and Survival in Colonial America.* Berkeley: University of California Press, 1981.

Tedlock, Dennis, and Barbara Tedlock, eds. *Teachings from the American Earth: Indian Religion and Philosophy.* New York: Liveright, 1975.

Thatcher, Benjamin. *Indian Biography: Or, An Historical Account of Those Individuals Who Have Been Distinguished Among the North American Natives as Orators, Warriors, Statesmen, and Other Remarkable Characters.* 2 vols. New York: J & J Harper, 1832. Chicago: Elliott-Madison, 1910.

Thirsk, Joan, ed. *1500-1640.* Vol. 4 of *The Agrarian History of England and Wales,* edited by H.P.R. Finberg. London: Cambridge University Press, 1967.

Thompson, Michael, Richard Ellis, and Aaron Wildavsky. *Cultural Theory.* Boulder, Colorado: Westview Press, 1990.

Thornton, Russell. *American Indian Holocaust and Survival: A Population History Since 1492.* Norman: University of Oklahoma Press, 1987.

Thwaites, Reuben Gold, ed. *The Jesuit Relations and Allied Documents: Travels and Explorations of the Jesuit Missionaries in New France, 1619-1791.* 73 vols. Cleveland: Burrows Brothers, 1900.

Tilton, Robert S. *Pocahontas: The Evolution of an American Narrative.* New York: Cambridge University Press, 1994.

Time-Life Books. *Algonquians of the East Coast.* Alexandria, Virginia: Time-Life, 1995.

Todorov, Tzvetan. *The Conquest of America: The Question of the Other.* Trans. Richard Howard. New York: HarperPerennial, 1984.

Tompson, Benjamin. *New Englands Crisis: Or a Brief Narrative of New-Englands Lamentable Estate . . . by the Barbarous Heathen Thereof; Poetically Described.* Boston: John Foster, 1676.

Travers, Milton A. *The Last of the Great Wampanoag Indian Sachems.* Boston: Christopher, 1963.

―――. *The Wampanoag Indian Federation of the Algonquin Nation, Indian Neighbors of the Pilgrims.* New Bedford, Massachusetts: Reynolds-De Walt, 1957.

―――. *The Wampanoag Indian Federation: Indian Neighbors of the Pilgrims.* Revised edition. Boston: Christopher, 1961.

Treuer, David. *Native American Fiction: A User's Manual.* St. Paul: Graywolf Press, 2006.

True Account of the Most Considerable Occurrences that Have Hapned in the Warre between the English and the Indians in New England. . . . Edited by Samuel Gardner Drake. London: Billingsley, 1676.

Trumbull, James Hammond. *Natick Dictionary.* Washington, D.C.: Government Printing Office, 1903.

Turner, Frederick Jackson. *The Significance of the Frontier in American History.* New York: Holt, Rinehart, and Winston, 1962.

Turner, George. *Traits of Indian Character: As Generally Applicable to the Aborigines of North America.* 2 vols. Philadelphia: Key and Biddle. 1836.

Twain, Mark. *The Adventures of Huckleberry Finn.* London: Chatto and Windus, 1884.

———. *The Adventures of Tom Sawyer.* Hartford, Connecticut: American Publishing Company, 1876.

———. *Roughing It.* Hartford, Connecticut: American Publishing Company, 1872.

Tyler, Lyon Gardiner, ed. *Narratives of Early Virginia: 1606-1625.* New York: Scribner's, 1907.

Underhill, John. *Newes from America; or, A New and Experimentall Discoverie of New England; Containing a True Relation of Their War-like Proceedings. . . .* London: J. D., 1638.

"U.S. Presidents with *Mayflower* Lineages." *Presidential Mayflower Lineage.* Web site. http://reocities.com/hawaii1620/prez.html.

Utley, Robert M., and Wilcomb E. Washburn. *Indian Wars.* Boston: Houghton Mifflin, 1977.

Vanderwerth, W. C. *Indian Oratory: Famous Speeches by Noted Indian Chieftains.* Norman: University of Oklahoma Press, 1971.

Vaughan, Alden T. *New England Frontier: Puritans and Indians 1620-1675.* Boston: Little, Brown, 1965.

———. *Roots of American Racism: Essays on the Colonial Experience.* New York: Oxford University Press, 1995.

Vaughan, Alden T., and Edward W. Clark. *Puritans Among the Indians: Accounts of Captivity and Redemption, 1676-1724.* Cambridge, Massachusetts: Harvard University Press, 1981.

Vaughan, Alden T., ed. *Early American Indian Documents: Treaties and Laws, 1607-1789.* 20 vols. Washington, D.C.: University Publications of America, 1983.

Velie, Alan R., ed. *American Indian Literature: An Anthology.* Norman: University of Oklahoma Press, 1979.

Vincent, P. "A True Relation of the Late Battell Fought in New England, between the English and the Pequet Salvages. . . ." *Collections of the Massachusetts Historical Society,* 3rd series, vol. 6, 29-44. Boston: 1837.

Viola, Herman. *After Columbus: The Smithsonian Chronicle of the North American Indians.* New York: Orion, 1990.

Vizenor, Gerald. *Earthdivers: Tribal Narratives on Mixed Descent.* Minneapolis: University of Minnesota Press, 1981.

Vogel, Virgil. *American Indian Medicine.* Norman: University of Oklahoma Press, 1970.

Warhus, Mark. *Another America: Native American Maps and the History of Our Land.* New York: St. Martin's, 1997.

Waters, Frank. *Book of the Hopi*. New York: Ballantine, 1963.

Weatherford, Jack. *Indian Givers: How the Indians of the Americas Transformed the World*. New York: Fawcett Columbine, 1988.

———. *Native Roots: How the Indians Enriched America*. New York: Fawcett Columbine. 1991.

Weaver, Jace. *Other Words: American Indian Literature, Law and Culture*. Norman: University of Oklahoma Press, 2001.

———. *That the People Might Live: Native American Literatures and Naïve American Community*. New York: Oxford University Press, 1997.

Weaver, Jace, Craig S. Womack, and Robert Warrior. *American Indian Literary Nationalism*. Albuquerque: University of New Mexico Press, 2005.

Weeden, William. *Indian Money as a Factor in New England Civilization*. Baltimore, Maryland: Johns Hopkins University Press, 1884.

Weeks, Alvin G. *Massasoit of the Wampanoags*. Norwood, Massachusetts: Plimpton, 1919.

Weiner, Annette. *Inalienable Possessions: The Paradox of Keeping-While Giving*. Berkeley: University of California Press, 1992.

Weinstein, Laurie. *Enduring Traditions: The Native Peoples of New England*. Westport, Connecticut: Greenwood Press, 1994.

Weinstein-Farson, Laurie. *The Wampanoag*. New York: Chelsea House, 1989.

Welch, James. *Winter in the Blood*. New York: Penguin, 1974.

Westbrook, Perry. *William Bradford*. Boston: Twayne, 1978.

Wheeler, Thomas. *A Thankfull Remembrance of Gods Mercy. . . .* Cambridge, Massachusetts: Samuel Green, 1676.

White, Richard. *The Middle Ground: Indians, Empires, and Republics in the Great Lakes Region, 1650-1815*. New York: Cambridge University Press, 1991.

Whitfield, John. "The Light Appearing More and More To-ward the Perfect Day: Or, A Farther Discovery of the Present State of the Indians in New-England, Concerning the Progress of the Gospel Amongst Them; Manifested by Letters from Such as Preacht to Them There." *Collections of the Massachusetts Historical Society*, 3rd series, vol. 4, 101-47. Boston: 1834.

Wiget, Andrew. "Oral Literature of the Southwest." *Dictionary of Native American Literature*. Edited by Andrew Wiget. New York: Garland, 1994.

Wilberforce, Samuel. *A History of the Protestant Episcopal Church in America*. London: J. Burns, 1844.

Williams, John. *The Redeemed Captive*. Edited by Edward W. Clark. Amherst: University of Massachusetts Press, 1976.

Williams, Roger. *A Key into the Language of America*. 5th edition. London: Gregory Dexter, 1643.

Williams, William Carlos. *In the American Grain*. Norfolk, Connecticut: New Directions, 1925.

Willison, George. *Saints and Strangers: Being the Lives of the Pilgrim Fathers & Their Families, with Their Friends & Foes; & an Account of Their Posthumous Wanderings in Limbo, Their Final Resurrection & Rise to Glory, & the Strange Pilgrimages of Plymouth Rock.* Orleans, Massachusetts: Parnassus, 1945.

Wilson, Edmund. *Apologies to the Iroquois: With a Study of the Mohawks in High Steel by Joseph Mitchell.* New York: Farrar, Straus, and Cuddahy, 1960.

Winslow, Edward. *Good Newes from New England: Or a True Relation of Things very Remarkable at the Plantation of Plymouth in New England. . . .* London: I. D., 1624.

———. *Hypocrisie Unmasked: A True Relation of the Proceedings of the Governor and Company of the Massachusetts Against Samuel Gorton of Rhode Island.* New York: B. Franklin, 1968.

———. *New-Englands Salamander, Discovered by an Irreligious and Scornefull Pamphlet, Called New-England's Jonas Cast up at London, etc. Owned by Major John Childe, but not probable to be written by him. Or, a Satisfactory Answer to Many Aspersions Cast upon New-England Therin. . . .* London: Ric. Cotes, 1947.

Winslow, Ola. *John Eliot, "Apostle to the Indians."* Boston: Houghton Mifflin, 1968.

Winthrop, John. "Reasons for the Plantation in New England." Winthrop Society Web site. http://www.winthropsociety.org/doc_reasons.php.

———. *Winthrop's Journal: History of New England, 1630-1649.* James K. Hosmer, ed. 2 vols. New York: Barnes and Noble, 1908.

Womack, Craig S. *Red on Red: Native American Literary Separatism.* Minneapolis: University of Minnesota Press, 1999.

Womack, Craig S., Daniel Heath Justice, and Christopher B. Teuton, eds. *Reasoning Together: The Native Critics Collective.* Norman: University of Oklahoma Press, 2008.

Wood, William. *New Englands Prospect: A True, Lively, and Experimentall Description of That Part of America, Commonly Called New England: Discovering the State of That County, both as it Stands to Our New-Come English Planters; and to the Old Native Inhabitants.* London: Thomas Cotes, 1634.

Woodard, Charles L. *Ancestral Voice: Conversations with N. Scott Momaday.* Lincoln: University of Nebraska Press, 1989.

Wyman, Leland, ed. *Beautyway: A Navajo Ceremonial.* Myth recorded and translated by Berard Haile. Bollingen Series 53. New York: Pantheon, 1957.

Young, Alexander, ed. *The Chronicles of the Pilgrim Fathers of the Colony of Plymouth From 1602-1625.* 2nd edition. Boston: Little and Brown, 1844.

Zolbrod, Paul G. *Dine bahane: The Navajo Creation Story.* Albuquerque: University of New Mexico Press, 1984.

INDEX

Betty Booth Donohue ᏯᏧ ᏪᏧ ᎧᏅᏁ is an independent scholar and a member of the Cherokee Nation. She has published articles on Alexander Posey and nineteenth-century American Indian poetry. She has recently written the opening chapter, "Remembering Muskrat: Native Poetics and the American Indian Oral Tradition," for the Cambridge History of American Poetry 2014 and articles on the Indianization of American literature and the emebedded Algonquian text in Mary Rowlandson's captivity narrative. *Bradford's Indian Book* won the Wordcraft Circle of Native Writers and Storytellers' award for best history written by a Native in 2012.

www.ingramcontent.com/pod-product-compliance
Lightning Source LLC
Chambersburg PA
CBHW021358090426
42742CB00009B/914